The Hambro
TAX GUIDE 1979-80

By
Professor A. S. Silke
M.Com., Ph.D. (Cape Town), F.C.A., C.A. (S.A.)
and
W. I. Sinclair
F.C.A.

Consulting Editor and Author of VAT Chapter
Professor G. S. A. Wheatcroft
M.A. (Oxon), Professor Emeritus of English
Law of the University of London, Consulting
Editor of the British Tax Review and
British Tax Encyclopaedia

MACDONALD GENERAL BOOKS
MACDONALD & JANE'S · LONDON AND SYDNEY

Key to References

S	Section (of Income and Corporation Taxes Act 1970 unless otherwise stated)
Sch	Schedule (of Income and Corporation Taxes Act 1970 unless otherwise stated)
FA	Finance Act
T.M.A.	Taxes Management Act 1970
C.A.A.	Capital Allowances Act 1968
F2A	Finance (No. 2) Act
D.L.T.A.	Development Land Tax Act 1976
C.G.T.A.	Capital Gains Tax Act 1979

First published in Great Britain in 1979
by Macdonald General Books,
Macdonald and Jane's Publishing Group Limited,
Paulton House, 8 Shepherdess Walk, London N1

Printed and bound in Great Britain by Billing & Sons Limited,
Guildford, London and Worcester

ISBN 0 354 08553 0

About this book

This book has been designed to be used both by the professional and non-professional. Solicitors, accountants and company secretaries will find it especially useful as a concise ready reference. Many others, company directors and executives, partners and sole-traders, employers and employees, will find in it much helpful information and advice when dealing with problems of personal and company taxation.

It illustrates the working of income tax, capital gains tax, corporation tax, capital transfer tax, development land tax and VAT, in the United Kingdom.

It is intended to revise the book annually in order to keep it up to date, in accordance with the annual changes to the law. This is the eighth edition which is based on the law as at 1 August 1979, including the Finance Act 1979 and Finance (No 2) Act 1979.

We are most grateful to all those who have written to us with kind and helpful comments concerning the previous editions, some of which have been taken into account in the preparation of this volume.

Because the book concisely covers a very wide field, it has been necessary to omit some of the exemptions and qualifications with which tax law abounds: to adopt a familiar saying, 'When I say never, I mean hardly ever and when I say always, I mean almost always'.

The book is intended to be only a general tax guide. If it cannot solve a problem, the time has come to look at one of the multi-volume tax textbooks or to consult a tax specialist.

We acknowledge with thanks the very valuable assistance and guidance given to us by Professor G. S. A. Wheatcroft, M.A. (Oxon), J.P., as well as the considerable help and work done in connection with this edition by Messrs A. N. Homburger, B.Com., F.C.A., A.C.M.A., J. F. Avery Jones, M.A., LL.B., F.T.I.I. and R. C. P. Coombs, A.C.A., and also by Messrs M. A. Weinberg, B.Com., LL.M., M. S. Lipworth, B.Com., LL.B., P. B. Hamilton, M.A. (Cantab), K. A. Bulgin, M.A. (Oxon), B. J. Blackburn, M.A. (Oxon), S. R. Lippiatt, M.A. (Oxon) and P. C. Howe, LL.B. of Hambro Life Assurance Limited. Our special thanks are due to Professor Wheatcroft and Mr Lipworth respectively for contributing the chapters on VAT and Life Assurance Taxation. We also acknowledge with thanks the permission granted by the Controller of Her Majesty's Stationery Office to make use of certain of their publications and Inland Revenue forms in this book.

A. S. Silke
W. I. Sinclair

Contents

4. The Unified System of Personal Taxation

5. Husband, Wife and Children

6. Income from Land and Property

7. Income from Dividends and Interest

8. Income from Businesses and Professions

9.   Income from Employments and PAYE

10.   Domicile and Residence

11. Tax on Foreign Income

12. Non-residents, Visitors and Immigrants

13. Miscellaneous Aspects

14.   Capital Gains Tax

15. Capital Taxes on Land

16. Partnerships

17. Returns, Assessments and Repayment Claims

18. The Taxation of Trusts and Estates

19. Companies

20. Capital Transfer Tax

21. Tax Aspects of Life Assurance
by M. S. Lipworth

CONTENTS

22.   An Outline of VAT
by Professor G. S. A. Wheatcroft

23. Tax Saving Hints

24.   Tax Tables

Introduction

This, the eighth edition of the *Hambro Tax Guide,* deals with the tax system at the time of writing for the 1979–80 fiscal year. Every chapter has been amended to reflect the many tax changes which have been made since the previous edition including those relating to personal allowances, tax rates, stock relief, car leasing, development land tax, VAT and capital transfer tax.

Because of the volume of changes, it is not possible to retain in each new edition full information for previous years. Thus for the tax rules for previous years, reference to past editions is sometimes necessary.

In every year since its first publication, there have been numerous new rules covered in the book. This year is exceptional, however, in marking a complete change in direction in our tax system. The higher rate of VAT has been abolished but the standard rate has been nearly doubled, thus substantially increasing the burden of indirect taxation. However, this is more than offset by reductions in direct taxation, so that, for example, the former 98% taxpayer now pays no more than 75% on investment income, representing a $12\frac{1}{2}$ times increase in his or her top slice of after-tax income.

Similarly, the top income tax burden on earned income is reduced from 83% to 60% and so tax planning at higher income levels requires thorough re-examination, as is reflected within. This re-examination is in fact necessary at all levels of income in view of the new tax rates and allowances, the abolition of most income tax child relief and the more favourable life assurance relief provisions now in force and considered in this edition.

The 1979–80 *Hambro Tax Guide* brings together in a single volume all of the main taxes which are operating at present, enabling their total effect to be borne in mind. In planning for the future, however, account should be taken of the various avenues for reform already indicated by the Government, including capital gains tax, capital transfer tax, interest relief and fringe benefits. Because of likely relaxations in the field of the capital taxes mentioned, it may be advisable to delay, for example, realising substantial capital gains until the new rules are known, naturally subject to commercial considerations. As new developments are crystallised, they will be covered in the future annual editions of this book.

1. The Basis of your Tax Liability

Who is Taxable?

Individuals, partnerships, estates, trusts, companies, and certain other organisations that are resident in the United Kingdom are taxable on their income arising here. They are also liable on income arising abroad subject to the rules outlined later in this book. The taxation of the income of individuals is covered first; partnerships, estates, trusts and companies being dealt with in later chapters.

The United Kingdom income of non-resident individuals, companies and other entities may also be subject to tax here (p 108).

Similarly capital gains tax is payable on certain capital profits made by United Kingdom residents anywhere in the world (p 121). Non-residents however are not normally liable to UK capital gains tax.

The Taxes Payable (S3 & F2A 1979 S5)

From 6 April 1973 a unified system of personal taxation operates under which there is, for 1979–80, a basic rate of 30%, a lower rate of 25% and various higher rates from 40% to 60% (p 22). Different rates apply for previous years (p 249). Additional tax is payable on your investment income if the latter is sufficiently high (p 25).

Until 5 April 1973 your assessable income after deducting personal reliefs and other permissible deductions was taxed at the standard rate of income tax which was 38.75%. If your income was sufficiently high then you were also charged additional tax known as surtax at rates varying from 10% to 50% (see previous editions).

The rate of capital gains tax is 30%. If your capital gains are not more than £9,500 however, a lower percentage is paid (p 122).

What Income is Taxable? (S1)

The following table summarises the classes of income that are subject to income tax, or corporation tax for companies. The table also shows the 'Schedules' and 'Cases' under which the income is classified and taxed in terms of the law.

Table 1: Classes of Income

Schedule A. Income from land and buildings including rents and certain premiums from leases (p 39).

Schedule B. The 'assessable value' of woodlands that are managed on a commercial basis (p 44).

1

Table 1 continued

Schedule C. Income from 'gilt-edged securities', payable in the United Kingdom as well as certain overseas public revenue dividends that are paid through a banker or other person here (p 49).

Schedule D. This is divided into the following separate 'Cases':

Case I	Trades (p 55).
Case II	Professions or vocations (p 55).
Case III	Interest received, annuities and other annual payments (p 50).
Cases IV and V	Overseas income from certain investments, possessions and businesses (p 99).
Case VI	Miscellaneous profits not falling within any of the other Cases of Schedule D (p 113).

Schedule E. Wages and salaries from employments (including directorships). There are the following 'Cases':

Case I	This normally applies where the employee is resident in the United Kingdom and the work is done here (p 75).
Case II	Work done here by a non-resident etc. (p 109).
Case III	Work done wholly abroad by a United Kingdom resident whose salary is sent here during the course of the overseas employment excluding however income taxed under Case I or Case II (p 104).

Schedule F. Dividends paid by companies and certain other distributions that they make (p 48).

Deduction of Tax at Source and Tax Credits

Tax under Schedules C and F is deducted at source at the basic rate (30%) by the payers and the recipients get the net amount. The former pay the tax over to the Revenue. Company dividend payments, however, are made without any tax deductions although the recipients are 'imputed' with a tax credit of 3/7ths of the dividend. (The company pays tax of 3/7ths of its dividend payments by way of Advance Corporation Tax, p 173.) Thus suppose you receive a dividend of £70: you will get a tax credit of £30 (£70 × 3/7ths) which you may be able to reclaim if your income is sufficiently low (p 158). If your income is high enough however, you may be taxed at higher rates (p 22) on £100 (70 + 30); but you deduct the £30 tax credit from your total bill.

Tax is also deducted at source in the case of certain annual payments (p 16) and income from wages and salaries under Schedule

E (see above). In the former case the payer of the income is entitled in certain circumstances to retain the tax deducted and need not pay it over to the Revenue.

The Distinction between Capital and Revenue Profits

Most of your income is subjected to income tax at the lower, basic and higher rates, whereas normally, capital profits are only liable to capital gains tax or are tax free. The question is then: What is a capital profit?

Generally speaking, a capital profit is a profit which you realise on the sale of an asset where it is clear that you are not making it your business to buy and sell assets of that type. On the other hand, if you conduct a business in such assets your profits will be income.

Examples of Capital Transactions

The sale of the house in which you live (also normally free of capital gains tax unless used for business) (p 135).
The sale of your private motor car (also free of capital gains tax).
The sale of shares you held as investments.
The sale of a plot of land you inherited.
The sale of the goodwill of your business.
The receipt of an inheritance (also free of capital gains tax).
The sale of a property which you had bought for investment purposes.
The sale of a picture unless you are a picture dealer.
The receipt of the proceeds of a 'qualifying' life assurance policy (p 206). This is also normally free of capital gains tax.

Examples of Revenue Transactions

The sale of houses and land if you are a property dealer.
The sale of motor cars if you are a car dealer.
The sale of shares if you are a share dealer.
The sale of pictures if you are a picture dealer.
The receipt of salaries, commissions, interest, dividends, rent, royalties, etc.

Revenue and Capital Expenses

In the same way as income and capital profits must be distinguished, you must separate revenue and capital expenses for tax purposes. The latter can only be charged against capital profits and the former against income. For example the commission on the sale of shares acquired for investment is deducted in calculating your capital gains but if you are a share dealer then it is a revenue expense.

Also, in determining the assessable profits of a business, only revenue expenses may be deducted and capital expenses are prohibited as a deduction (p 57).

3

Tax Free Income

Certain items in your income may be entirely free of tax. These are listed here.

Table 2: Tax Free Income (Ss360–377)

(1) Casual gambling profits (e.g. pools, horse racing, etc.).
(2) Premium Bond winnings.
(3) Lottery prizes.
(4) Interest on National Savings Certificates.
(5) Bonuses paid at the end of 'save as you earn' contracts.
(6) Maturity bonuses payable on Defence Bonds, British Savings Bonds and National Development Bonds.
(7) Interest on Post-War Credits.
(8) Wedding and certain other presents from your employer that are in truth not given in return for your services as an employee.
(9) Certain retirement gratuities paid by your employer (p 86).
(10) Any scholarship or other educational grant that you receive if you are a full-time student at school, college, etc.
(11) Any grant you receive from your employer solely because you passed an examination or obtained a degree or diploma.
(12) War widows' pensions (prior to 6 April 1979 50% taxable) ; also comparable payments overseas (F2A 1979 S9).
(13) Certain social security benefits including :
    (a) unemployment benefit
    (b) sickness benefit
    (c) maternity benefit and grant
    (d) death grant
    (e) attendance allowance
    (f) child benefit (but not the previous family allowances)
    (g) family income supplement (but retirement pensions under the National Insurance Scheme and family allowances are assessable).
(14) Housing grants paid by local authorities, etc.
(15) German compensation payments to victims of National-Socialist persecution where such amounts are tax exempted by German law.
(16) Wounds and disability pensions.
(17) Allowances, bounties and gratuities paid for additional service in the armed forces.
(18) The capital part of a purchased life annuity (but not the interest portion).
(19) Your first £70 of interest each year from Post Office Savings Bank or Trustee Savings Bank deposits. This £70 exemption from tax applies separately to your wife and yourself. For 1976–77 the exemption was £40.
(20) Allowances paid under job release schemes from 1977 onwards, as described in the Job Release Act 1977.
(21) Compensation for late payments by the Department for National Savings due to industrial action in 1979 (F2A 1979 S17).

Income free of Tax at Basic but not Higher Rates

Any building society interest which you receive is free of basic rate income tax. If your income is sufficiently high however, you will be charged to additional tax on the grossed up equivalent of the interest as if you had suffered tax on it at the basic rate (30%). The additional tax payable consists of higher rate income tax and the investment surcharge (p 25) if applicable on the grossed equivalent of the income, less tax on it at the basic rate. Thus if you receive building society interest of £70 in the year then £100 (the grossed up equivalent) will be included in your total taxable income. The grossed up equivalent is determined by the formula:

Interest received $\times \dfrac{100}{70}$ (100 less 30%)

Year of Assessment

Income tax is an annual tax; thus it is your total income over each twelve month period that is assessed to tax. The year of assessment runs from 6 April to the following 5 April and so the tax year 1979–80 means the year ending 5 April 1980.

The income chargeable to tax for each year of assessment is computed according to the rules relevant to the various Schedules (see Table 1) as described later in this book. Sometimes an 'actual' basis is required in which the income received during a particular year is assessable for that year. Sometimes it is the income of the preceding year of assessment or of the accounting year ending in the preceding year of assessment that is assessed. This 'preceding year basis' is normally used for the profits from trades and vocations, as well as interest assessed under Schedule D.

The year to 5 April also forms the year of assessment for capital gains tax.

Period of Assessment less than Full Year

It is possible for a taxpayer to have a period of assessment of less than twelve months. For example, a baby born during any year has a period of assessment running from the date of his birth until the next 5 April. If a taxpayer dies, his period of assessment runs from 6 April to the date of his death.

Another example of a period of assessment shorter than a year is the case of a woman who is widowed or divorced during the year.

Notwithstanding that the period of assessment may be less than a year, the taxpayer receives the personal reliefs applicable to a whole year of assessment. But see page 8 for the restriction of the married man's personal relief in the year of marriage.

2. Personal Reliefs

According to your circumstances you can claim certain personal tax reliefs which are deducted from your total income in arriving at the amount on which you pay income tax.

Table 3: Your Personal Reliefs at a Glance – 1979-80

Type	Circumstances		Relief	
Personal allowance (p 7)	Married Single		£1,815* £1,165*	
Wife's earnings allowance (p 8)	Wife's earned income		Maximum £1,165*	
		A	*B*	
Children (p 9)	Age under 11 at 6 April in year of assessment	£300	NIL	
	Age 11–15 at 6 April in year of assessment	£335	NIL	
	Age 16 and over and studying	£365	NIL	
	A Certain overseas children and some older students (p 9) *B* Others			
Life assurance relief (p 10)	Policy on your own or wife's life – deduction from premium		17.5% of premiums	
Dependent relatives (p 11)	Incapacitated relative or widowed mother of self or wife		£100	
Housekeeper (p 12)	Claim by widow or widower		£100	
Additional personal allowance for children (p 12)			£650*	
Services of son or daughter (p 13)	You are old and maintain son or daughter who looks after you		£55	
Blind person's allowance (p 13)	Either you or your wife is blind Both you and your wife are blind		£180 £360	

6

Table 3 continued

Age allowance (p 13)	Age 65 or over Single	£1,540*
	Married	£2,455*
	Reduced by £2 for every £3 of excess income over £5,000 down to personal reliefs level	

*Note : These allowances will be increased for future years in line with the retail price index (unless the Treasury otherwise order).

Earned and Unearned Income

For tax purposes income is classified as being either 'earned' or 'unearned'. Earned income is usually taxed on a more favourable basis and includes the following :

(a) The salary or wages from your job including any taxable benefits.
(b) Any pension or retirement annuity paid to you or your wife under a Revenue approved scheme (p 87).
(c) Any income from a trade or profession in which you engage.
(d) Any income from a partnership provided that you work in it and are not merely a sleeping partner.
(e) Family allowances, old age pensions and widow's pensions received under the National Insurance Act.
(f) Income from a patent or copyright if you actually created the subject matter.
(g) After leaving your employment, trade or profession; any taxable amounts that you receive from that source.

The rest of your income is 'unearned' and includes :

(a) Dividends.
(b) Bank deposit interest.
(c) Building society interest received.
(d) Rents from property investments.
(e) Income from trusts.
(f) Interest from government or local authority stock.

Personal Allowance (S8 & F2A 1979 S8)

Single Personal Allowance

If you are 'single', you will get a personal allowance of £1,165. This will apply if you are a widow or widower or are divorced or separated from your husband or wife. If, however, you are separated from your wife but voluntarily wholly maintain her (p 37) you will qualify for the married personal allowance and so neither of you will obtain the single personal allowance.

A married couple will each get only the single allowance if they elect that their earnings should be separately taxed (p 31).

7

PERSONAL RELIEFS

Married Personal Allowance (also p 28)

You will get the full married man's personal allowance of £1,815 if you are married at the start of the tax year. If you are married during the year, however, for every completed month from 6 April until your date of marriage, your relief is reduced by one-twelfth of £650 (£1,815 *less* £1,165). Thus if you marry on 21 October 1979 your relief is £1,815 *less* 6/12ths × £650 = £1,490. You only get this allowance (£1,815) if your wife is living with you or if you are wholly maintaining her by voluntary contributions in the event of your being separated.

Wife's Earned Income Allowance (S8 & F2A 1979 S8)

If your wife works and her earnings are not separately taxed (p 31) you will get this relief comprising her earned income with a maximum of £1,165. Earned income for this purpose includes national insurance pensions where your wife has made her own contributions (but not otherwise).

Any housekeeping money paid to your wife is not taxable but if she works for your business then her wages are allowed as earned income and qualify for the wife's earned income allowance. Provided that her salary is in line with the work done, you will be able to deduct her wages from your taxable business profits.

Child Relief (S10 & FA 1979 S1)

For 1979–80 you will get relief for each of your children as follows:

Age on 6 April 1979	General	Special (p 9)
Under 11	NIL	£300
11 or over but under 16	NIL	£335
16 or over and a full-time student	NIL	£365

Before the introduction of child benefit (p 10), higher child relief generally applied (p 249). Certain special categories of children (p 9) still qualify for relief at the 1976–77 levels.

The following conditions must be satisfied to obtain the relief:

(a) It must be your own child (including a legally adopted or legitimated child or a stepchild). Alternatively, the child must be in your custody and maintained by you.

(b) The child must be under 16 on 6 April 1979 or a full-time student if over 16. If over 16, the child must be studying at school or university, etc. or studying full-time for not less than two years for a profession or trade.

(c) The child's income must be no more than £500 or else the relief will be restricted by £1 for every £1 by which his income exceeds £500. (The 'child's income' includes earnings from holiday jobs etc., and certain investment income.) If the child is under 18 on 5 April 1980 (and not married) only £115 of this £500 can be unearned and any excess causes a restriction.

Because of the introduction of tax free child benefit in place of taxable family allowances (p 10), child relief has now in general ceased. If you do not receive child benefit for certain of your children, however, you might obtain child relief at the 1976–77 rates. This broadly applies to certain older students and children living abroad for whom you are not eligible to claim child benefit.

Children Living Abroad (FA 1977 S25 & FA 1978 S20)

You get child relief for 1979–80 provided the above rules and also the following are satisfied:

(a) Your child is outside the United Kingdom for the whole of 1979–80 (apart from visits totalling no more than 30 days) and does not live in certain specified countries including Australia, Canada, New Zealand, Ireland, Jersey, Isle of Man and the E.E.C.
(b) He or she is under 19 at 5 April 1980.
(c) No child benefit is paid to you for that child during 1979–80.

Child Relief for Students (FA 1977 S26)

Subject to the following additional rules, you will obtain child relief at the 1976–77 rates for 1977–78 and the next three tax years. This applies to any child who on 31 December 1976 was following a full-time course at a university, college, school or other educational establishment who is:

(a) Over 19 on 31 December 1976 or following an 'advanced course' (broadly above advanced level or its equivalent) at that date, and
(b) following an 'advanced course' in an academic year beginning in the tax year in question, and
(c) getting no grant or a full grant but not one partially reduced because of the level of your income.

Example 1: Child Relief – 1978-79

Mr A has 3 sons, B, C and D (who live in the United Kingdom). Their respective ages on 6 April 1978 are 4, 12 and 17. Their incomes are B £50, C £200 (unearned) and D £545. D is still at school. Mr A gets child relief as follows for *1978–79*:

B	£100
C £135 – (£200 – £115)	50
D £165 – (£545 – £500)	120
	———
Total relief	£270

Note: D will be 18 by 5 April 1979 and so gets the full £500 margin whether his income is earned or unearned.

Child Benefit and Family Allowances
(S24, FA 1974 S14 & FA 1977 S23)

For all children except the first you obtained social security family allowance prior to 4 April 1977. This applied to children under 19 who received full-time education and all children under 16. The rate was 150p weekly for each child apart from the first.

The family allowances were taxed as part of your earned income. Also your total tax reliefs were reduced by £52 for each child for whom you received the family allowance.

On 4 April 1977 the family allowance was replaced by child benefit at the rate of £1 weekly for your first child and £1.50 for each of the others satisfying the relevant rules. From April 1978, a single rate of £2.30 operated, which has been increased to £3 in November 1978 and £4 in April 1979.

Although high rate tax payers saved money by not claiming family allowances, this does not apply to child benefit, because it is *tax free*.

Life Assurance Relief
(Ss 19–21 & Sch 1, FA 1975 Sch 2 & FA 1976 S34 & Sch 4 & FA 1978 Sch 3)

Tax relief in respect of life assurance is given based on the premiums paid in the tax year. You now normally deduct the relief from your premium payments (see below).

Table 4: Rules for Life Assurance Relief

(a) The policy benefits must include a sum payable on death or in certain circumstances provide for a deferred annuity.

(b) The policy must be effected with a United Kingdom, Dominion or Irish insurance company or one carrying on business here; or a Lloyds Underwriter; or a registered friendly society.

(c) The policy must be on your own or your wife's life and either of you may pay the premiums. (If, however, you had elected that your wife's earnings should be taxed separately (p 31) neither of you obtained relief for any premiums paid on policies on the other's life up to 5 April 1979.)

(d) Special rules related to policies taken out up to 22 June 1916. For premiums paid before 6 April 1979 only, relief was given according to your income level by deducting the following percentages of the premiums from your tax bill:

Total Income	% Relief
Not over £1,000	half of basic rate of income tax.
£1,001–£2,000	three-quarters of basic rate.
over £2,000	basic rate of income tax.

(e) Special relief is still given for sums paid under an Act of Parliament or under the rules of your employment to secure a deferred annuity for your widow or children after your death. The relief is as shown in (d) above.

Table 4 continued

(f) New policies taken out after 19 March 1968 or old policies changed after that date have to be 'qualifying policies' (p 207).

(g) Subject to the restriction in (h) below, the following relief was deducted from your total tax bill for premiums paid prior to 6 April 1979 :
   (i) If your total premiums were between £10 and £20 then your relief was £10 at the basic tax rate.
   (ii) If your total premiums were under £10 then your relief was equal to your total premiums at the basic rate.
   (iii) If your total premiums exceeded £20 then your relief was your total premiums at half of the basic rate of income tax.

(h) Prior to 6 April 1979 your total income (after annual charges) needed to be at least six times as much as your total life assurance premiums during the year — otherwise your relief was restricted by using 1/6th of your total income instead of your actual premiums.

(i) After 5 April 1979 under the new system of relief for life assurance premiums, broadly 17.5% of each premium is deducted by you on payment and you keep this relief. The premium limit is the larger of 1/6th of your total income (after charges) and £1,500. Any over-deduction by you will be adjusted in your assessment at the end of the tax year or you may be directed by the Revenue to pay premiums without the deduction of tax relief.

Example 2: Life Assurance Relief Restrictions for 1979-80

Policy A — Capital sum £10,000 Premium	£1,000
Policy B — Capital sum £20,000 Premium	1,500
	£2,500

But total income for year = £12,000
Therefore premium restricted to
1/6th × £12,000   = £2,000

Life assurance relief for year = £350 (17.5% × £2,000)

Note: Normally the proceeds of qualifying policies are tax free. The profit element of the proceeds of non-qualifying policies may be liable to tax however (p 208).

Dependent Relative Relief
(S16, FA 1971 S33 & FA 1973 S12)

(a) You get this relief for each of your own or your wife's relatives whom you maintain. The relative must either be incapacitated by old age or infirmity or be your own or your wife's widowed, divorced or separated mother.

(b) The relief is normally £100 for each relative.

11

(c)   If the relative's own income exceeds the basic retirement pension, your relief is reduced by £1 for each £1 of the excess. Thus if the relative's income is more than £100 in excess of the basic pension you get no relief.

(d)   If you are a woman, your relief for each dependent relative is increased to £145. This means that if the relative's income is more than £145 in excess of the basic pension you get no relief. This does not apply if you are married and living with your husband.

(e)   Where two or more people maintain a dependent relative, the relief is split between them in proportion to their payments for the relative's keep.

Housekeeper Relief
(S12 & FA 1971 S33 & FA 1978 S19)

You get £100 relief if you are a widow or widower and you have a relative staying with you as your housekeeper. (Prior to 1978-79 this only applied to female relatives.) Alternatively, you get the relief if you employ a housekeeper who is not a relative. If the housekeeper is your relative and is married however, you do not get the relief if her husband is getting the £1,815 married man's personal allowance. From 1978-79, this relief extends to males.

Person looking after Children
(S13, FA 1971 S33 & F2A 1979 S8 & Sch 1)

(a)   Prior to 1979–80 if you had any brothers and sisters living with you and you maintained a relative to look after them, you got relief of £100 each year.

(b)   For 1978-79 this relief was available in respect of the services of male or female relatives, but for earlier years, only females.

(c)   You only got £100 relief no matter how many children resided with you.

(d)   The child or children needed to qualify for child relief.

(e)   You did not get this relief if you were getting the additional personal relief for children which is described next.

(f)   This relief does not apply for 1979-80 or later years.

Additional Personal Relief for Children
(S14 & F2A 1979 S8 & Sch1)

(a)   This relief of £650 each year applies to widows, widowers and others not entitled to married personal allowance. You also get it if you are married but your wife is totally incapacitated for the year.

(b)   Before 1979–80, this relief was only available to you if you were entitled to child relief or only lost this because the child had too much income.

(c)   For 1979–80 and future years, the link with child relief no longer applies but there must be at least one child who fulfills requirements (a) and (b) but not (c) on page 8. Further, even if the child is not your own, the custody requirement does not apply.

(d)   You only get £650 relief no matter how many children reside with you.

Son's or Daughter's Services
(S17 & FA 1971 S33 & FA 1978 S19)

If you are aged or infirm and so have to depend on the services of a son or daughter you get this relief of £55 each year. The son or daughter must live with you and you must maintain him or her. Before 1978–79, this relief only covered daughters.

Blind Person's Relief
(S18 & F2A 1975 S30 & FA 1978 S19)

(a)   The relief is given to registered blind persons.
(b)   The relief is £180 for a single person or for one of the partners to a marriage.
(c)   If both husband and wife are blind then the relief is £360.
(d)   If tax free blindness disability pension is received, the relief is reduced by that pension.
(e)   Anyone who also qualifies for daughter's services relief (£55) must disclaim it or else he will not be allowed blind person's relief.

Age Allowance (F2A 1975 S31 & F2A 1979 S8)

(a)   This applies for 1979–80 if either you or your wife is over 65 by 5 April 1980.
(b)   If you are single, your personal relief (p 7) is increased to £1,540.
(c)   If you are married, your personal relief (p 8) is increased to £2,455.
(d)   The above allowance figures are restricted if your combined incomes exceed £5,000. The restriction is two-thirds of the excess of your incomes over £5,000. (This figure was £3,250 for 1976–77 and earlier years, £3,500 for 1977–78 and £4,000 for 1978–79.) Thus if your income is £5,300 and you are not married, your allowance is restricted to £1,540 – £200 = £1,340. If you are married and your combined income is £5,600, your age allowance is £2,455 – £400 = £2,055.
(e)   If your income is sufficiently high, your personal relief is restricted to the normal £1,165 (single) or £1,815 (married) rate; but not below this.

Indexation of Personal Reliefs (FA 1977 S22)

For 1980–81 and subsequent years, certain personal reliefs are to be increased from their 1979–80 levels by not less than the proportionate increase in the retail index for the previous calendar year. With Parliamentary approval, however, a lower increase may be ordered by the Treasury.

The reliefs concerned are single personal allowance (£1,165),

PERSONAL RELIEFS

married personal allowance (£1,815), wife's earnings allowance (£1,165), additional personal allowance for children (£650), single age allowance (£1,540) and married age allowance (£2,455).

Example 3: Personal Reliefs — General Illustration

Mr A lives with his family at 1 Bridge Street. The family are:

Name	Age on 6.4.79	Income Assessable for 1979–80 Earned	Unearned
Mr A	45	£3,500	£4,000
Mrs A	42	2,400	500
Mrs F (the widowed mother of Mrs A maintained by Mrs A)	63	—	300
Children:			
B	10	—	—
C	14	50	—
D (at Oxford University since October 1976 on no grant)	21	545	—

Mr A pays £500 interest during 1979–80 on a mortgage of 1 Bridge Street. The mortgage was arranged to purchase the house and so the interest is wholly allowable. Mrs A pays an annual premium of £200 on a qualifying life assurance policy on Mr A's life. How much income tax is payable by Mr A for 1979–80?

1979–80

Earned income	Mr A	£3,500	
	Mrs A	2,400	
		———	£5,900
Unearned income	Mr A	4,000	
	Mrs A	500	
		———	4,500
			£10,400
Less: Mortgage interest			500
Total income			£9,900

Less:

Personal allowance	£1,815	
Wife's earned income allowance	1,165	
Child relief		
D 365 – (545 – 500)	320	
Dependent relative relief (unrestricted)	100	
	———	£3,400
		£6,500

14

Example 3 continued

Income tax payable (p 20) £1,500 at 25%   375.00
                   5,000 at 30% 1,500.00
                                   ———   £1,875.00

Notes: (a) On the levels of income shown above Mr A is not liable to higher rates (p 22) or investment surcharge (p 25).
(b) Life assurance relief of 17.5% × £200 = £35 normally will be obtained by deduction from the premium payment each year.

3. Annual Payments and Interest

Annual Payments apart from Interest (Ss52 & 53)

If you make an annual payment it is normally considered for tax purposes as being the income of the recipient and is usually subject to income tax at the basic rate (30%) by deduction at source. You should therefore deduct this tax in making each payment. You will be allowed to retain all of the tax deducted provided that your income taxed at the basic or higher rates is sufficient to cover the amount of the payment. For example if you have suffered basic rate income tax of £200 in the tax year and you made an annual payment of £100 you deduct tax from the latter amounting to £30. You thus pay only £70 when making your annual payment. Your effective income tax bill is £200—£30 = £170. If, however, your taxed income is less than your annual payments you will have to pay to the Revenue income tax at 30% on the difference. So if your taxed income is nil in any tax year, you will have to account to the Revenue for basic rate income tax on your entire annual payments for that year. The result of this procedure is to give you basic rate income tax relief on your annual payments provided your income taxable at the basic rate exceeds those payments.

If any part of your annual payments is covered by the new 25% lower rate band (p 22), your relief is restricted to this rate and so you will pay to the Revenue income tax at 5% (30%—25%) on the appropriate part.

Under certain circumstances relief is available for tax at the higher rates as well as the basic rate.

Examples are as follows:

(a) Annual payments under court orders for maintenance or alimony (p 37).

(b) Annual payments under deeds of covenant to individuals that were entered into before 7 April 1965, such individuals not including your infant children (p 17).

(c) Certain annual payments under partnership agreements to retiring partners or their widows.

(d) Certain annual payments which you make in connection with the purchase of a business where the payments are made to the former owner of the business or his widow or dependants.

What are Annual Payments?

(a) Examples of annual payments are annuities, alimony payments, maintenance payments to your divorced or separated wife, payments under deeds of covenant and certain interest payments which are subject to special tax rules (p 17).

(b) They are normally paid under a binding legal obligation such as a contract or deed of covenant.

16

(c)   The payments must be recurrent although repeated gifts (unless under covenant) are not annual payments.

(d)   In the hands of the recipient an annual payment must neither form part of his trading profits nor consist of a payment for services rendered.

(e)   Payments consisting of instalments of capital are not annual payments for tax purposes. In the case of life annuities however each payment is split between an income element (which is treated as an annual payment) and a capital element which is tax free.

Deeds of Covenant

This class of annual payments is very popular and can be used to great advantage in making regular payments to charities and individuals with low incomes. The deed must be properly drawn up – most charities have prepared forms for covenanted donations – otherwise seek professional advice.

The deed must provide for payments at annual or more frequent intervals for a period capable of exceeding six years (or until your death if earlier). You will then be required to deduct income tax at 30% from each payment according to the rules for annual payments (p 16). This does not apply to payments made by you under deed of covenant to any of your children who are less than eighteen years of age and unmarried – these payments are disregarded for tax purposes.

If any of your children are eighteen or over, it may be beneficial from a tax viewpoint to enter into deeds of covenant in their favour. This is particularly useful in the case of students. The £500 income rule (p 8) should be considered, however, since if the child's income exceeds this amount you will partially or completely lose child relief, if, in fact, you had been obtaining this.

Payments to individuals under deeds of covenant entered into before 7 April 1965 are allowable deductions for higher rate tax. Any such payments that you make to charities however are not deductible from your total income for higher rate tax purposes.

An approved charity (p 113) is able to reclaim the basic rate income tax that you deducted in making a payment to it under a deed of covenant. This also applies in the case of an individual whose income (including gross payments to him under deeds of covenant) is too low for him to pay any income tax. Thus if you covenant to pay a charity £100 gross each year, you will deduct income tax at the basic rate (30%) and only pay £70. The charity will then reclaim the income tax amounting to £30. The charity thus gets a total of £100 each year. Even if the basic rate of income tax is changed, the charity will still get a total of £100 each year from your payment.

Interest Payments (S54 & FA 1972 S75)

Subject to the following, you must not deduct income tax from any payments of interest that you make. This means that nearly all interest payments made by you personally will be gross without any tax deduction.

If you pay 'annual interest' to anyone who lives outside the United Kingdom (unless you get permission to pay gross under a double tax agreement) you must deduct income tax at the basic rate (30%) in making the payment.

If however you pay 'annual interest' in this country on an advance from an overseas bank carrying on business in the United Kingdom, you should not deduct income tax.

'Annual interest' is interest paid on a loan which is capable of continuing for a period exceeding one year. If at the start of a loan, you agree that it should last for a stated period of less than one year then any interest arising will not be 'annual interest'.

Companies and local authorities must normally deduct income tax in making 'annual interest' payments and this applies to a partnership of which a company is a member. Interest paid by a bank in the normal course of its business however is normally paid without any deduction for income tax even if the payments are made to persons living outside this country.

Subject to the rules which are outlined in the following pages, certain interest payments are allowed as deductions from your total income for income tax at basic and higher rates. (Also see p 216 for loans to pay life policy premiums.)

Prior to April 1969, relief was available in respect of most forms of interest payments. In the period from *April 1969 to 5 April 1972*, interest relief was only available subject to specific rules, in respect of interest payments on loans for certain 'qualifying purposes'. These included purchases of land, buildings plant, partnership interests and close companies, etc.

For the period from *6 April 1972 to 26 March 1974* you were entitled to relief provided you made the required claim (normally by entering the details in your tax return). You got relief for:

Annual interest, and interest paid to banks, stockbrokers and discount houses carrying on business in this country.

You got no relief for the first £35 of interest apart from 'protected interest' paid each year. This consisted of interest on loans for the purchase and improvement of buildings and land in the United Kingdom or Eire; and interest on loans for the purchase of plant and machinery for use in partnerships or employment. Bank overdraft interest however was not classified as 'protected interest'.

Interest Paid for Business Purposes

Note that interest paid for business purposes is allowable against your taxable business profits provided the loan is used wholly and exclusively for the purposes of your business, profession or vocation. This basic rule applies to interest paid both before and after 26 March 1974 and includes interest on bank overdrafts as well as that on other loans.

Rules for Interest Payments after 26 March 1974
(FA 1974 S19 & Sch 1)

Subject to transitional relief (p 20) in order to obtain relief for interest paid after 26 March 1974 you must show that it is 'eligible for relief'. This term is used in place of 'protected interest' (see previous page). It specifically excludes bank overdraft or credit card interest.

Table 5: Tax Relief for Interest Payments

Your interest is 'eligible for relief' if it is paid on loans raised for the following purposes:

(1)   Subject to various restrictions, the purchase and improvement of buildings and land in the United Kingdom or Eire (p 19).
(2)   Buying plant and machinery for use in a partnership which gets capital allowances on it, where you are one of the partners.
(3)   Buying plant and machinery (e.g. a motor car) which is used in connection with an office or employment that you hold and for which you personally get capital allowances.
(4)   Acquiring ordinary shares in a close company (p 180) or lending it money for use in its business if you own more than 5% of its shares. (This does not apply to a close investment company.) You must work for the greater part of your time for the company.
(5)   Purchasing a share in a partnership, or lending it money for use in its business.
(6)   Paying capital transfer tax arising on death or estate duty. The personal representatives of the deceased obtain relief for interest paid within a year of raising the loan. If the interest cannot be relieved wholly in the year of payment it can be spread forward or backwards.

Note: Relief for interest on loans to purchase plant and machinery (see (2) and (3) above) is given for three years after the year of assessment in which the loan is taken out.

Loans for Purchase and Improvement of Buildings and Land
(FA 1972 Sch 9, FA 1974 S19 & Sch 1 & FA 1977 S36)

Within the limits mentioned below, any interest which you pay on a loan raised to buy land or buildings, or to improve them, is 'eligible for relief'. This does not include overdraft interest but covers fixed bank loans and Building Society mortgages, etc. When you pay the interest you must still own the property. The interest on any loan that you raise to pay off another loan previously obtained to buy or improve property is also 'eligible for relief'.
'Property improvements' include:

Central heating installations.

Garages and garden sheds.
Garden construction and landscaping.
Double glazing installations.
Plumbing improvements (excluding maintenance).
Conversions of houses into flats.
Construction of swimming pools, tennis courts, etc.

If however you merely carry out repairs to existing property without improving it then any loan interest incurred will not normally be treated as 'eligible for relief'.

The Revenue gives sympathetic consideration to cases where for example the husband buys the property and the wife pays the interest – the couple would usually get tax relief.

If you elect to make your mortgage payments under the 'option mortgage scheme' then your rate of interest will be reduced but you will get no tax relief for the interest paid.

Concerning a new property loan raised after 26 March 1974, you only obtain tax relief if either (a) it is to purchase or improve your only or main residence or (b) you let the property at a commercial rent for at least 26 weeks in the year and it is available for letting at other times.

Under (a) your interest is restricted to that on a loan of £25,000 and if your borrowing exceeds this figure your interest relief is proportionately reduced. You also get relief for interest on a loan which you obtain to buy a house for a former or separated spouse, or a dependant relative of your wife or yourself. A dependant relative is broadly an elderly or infirm relative; also your widowed, divorced or separated mother. This interest counts however towards the £25,000 limit. You also obtain relief for interest on a bridging loan of up to £25,000 for normally up to one year when you change houses.

For interest paid after 5 April 1977, your relief is not restricted because you do not reside in your property, if you live in job-related accommodation (p 81) and intend to make your property your main residence in due course (FA 1977 S36).

Under (b) you are only allowed interest relief against your income from letting property.

Rules for Transitional Interest Relief
(FA 1974 S19 & F2A 1979 S10)

If you pay interest under an obligation entered into before 27 March 1974, you still get tax relief as follows:

(a)   If you had an overdraft or credit card arrangement you got relief for interest paid before 6 April 1975, provided it was due for payment. This relief was restricted however to the interest which would have been paid up to that date on a loan equal to your debit balance at 26 March 1974, at the then prevailing rate.

(b)   If before 6 April 1975 you replaced by a loan an overdraft which existed at 26 March 1974 you will continue to get some interest relief up to 5 April 1982. This relief is restricted to interest on the balance of the overdraft at 26 March 1974.

(c) For loans apart from overdrafts and credit card arrangements, you will get relief for all interest which is payable before 6 April 1982.

(d) Even if you had not taken out a mortgage by 26 March 1974 if you contracted to do so by that date, and also contracted to buy a house, you will get full interest relief until 5 April 1982. This applies even if it is not your main residence.

(e) If you get transitional relief on a loan which you obtained to buy or improve a property this is counted against the £25,000 maximum for loans obtained after 26 March 1974 on which you get relief. This even applies if the old loan is not for your main residence.

(f) Originally, transitional relief applied up to 5 April 1980, but this was extended for two years by F2A 1979 S10.

4. The Unified System of Personal Taxation

Your 'total income' (see below) less your allowances for the tax year (p 6) will be subjected to income tax at the basic and other rates according to the following table:

Table 6: Basic and Higher Rates for 1979-80

Slice of income	Rate	Total income (after allowances)	Total tax
£750 (£0–750)	25%	£750	£187.50
9,250 (750–10,000)	30%	10,000	2,962.50
2,000 (10–12,000)	40%	12,000	3,762.50
3,000 (12–15,000)	45%	15,000	5,112.50
5,000 (15–20,000)	50%	20,000	7,612.50
5,000 (20–25,000)	55%	25,000	10,362.50
Remainder	60%		

Note: If you have over £5,000 of investment income, it is normally subjected to 15% surcharge. The top investment income rate is thus 60%+15% = 75%.

Lower Rate of Income Tax (FA 1978 S14 & Sch 2)

For 1978-79 and subsequent years, the first £750 of your taxable income is subjected to a lower rate of income tax of 25%.

Any earned income of your wife, after her wife's earned income allowance (p 8) also qualifies for the 25% rate on the first £750. (This broadly applies whether or not an election is made for the separate taxation of her earnings.) Where £750 of your wife's income attracts the 25% rate, however, your 30% rate band is reduced from £9,250 to £8,500.

What is Total Income? (S528 & FA 1971 Sch 6(78))

Your total income comprises your income for the tax year less specified deductions (p 24). The following classes of income will be included for each tax year:

(a) Income as assessed for the tax year under the following schedules:

THE UNIFIED SYSTEM OF PERSONAL TAXATION

(b) The gross income actually paid to you in the tax year under the deduction of basic rate income tax (30%) at the source. This will include income taxed at source under Schedules C and F. You will receive the net amount after suffering basic rate income tax (30%) but you will pay higher rates of tax if appropriate on the gross amount. You will obtain a tax credit for the basic rate tax suffered at source which will be deducted from your tax bill. The following would come within this category:

> The income portion of annuities.
> Interest on certain investments.
> Alimony and maintenance payments under court order (p 37).
> Any annual payments which you receive (p 16).

(c) Income distributions from discretionary and accumulating settlements (p 167). Net payments made to you must be grossed up at 45% and carry with them a tax credit of this amount which represents basic rate income tax (30%) and additional rate tax (15%) effectively suffered by the settlement. Thus if you receive £55 this is included in your total income together with a tax credit of £45.

(d) Dividends received together with the relevant tax credits. Your dividends from United Kingdom companies carry with them tax credits of 3/7ths of the actual payments. Thus if you receive a dividend of £70 during the tax year, this is included in your total income together with the tax credit of £30 (£70 × 3/7ths).

(e) Your gross income taxed at source under PAYE (p. 90). This consists of your salary, etc., derived from your employment; it is subjected to lower rate, basic rate and higher rate income tax at source. No additional rate (p 25) is payable because the income in question is all earned. The tax suffered at source is naturally deducted from the tax bill on your total income.

(f) The grossed up equivalent of any building society interest received. This income is paid free of basic rate income tax but must be included in your total income as if such tax had been deducted at source. You must thus gross it up by multiplying the income received by $\frac{100}{100-30}$ (i.e. $\frac{100}{70}$). You obtain a credit for the notional tax. For example if you receive £70 building society interest, your total income will include $£70 \times \dfrac{100}{70} = £100$ and you obtain a notional tax credit of £30. This credit is not repayable but effectively exempts you from the first 30% of tax on the grossed interest.

Total Income – Deductions

As well as normal business expenses, etc., which are deducted in arriving at the various income tax assessments, the following are deductible:

(a) Loan interest subject to the relevant rules (p 17). As previously mentioned however, since 26 March 1974, tax relief for loan interest payments has been much reduced in scope.

(b) Business losses and capital allowances.

(c) Annual payments under court orders for maintenance or alimony (p 37).

(d) Annual payments under deeds of covenant to individuals that were entered into before 7 April 1965, such individuals not including your infant children (p 17).

(e) Certain annual payments under partnership agreements to retiring partners or their widows.

(f) Certain annual payments which you make in connection with the purchase of a business where the payments are made to the former owner of the business or his widow or dependants.

(g) Allowable retirement annuity premiums (p 216).

(h) A proportion of certain transfers to reserves made by underwriters at Lloyds or other approved underwriters.

(i) Personal reliefs and allowances (see Chapter 2). (These are strictly speaking deductions which are made from your total income rather than in its computation.)

Charges on Income (FA 1971 S33(5))

The annual payments mentioned above (c–f) as well as various other charges on income (p 16) are paid under the deduction of basic rate income tax (30%). To the extent that your income less allowances is not sufficient to cover your annual charges payments, your personal allowances, etc., must be restricted.

Thus, if your income for 1979–80 is £2,200 and your personal allowances and reliefs total £1,200, you can pay up to £1,000 annual charges without restriction. The £1,000 is paid by you under deduction of basic rate income tax. Thus you actually pay only £1,000 − 30% × £1,000 = £700. You also pay to the Revenue tax at 30% on £1,000 = £300. In these circumstances you would lose the effective benefit of the lower (25%) tax band. If your annual charges were £1,200, your total reliefs would be reduced to £1,000 so that your taxable income after allowances (£1,200) would be sufficient to cover your charges.

The basic rate tax which you deduct from your annual payments must effectively be paid over to the Revenue. This is done by paying basic rate tax on that part of your income which is equal to such annual payments. Where however the payments in question are allowed as deductions in computing your total income (e.g. c–f above) you get relief for the excess of your higher rate tax over basic rate tax on income covered by those charges.

Thus, if your top rate is 60% and you pay gross alimony of £2,000 during 1979–80 you will pay £2,000–30% × £2,000 = £1,400 to your ex-wife. You will deduct £2,000 in arriving at your total income for 1979–80 and thus get relief for this at 60%, i.e. £1,200. You will however be required to pay to the Revenue basic rate tax at 30% × £2,000 = £600. What is really happening is that you are obtaining relief at 30% when you pay your ex-wife and 30% (60%–30%) when your own tax liability is settled.

Deductions from Tax Payable

When your total tax liability is computed certain deductions from the tax payable must be made, either because you have already paid part of it or because of special reliefs. These deductions include the following:

(a) Life assurance relief (p 10). Normally 17½% of your qualifying premiums (p 207) (subject to the various rules) is deductible from your tax payable. After 5 April 1979, you normally obtain this relief by deducting 17.5% from each premium payment.

(b) 3/7ths of your building society interest received (p 53). This notional basic rate tax is not repayable but you deduct it from your total tax bill.

(c) Tax credits on dividends received (p 48). The tax credit is 3/7ths of each dividend received.

(d) Tax paid under PAYE (p 90).

(e) Basic rate tax deducted at the source on certain investment interest paid to you (such as on company debentures).

(f) Basic rate tax deducted from annual payments made to you during the year which are included in your total income.

(g) Tax at the basic rate (30%) and the additional rate (15%) on income distributions made to you during the tax year by discretionary settlements (p 167). The tax is computed on the gross equivalent of the distributions.

Investment Income Surcharge (Additional Rate)
(FA 1971 Ss32 & 34, FA 1974 S15 & F2A 1979 S5)

For 1979–80 you will be charged an additional rate of 15% on so much of your investment income as exceeds £5,000. The 10% rate which applied to a limited band of investment income up to 5 April 1979 has been removed, as has the different threshold for those over 65 (p 250).

THE UNIFIED SYSTEM OF PERSONAL TAXATION

Your investment income is sometimes referred to as unearned income (p 7) and for the purposes of ascertaining the amount which is charged to the additional rates, the following rules are applied:

(a) Deduct all charges on income (p 16) including interest, in the order which produces the lowest tax charge on your income. This would normally be first from your investment income, apart from building society interest.

(b) Deduct your personal reliefs and allowances (p 6) first from your earned income (p 7) and then from your investment income.

(c) Any of your personal reliefs and allowances which in accordance with (b) above are set against your investment income first go against the part which is free of the additional rates and then against the balance. With the higher (£5,000) free band which applies from 6 April 1979, however, this rule is now most unlikely to produce any benefit.

(d) If you are a divorced or separated wife, the first £1,500 of maintenance payments which you received for 1977–78 was not regarded as investment income. (Before 6.4.77, this figure was £1,000.) After 5 April 1978, however, such maintenance is completely exempted from investment income surcharge.

Certain discretionary and accumulating settlements (p 167) are also subjected to the additional rate (15%). In this case however the charge is made on both investment and earned income including the first £5,000. Higher rate tax is not normally charged on the trust income however unless it is distributed to beneficiaries who are themselves liable to higher rates of tax. (See Chapter 17, p 150, for fuller details.)

Example 4: Computation of Investment Income Liable to Additional Rate

Mr A, who is under 65, has the following income assessable for 1979–80:

Earned income		£5,000
Investment income:		
Bank deposit interest	£2,500	
Dividends – received	4,200	
– tax credits	1,800	
	———	
		8,500

During 1979–80 Mr A pays £800 of mortgage interest on his house and gross alimony of £1,000 to his ex-wife. He has personal reliefs and allowances amounting to £1,200. How much additional rate tax does Mr A pay for 1979–80?

Example 4 continued

Mr A 1979–80	Earned income		Unearned income
Income	£5,000		£8,500
Less:			
Mortgage interest		800	
Alimony		1,000	
		——	1,800
Personal reliefs	1,200		
Taxable income	£3,800		£6,700
Less: Free band			5,000
Investment income liable to additional rate			£1,700
Additional rate payable at:			
15% on £1,700			£255

Example 5: Unified Income Tax Computation

Mr B has his own business from which his assessable profit for 1979–80 is £8,835. His other income for 1979–80 consists of £700 building society interest and £4,200 dividends received (tax credits £1,800). His wife's only income consists of £350 building society interest. He pays £1,500 interest on a mortgage for the purchase of his house. From the above particulars, compute Mr B's income tax liability.

Mr B – Income tax computation for 1979–80

Earned income – business assessment			£8,835
Investment income – Building Society interest:			
Mr B		£700	
Mrs B		350	
		£1,050	
Add: Notional basic rate tax			
£1,050 × 3/7ths		450	
		£1,500	
Dividends, Mr B		4,200	
Add: Tax Credit		1,800	
		——	7,500
			£16,335
Less: Mortgage interest			1,500
Total income before personal reliefs and allowances			£14,835

Example 5 continued

Less: Personal allowance	1,815
Taxable balance	£13,020

Tax payable:

£750 at 25%	£187.50
9,250 at 30%	2,775.00
2,000 at 40%	800.00
1,020 at 45%	459.00
£13,020	4,221.50

Additional rate: 15% × (£7,500 − £1,500 − £5,000)	150.00
Total Tax	4,371.50

Less: Tax credit on dividends	£1,800	
Notional credit on building society interest	450	2,250.00
Net further tax payable		£2,121.50

The Assessment and Payment of your Income Tax
(Ss3 & 4, FA 1971 Sch 6(3) & F2A 1975 Ss44 & 45)

This matter is considered in Chapter 17 (p 150). As a general rule you must pay income tax at the basic and higher rates (including the additional rate) by 1 January in the year for which the income is assessed, if the income has not already been taxed. If, however, your assessment based on the income has not been agreed in time, then you are due to pay the tax normally 30 days after the assessment is issued. Special rules apply where you appeal (p 156).

An exception to the above rule concerns your tax on business profits (p 55) which is payable in two equal instalments on 1 January in the year of assessment and the following 1 July.

Tax at higher rates including the additional rate is due for payment by 6 July following the year of assessment on any income which has already been taxed. This includes income treated as notionally taxed like building society interest as well as dividends, etc. If the assessment is not agreed by 6 June following the year of assessment, you are due to pay the tax no earlier than 30 days after the date of issue, special rules applying if you appeal (p 156).

Interest on Overdue Tax
(T.M.A. S86, FA 1971 Sch 6(86) & F2A 1975 S46)

If you are late in paying your income tax you may be charged interest at the rate of 6% for the entire period that payment is overdue prior to 1 July 1974 and 9% after that date. This interest is not deductible for income tax purposes. The exact rules are given later (p 161).

Interest is also charged according to the above rules on overdue basic rate tax payable under Schedules A and D (p 161).

Fluctuating Income

Because of the graduated nature of income tax rates, if your income greatly fluctuates from year to year you may find that your tax liability is high in some years and low in others. The result is that your total income tax over the years is more than it would have been had your income been spread evenly over those years. Certain special rules exist which have the effect of spreading lump sums of income over the period during which they have been earned. For example, lump sum payments received for the copyright, etc., of artistic works may be taxed as if spread over up to three years, depending on the time taken to produce the work (p 114).

So-called 'top slicing' relief is obtained when you receive certain large taxable sums in one tax year. You may effectively spread these sums over a stated period and recompute your tax liability on the basis that the income had been paid in this way. (The tax is payable for the year when you receive the income but the rate is normally lower.) What you do is to divide the lump sum (L) by the stated period (P) and calculate the tax payable (T) for the year on your other income plus L/P. You then calculate the tax payable on your other income by itself and deduct it from (T). This gives the tax payable on (L/P) and this tax is multiplied by P to give the total tax payable on (L).

Particular examples of receipts to which 'top slicing' would apply are compensation for loss of office payments and the profit elements in the proceeds of non-qualifying life assurance policies (p 208). Such policy proceeds are taxed at the excess of higher rate income tax and additional rate tax over income tax at the basic rate, subject to the relief outlined above.

5. Husband, Wife and Children

When You Marry

As a married person you will be taxed not only on your own income but also normally on that of your wife. If you marry after 6 April 1976, you will not be taxed however, on your wife's income for the tax year during which you marry. You will obtain personal relief at a higher rate (£1,815) than a single person (£1,165) (p 7). If your wife is working then against her earnings will be set her (wife's) earned income relief (maximum £1,165).

At the end of the year in which you marry both you and your wife will have to complete an income tax return.

Your Wife's Return

If the date of your marriage was before 6 April 1976, your wife's return covered the period before your marriage, i.e. from 6 April to the date of your marriage. She was taxed on her income for this period as a single person and so she obtained single personal allowance.

In the year of your marriage (after 6 April 1976) your wife obtains her own personal relief (£1,165) but no wife's earned income relief (p 8).

Your Own Return

Your own return on the other hand, will cover the full tax year and you must include:

(a)   Your own income for the year, and
(b)   Your wife's income from the date of your marriage to 5 April, only if the date of your marriage was before 6 April 1976.

Even though you were single for part of the year you will be taxed as a married person for the whole of that year. But your personal allowance is restricted by £54.17, for every completed month during that tax year prior to your date of marriage (p 8), provided your marriage is after 5 April 1979.

Separate Assessment
(Ss38 & 39 & FA 1971 Sch 6 (18 & 19))

Despite the fact that it is the husband who is taxed on both his own and his wife's income, it is nevertheless possible for a married couple to be assessed separately and to pay their respective shares of tax separately.

Separate assessment is not the same as the separate taxation of your wife's earned income (p 31) under which your wife is taxed separately on her earnings as if she were a single person. Separate assessment merely has the effect of apportioning to your wife her share of the total income tax bill so that you each pay your own share according to your own income.

The tax which you each pay is calculated by taking the total tax payable on your combined incomes at the lower, basic, higher and additional rates. This is then apportioned between your wife and yourself in the ratio of your incomes. You then deduct from the tax share of each the tax equivalent of the personal reliefs attributable to you and your wife. The tax equivalent of the personal reliefs is found by calculating tax on them at your top rate(s). Your personal reliefs are split between you and your wife according to the following rules:

(a) Life assurance relief is given to the payer of the premiums.
(b) Relief for children not of the marriage and dependent relatives goes to the one who maintains them and could be apportioned if appropriate.
(c) The remaining allowances are split in the ratio of the tax on your incomes before allowances. This includes allowances for your own children.
(d) The allowances allocated to your wife must not be less than the £1,165 additional personal relief.
(e) If your wife's allocation of allowances exceeds her taxable income then you get the benefit of her excess allowances and vice versa.

In order to be assessed separately for a tax year you or your wife simply have to make application to your Inspector of Taxes within six months before 5 July in that tax year. You will then both be separately assessed for that year and subsequent years until you or your wife give notice of revocation to the Inspector of Taxes. (Separate assessment can also be required by the Inland Revenue if the husband does not pay his tax promptly.)

If you are being assessed separately the total tax payable by you and your wife will be exactly the same as if you had been assessed in the normal way. Since there is no tax advantage to be gained you should only apply for separate assessment if you consider it convenient. Your application should be made in good time, pre-ferably before you receive your tax return. On approval of your application, you and your wife will each receive a return for completion. You should *not* include her income with yours as would normally be necessary.

Separate Taxation of Wife's Earnings
(FA 1971 S23 & Sch 4 & FA 1976 S36)

If you and your wife jointly make the required election then she will be taxed separately on her 'earnings' as if she were a single person. You will then be taxed on the balance of your joint incomes (including your wife's unearned income) as if you also were single.

The necessary joint election must be made not earlier than six months before the start of the year of assessment, nor later than twelve months after the end of the year of assessment; it is then valid for that year of assessment and each subsequent one until revoked. The revocation must also be jointly made by you and your wife not later than twelve months after the end of the year of assessment to which it applies.

For this purpose your wife's 'earnings' means all of her earned income (p 7) apart from:

(a) Any pension or other allowances given in respect of your past employment.

(b) Any family allowances payments (up to 5 April 1976).

(c) Any National Insurance benefits payable to your wife otherwise than by virtue of her own insurance.

The rules for the allocation of your personal reliefs are as follows:

(a) You get the single man's allowance of £1,165 (not £1,815) and your wife also gets £1,165 personal allowance.

(b) You get all of the child relief for your own children.

(c) Reliefs in general are allocated as if you and your wife were not married. For example you each got life assurance relief for any premiums that you pay on qualifying policies on your own respective life but not for premiums that you pay if the policy is on your wife's life or vice versa. This particular rule only applies prior to 1979–80, however.

(d) Certain reliefs will not be available to either you or your wife. These include additional personal relief for children and age allowance.

If you elect for the separate taxation of your wife's earnings then any deductions which are normally directed to be made in priority against your wife's earnings before your own may only be set off against her earnings. This applies to items like losses and capital allowances; also deeds of covenant made by her. For example trading losses of one of you that could normally be set off against the other income of either of you will only be usable against the income of the one who makes the particular losses. Interest paid by your wife can only be set off against her income.

If you elect for your wife's earnings to be taxed separately then she will pay the tax or get any tax repayment relative to those earnings.

This applies whether or not you have elected for separate assessment (p 30).

Whether it will pay you to elect for the separate taxation of your wife's earnings depends on the amounts of your respective incomes and your particular circumstances. You should thus compute the effect in your own case and decide accordingly. Normally both you and your wife will need to have reasonably substantial earnings before the exercise becomes worthwhile. (For 1979–80, you will need earnings of at least £14,930 between you, on the assumption that you have no tax reliefs except the personal allowances. Of this amount you must each have at least £3,765.) The biggest savings result where both your own income and your wife's earnings are high; for the following reasons:

Example 6: Separate Taxation of Wife's Earnings

Using the particulars given for Mr and Mrs A below, how much income tax would be saved if an election were made for the separate taxation of the earnings of Mrs A? (Allowances are available for one young child and a dependent relative of Mrs A.)

	Mr A 1979–80		Mrs A 1979–80		combined	
Earned income		£8,000		£6,000		£14,000
Investment income Mr A		2,000		—		2,000
Mrs A		1,000		—		1,000
Total income		£11,000		£6,000		£17,000
Less: Personal allowance	£1,165		£1,165		£1,815	
Wife's earnings allowance	—		—		1,165	
Dependent relative relief (higher rate)	—		145		100	
		1,165		1,310		3,080
Taxable amount		£9,835		£4,690		£13,920
Income tax payable:						
At 25%	750	187.50	750	187.50	1,500	375.00
30%	9,085	2,725.50	3,940	1,182.00	8,500	2,550.00
40%	—	—	—	—	2,000	800.00
45%	—	—	—	—	1,920	864.00
		£2,913.00		£1,369.50		£4,589.00

£4,282.50

£4,589.00 – £4,282.50 = £306.50

Saving by election:

33

(a) You will each pay only 30% basic rate on the first £9,250 of your taxable earned income after allowances and lower rate band.

(b) You will each be charged to higher income tax rates at the appropriate rate for each slice (i.e. £2,000 at 40%, £3,000 at 45%, etc).

(c) You will, however, lose £650 of your allowances, being the difference between the married and single personal allowances. Note that this difference has increased regularly in recent years resulting in higher earnings being necessary to make the election worthwhile.

The Income of Your Children

No matter how young they are, there is nothing to prevent your children earning income in their own right and being taxed on that earned income. This also applies to investment income for 1972–73, and later years unless the investments were given by your wife and yourself and the child is neither married nor over the age of eighteen at the time that the income is paid. (For 1971–72 and earlier years the relevant age was twenty-one.)

Settlements and arrangements made by you through which your child gets investment income result in your being normally taxed on that income if the child is neither married nor over eighteen. If the child's investment income which would otherwise be treated as your own is less than £5 however, you will not pay tax on that income.

You should obtain a tax return each year for each of your minor children who has any income (including trust income). Completing a return will often prove beneficial since if the child has suffered tax at source on any income this may be reclaimable in whole or part depending on how much other income there is to set against the child's tax allowances. In such circumstances a repayment claim form can be submitted instead of a normal tax return (p 158).

If the child has little or no other income then it is of benefit for it to be paid an annual amount under deed of covenant by a friend or relative (not its parents, unless the child is over 18 or married). The deed must be for a period capable of exceeding six years, hence seven year covenants are very popular. The covenant payments are made under the deduction of income tax at the basic rate (30%), thus costing the payer less unless he is not liable for tax (p 17). If the child's income is small enough then the tax can be reclaimed on its behalf. It should be remembered however that if the annual income of any of your children exceeds £115 then your child relief (if any) may be reduced (p 8). If the child is over 18, the income limit is £500 and so higher covenant payments are possible without any reduction of your child relief.

Example 7: Income of Child

Mr A has one child, B, aged 10 years, whose income for 1979–80 is as follows:

Example 7 continued

		Gross
(a)	Dividends, including tax credits, on shares given to B by Mr A	£200
(b)	Dividends, including tax credits, on shares given to B by his grandfather	£400
(c)	Annual payment under deed of covenant from B's uncle	£400
(d)	Interest on bank deposit assessable for 1979–80 (capital gifted by grandmother)	£375

How much income tax is reclaimable on behalf of B for 1979–80?

Item (a) is not treated as B's income for tax purposes because it is regarded as the income of Mr A who gifted the shares to his child B. The income tax payable by B for 1979–80 is calculated as follows:

		Gross	Income tax deducted or tax credits
(b)	Dividends including tax credits on shares from grandfather	£400	£120
(c)	Annual payment from B's uncle	400	120
(d)	Deposit interest	375	—
	Total income	£1,175	£240
	Less: Personal allowance of B	£1,165	
	Taxable amount	£10	

Income tax due £10 at 25%	£2.50
Less: Income tax suffered by deduction at source and tax credits	240.00
Net income tax reclaimable	£237.50

Death of Husband or Wife

If you are a widower or widow you are regarded as a single person for tax purposes. This means that the personal reliefs for single persons will apply to your income. You may however qualify for the £100 Housekeeper Relief (p 12) and the £650 Additional Personal Relief for Children (p 12).

If Husband Dies

If a husband dies during the tax year his income for the period from 6 April to the date of his death will be subject to tax. This income will, of course, include any income derived by his wife for the same period and must be returned by his executors who must arrange for payment of tax out of the estate funds.

Even though his period of assessment will be less than a full year, he will get the full married man's personal allowance (£1,815), and various other reliefs in full including the £1,165 additional personal allowance for his wife against her earned income. Child relief however is apportioned to the date of death and the widow receives relief for the appropriate fraction after her husband's death.

On his death, his widow becomes a taxpayer in her own right and will be taxed on the income derived by her during the period from the date of death to 5 April and she will complete a separate tax return for that period. She will receive the full £1,165 personal allowance as a single person for the period.

If Wife Dies

If a wife dies during the tax year this will not normally affect her husband's tax return. He will include with his own income for the full year the income of his wife up to the date of her death. He will get personal allowance as a married man for the full year (£1,815) and also £1,165 wife's additional personal allowance if appropriate.

Example 8: Death of Husband during the Tax Year

Mr A earned a salary of £2,000 from 6 April 1979 until 5 October 1979, the date of his death. Mrs A earned a salary of £900 from 6 April 1979 to 5 October 1979 and £800 from 6 October 1979 to 5 April 1980. She also received a pension of £100 per month for the latter period. How much income tax will be payable by Mr A (or his estate) and how much by Mrs A?

1. Mr A (Period of assessment 6.4.79 to 5.10.79 i.e. 6 months)

Salary – own		£2,000
Salary – wife's up to 5.10.79		900
Total income		2,900
Less: Personal allowance	£1,815	
Wife's additional personal allowance (restricted)	900	
		2,715
Taxable amount		£185
Income tax payable at 25%		£46.25

2. Mrs A (Period of assessment 6.10.79 to 5.4.80 i.e. 6 months)

Salary	£800
Pension (£100 × 6)	600
Total income	£1,400
Less: Personal allowance	1,165
Taxable amount	£235
Income tax payable at 25%	£58.75

Divorce or Separation

If you are divorced or permanently separated you are regarded as a single person for tax purposes. This means that the personal reliefs for single persons will apply to your income. If however, you are separated but maintain your wife by voluntary maintenance payments for which you get no tax relief, you will still get the married man's personal allowance (£1,815).

You are treated as being permanently separated from your wife if you are separated under a court order or deed of separation; also if you are separated in such circumstances that the separation is likely to be permanent.

Divorce or Separation during the Tax Year

On her divorce or permanent separation a woman becomes a taxpayer in her own right and will have to submit a return from the date of divorce or separation to 5 April. She will be taxed as a single person getting the full £1,165 personal allowance.

A man who is divorced or permanently separated during the year still submits a return for the full year in the usual way. He will include with his own income for the year that of his wife up to the date of the divorce or separation but will not include the income derived by her after that date. He gets the full married man's personal allowance (£1,815) for this year.

Who may claim the Child Reliefs? (Ss10 & 11 & F2A 1979 Sch 1)

For any tax year only one lot of child relief is allowable for any one child. If you are separated or divorced from your wife you must jointly agree as to who should claim the tax relief for your mutual children or you should agree a basis of apportioning the relief between you. If you do not agree on a basis then the relief will be split in proportion to the respective contributions made by you and your ex-wife (or separated wife) towards the child's maintenance and education for the tax year.

In the year of separation (or divorce) the husband gets the proportion of the child relief up to the date of separation and for the remainder of the tax year the balance is split on the basis described in the previous paragraph.

After 5 April 1979, child relief only applies in special cases, but the question may still arise of apportioning additional personal relief (£650). Previously, the sharing of this relief followed the division of child relief. Now, however, additional personal relief is available without any link with child relief, but is split between more than one claimant according to similar principles.

Alimony and Maintenance Payments

If you are separated or divorced and you make any payments under a court order or a binding agreement for the maintenance of your children or your separated or ex-wife, then you should deduct income tax at the basic rate (30%) from the gross payments.

The full gross payments however are treated as annual charges (p 16) and are deducted from your total income for income tax purposes (p 22), although you make good to the Revenue the basic rate tax which you deducted. If the court order directs that the payments should be made 'tax free' then you should include in your income tax return the 'grossed up' amount taking into account tax at the basic rate.

Purely voluntary payments of maintenance should be paid without any tax deductions and these are not allowable as annual charges against your income. As indicated however (p 37), if you maintain your separated wife by voluntary payments only, then you still get the married man's personal allowance (£1,815). This does not apply if you are divorced. Voluntary payments are not taxed on the recipient as income but payments under court orders to the wife, ex-wife or children are treated as their income. Thus if the income of the recipient is sufficiently small then some repayment might be due along the lines indicated in Example 8 (p 36).

If maintenance payments under a court order are made direct to the children, then these are treated as their own income. If however the payments are made to the mother for the maintenance of the children then the income is treated for tax purposes as her income. Furthermore, where a deed of separation, as opposed to a court order, provides for payments to the children, such payments remain the payer's income for tax purposes.

Special rules exist for 'small maintenance payments'. These are payments made under a court order to a separated or divorced wife (or husband) or a child of the broken marriage, where the amounts do not exceed £21 weekly or £91 monthly. Such 'small maintenance payments' must be made without any deduction of tax. They will be allowed as deductions from the taxable income of the payer and assessed to tax in the hands of the recipient. For payments to, or for the benefit of children, the limits are £12 weekly and £52 monthly. These limits applied generally before 6 April 1978 for payments under old Court Orders and 1 May 1977 for payments under new ones.

If you are a divorced or separated wife, your maintenance payments up to 5 April 1978 were treated as your unearned income and subjected to the investment income surcharge. You were allowed however an extra £1,500 of such income before this tax was payable (p 26). After 5 April 1978 such maintenance payments are no longer liable to investment income surcharge in your hands.

Foreign Divorces

If the divorce is effected by a foreign court then completely different rules relate to the receipt or payment of alimony by residents of this country. Normally no tax will be deductible from the payments by a United Kingdom resident and a recipient resident in this country will be assessed to tax on the amount arising.

6. Income from Land and Property

The amount of income that you derive during the tax year from letting property such as a house, flat, factory or shop, less the deductions you may claim represents your net income from letting property and must be shown separately on your tax return. You must return your gross property income including certain lease premiums and also give full particulars of your expenses. If the income is derived from furnished lettings then the assessment will be under Schedule D Case VI (p 113) ; otherwise it will generally be under Schedule A.

Income Falling within Schedule A (S67)
Annual profits or gains (i.e. after deducting expenses) in respect of :

(a) Rents under leases of land (and buildings) in the United Kingdom.
(b) Rent charges, ground annual and feu duties, and any other annual payments arising out of land in the United Kingdom. (This includes some wayleaves, easements, etc.)
(c) Other receipts arising to a person from the ownership of land in the United Kingdom or from rights or interests in such land.

Exceptions
(a) Yearly interest.
(b) Income including royalties from mines, quarries, etc., which are charged under Schedule D.
(c) Income from various other sources charged under Schedule D such as ironworks, gasworks, canals, docks, fishing rights, railways, bridges, etc.
(d) Income from furnished lettings (i.e. tenant entitled to use of furniture). This is assessed under Schedule D Case VI unless you elect within two years of the end of the relevant tax year that it should be taxed under Schedule A.

Expenses Allowed against Schedule A Income (Ss71–79)
(a) Repairs and maintenance including redecorating the premises during the lease.
(b) Insurance premiums against fire and water damage, etc., to the building.
(c) Management costs including costs of rent collection, salaries, advertising for new tenants, legal and accountancy charges, etc. If your wife takes part in the management, consider paying her a salary (p 237).
(d) Services that you are obliged to provide for the tenants but for which you get no specific payment.

(e) Any payments that you make for general and water rates.

(f) Any payments that you make for any rent, rentcharge, ground annual, feu duty or other periodical payment in respect of the land.

(g) The cost of lighting any common parts of office blocks or flats and otherwise maintaining them.

(h) The upkeep of gardens of flats, etc., where the lease requires you to be responsible for this expense.

(i) Architects' and surveyors' fees in connection with maintenance but not improvements.

(j) Capital allowances (p 65), on any plant or machinery that you might use in the upkeep of your property.

(k) The upkeep of any private roads, drains and ditches, etc., on your land if part or all of the property is let and the expenditure is for the benefit of your tenants.

(l) In the case of an industrial building which is used by the tenant for industrial purposes (e.g. manufacturing) you may get capital allowances on the building (p 70). This also applies to some hotels (p 70).

(m) When you yourself live in a part of the premises you let to others you may not deduct the full amount of your expenditure from your income. Instead you must subtract from your expenditure some reasonable proportion because the premises were not wholly used to produce the income. You may calculate this proportion as being for example:

$$\frac{\text{Area (or rooms) used by you}}{\text{Total area (or rooms)}} \times \text{Expenses}$$

Special Rules Concerning Expenses

Your expenditure in respect of maintenance and repairs is deductible if incurred by reason of dilapidation attributable to a period falling within the duration of the lease. All other expenditure must be incurred in respect of that period. If however you bought the premises subject to a lease you normally get no relief for your expenses relating to the period prior to the purchase.

Special rules relate to a 'lease at full rent' which is one that produces sufficient income for you to pay for the maintenance, repairs, insurance and management of the premises in accordance with the undertakings in the lease. In that case you can charge expenses relating to a period that the premises were empty (void) immediately before you bought them. You can also deduct expenses relating to a previous letting that you made of the premises or a void period between lettings.

If you have a number of 'leases at full rent' that are not 'tenant's repairing leases', then you can set off expenses attributable to one such lease against the rents derived from another (a tenant's repairing lease is one where the lessee (tenant) is under an obligation to maintain the premises).

Losses

If in any year your expenses for any property exceed the rent and you do not get relief as above then you can carry the resultant loss forward to be set off against future Schedule A income from the same property, or against income from other properties provided that all of the properties concerned are let on 'leases at full rent' that are not 'tenant's repairing leases' (see above).

A loss from a property cannot be set off against income derived from a trade or business carried on.

Assessment under Schedule A (S69)

Tax under this schedule is charged by reference to the income to which you become entitled in the tax year. This applies whether or not you actually receive the rents, etc., unless:

(a) You did not receive an amount to which you were entitled because of the default of the person who owed you the money and you took reasonable steps to enforce payment; or

(b) you actually waived payment of the rent, etc. (without receiving any other benefit) for the purpose of avoiding hardship.

Thus your 1979–80 assessment will be based on the rents, etc., to which you are entitled in the year to 5 April 1980 less your allowable Schedule A deductions for that year.

Schedule A income tax is payable on 1 January in the tax year. Thus your 1979–80 demand will be payable on 1 January 1980. Since obviously your income less expenses for that year will not be known until after 5 April 1980 you are first assessed on the basis of the previous year (i.e. 1978–79). When your rents, etc., and expenses have been computed for the year 1979–80 and agreed with the Revenue, your assessment is adjusted and you will either pay over any additional income tax that is due or receive a repayment.

Income assessable under Schedule A is normally treated as investment income and is subjected to the 15% additional rate (p 25).

Example 9: Assessment under Schedule A

Mr A bought an old house some years ago and divided it into three flats each of which he let unfurnished at an annual rent of £700. Taking the expenses shown in the example, assuming that Mr A is not liable for higher rates of tax or the investment income surcharge, and assuming his personal reliefs and lower rate have been used against other income, his assessments are as follows:

Year ended 5 April:	1979		1980	
Rents receivable 3 × £700		£2,100		£2,100
Less: Expenses				
General rates	£315		£320	
Water rates	20		20	
Garden upkeep	220		250	

Example 9 continued

Maintenance, light and heat of hall and stairs	55		60
Exterior repairs and decorating	330		200
Fire insurance of structure of building	40		40
Accountancy	30		40
Agents' rent collection charges	140		140
	——	1,150	——	1,070
Net Schedule A assessments		£950		£1,030

	1978–79		1979–80
Income tax payable (33%)	£313.50	(30%)	£309.00

Note: Income tax will be payable for 1979–80 as follows:

On 1 January 1980 – provisional assessment based on 1978–79 £950 at 30%	£285.00
On agreement of 1979–80 assessment – additional demand	24.00
Total income tax liability under Schedule A 1979–80	£309.00

Furnished Lettings

Your income from furnished lettings is normally taxed under Schedule D Case VI on the actual income less expenditure for the tax year.

As well as expenses normally allowable for Schedule A purposes (p 40), you are also entitled to a deduction to cover depreciation on furniture and furnishings. This may be given to you as a deduction of the entire replacement cost from year to year.

More likely, you will obtain a yearly deduction of 10% of your rents. (For these purposes, your rents exclude amounts received to cover rates and services.) Thus if your annual rents are £1,000 you can deduct £100 yearly to cover the depreciation and replacement of furniture and furnishings.

If under the terms of a letting you provide services such as laundry, meals, domestic help, etc., then you can charge the cost of these items against your taxable profit. If you provide such services then your lettings income may well be treated as earned income. Otherwise it would be unearned income.

Losses (S176)

Furnished lettings losses can be set off against other Schedule D

Case VI profits (from lettings or miscellaneous income) during the tax year. Any losses that are not relieved in this way can be carried forward and set off against future assessments under Schedule D Case VI either in respect of furnished lettings or other income.

The Taxation of Lease Premiums
(Ss 80–85, FA 1972 S81 & FA 1978 S32)

If you obtain a premium in connection with the granting of a lease of not more than 50 years' duration on any property that you own then you will be assessed to tax (under Schedule A) on part of such premium. The amount to be included in your Schedule A assessment is the premium, reduced by 1/50th of its amount for each complete period of 12 months (other than the first) comprised in the duration of the lease (see Example 10, p 44). The balance of the premium which is not charged under Schedule A normally attracts capital gains tax (p 121).

If you sell a lease rather than grant one you will normally be assessed to capital gains tax on any profit unless you are a dealer (p 45) or it is an 'artificial transaction' (p 45).

The following are also included with your taxable premiums:

(a)   The value of any work that the tenant agreed to do to your premises to the extent that the value of your property is enhanced.

(b)   Any premiums paid to you in instalments. You include the aggregate of the instalments in the year that you grant the lease; but you can claim on grounds of hardship to pay the tax by instalments over a period not exceeding eight years, or ending with your last premium instalment if earlier.

(c)   If you are granted a lease at a premium (£P) that is less than its market value (£M) and you then assign the lease at a profit, the amount of your profit is taxed under Schedule D Case VI to the extent that it does not exceed (£M–£P).

Lease Premium Top Slicing Relief (Sch 3)

Having to pay income tax at basic and higher rates on a premium in one tax year might result in a very heavy tax bill. To relieve this situation individuals only are allowed to claim 'top slicing relief'. As a result of such a claim your premium will be spread evenly over the term of the lease to give a 'yearly equivalent'. Your allowable expenses are first set against your rents and then any balance is deducted from the 'yearly equivalent'. Tax is then calculated on the latter at your top income tax rates for the tax year. This will give a combined tax rate that is applied to the total premium so as to give your final tax liability on the premium.

Example 10: The Taxation of Lease Premiums

Mr A owns the freehold of a factory and grants a 21-year lease to B Ltd during the year to 5 April 1980 at a premium of £20,000.

Example 10 continued

Rent of £4,000 is receivable during 1979–80 and the relevant expenses are £4,500. After all deductions Mr A's taxable income for 1979–80 amounts to £10,000 excluding property income. Taking account of top slicing relief how much income tax is payable on the premium of £20,000? Assume that the 15% additional rate applies.

Term of lease	21 years		
Premium received			£20,000
Less: reduction	£20,000 $\times \dfrac{21-1}{50}$		8,000
Taxable proportion			£12,000

Top slicing relief:

'Yearly equivalent'*	$\dfrac{12,000}{21}$	571
Deduct: excess of expenses over rents (4,500–£4,000)		500
Balance		£71

Taxable income	10,000
Add: balance as above	71
	£10,071

Top income rate on £10,071 is	40%	(On £71)
Add: investment income surcharge	15%	
Combined tax rate applicable to premium	55%	

Schedule A liability for 1979–80	
Taxable portion of premium as calculated	£12,000
Add: Rents receivable	4,000
	£16,000
Less: Expenses	4,500
Schedule A assessment 1979–80	£11,500
Total tax payable at 55%	£6,325

Note: If B Ltd uses the factory in its trade it is entitled to an annual deduction of £571 from its taxable profits (p 53).

Woodlands (Ss91, 92 & 111)

(a) You will only be assessed to income tax in respect of woodlands if you occupy them with a view to obtaining a profit and manage them on a commercial basis.

(b) You are assessed under Schedule B on the 'assessable value' of the woodlands that you occupy in the tax year. The 'assessable value' is one-third of the woodlands' annual value (the annual rent that you would expect to obtain from letting the woodlands in their natural and unimproved state if you undertake to bear the costs of repairs and insurance, etc.).

(c) For the above purposes 'occupying' woodlands means having the use of them.

(d) As an alternative to being assessed under Schedule B you can elect to be assessed under Schedule D Case I on the actual profits derived from your woodlands. The election must extend to all of the woodlands that you own on the same estate. Note that for this purpose, you can treat any area as being a separate estate, if you so elect within 10 years of its being planted or replanted. An advantage of making the election is that any losses will then be available against your other income (p 71). Once you make the election you cannot switch back to Schedule B. This can be arranged, however, if you introduce the woodlands into a company.

Dealing in Property

Normally, when you sell a property which you acquired as an investment you will be liable to capital gains tax on any profit that you make (p 121). The maximum tax rate would then be 30%, unless the sale is after 17 December 1973 and development gains tax or development land tax applied (p 142).

If however you carry out a number of purchases and sales of land and/or buildings you are likely to be treated as dealing in property and you will be taxed accordingly. This means that your profits must be computed as if you were conducting a trade (p 58) and you will be taxed on your adjusted profits under Schedule D Case I. This income will be treated as being earned and you will be charged to income tax at basic and higher rates where applicable.

Artificial Transactions in Land

This is the heading of Section 488 of the 1970 Taxes Act.

The section may operate wherever you make a capital profit from selling land (or buildings) that you had purchased with a view to selling later at a profit. The Section also applies to sales of land held as trading stock and the sale of land (and buildings) that had been developed with the intention of selling them at a profit.

Any capital profit arising in the above circumstances can be treated by the Revenue as being income falling under Schedule D Case VI on which you will be liable to pay income tax instead of capital gains tax.

This section does not apply to any purchase or sale by you of the house or flat in which you reside provided that it is your principal private residence (p 135).

45

If you believe that Section 488 might apply to any property sale that you have made or are planning then you can apply for a clearance to the Inspector of Taxes to whom you submit your annual tax return. You should give the Inspector full written particulars of how the gain has arisen or how it will arise. He must then let you know within thirty days whether or not he is satisfied that your gain is outside the ambit of Section 488. If the Inspector does give you a clearance then provided your transaction proceeds exactly as you have described it to him, you will not be taxed under Section 488 in respect of your gain.

Agricultural Land, etc. (S79)

Farmers are basically chargeable to income tax in the same way as persons who carry on a trade or business (p 55). Certain special rules apply however (p 115).

If you own any sand or gravel quarries, any rents and royalties to which you are entitled will be payable to you under the deduction at the source of income tax at 30%.

Land Sold and Leased Back (FA 1972 S80)

Special provisions may apply when you sell a lease with less than fifty years to run and take a fresh lease on the same premises after 21 June 1971. if you had been obtaining tax relief for your rent payments under the old lease and your new lease is for a term of less than fifteen years, you will be charged to income tax on a proportion of the capital sum that you receive for your old lease.

The proportion is given by the formula $\frac{16-n}{15}$ where n is the term in years of your new lease. Thus if you have, say, a forty-year lease, which you sell for £15,000 and take back a ten-year lease you will be charged to income tax on £15,000 $\times \frac{16-10}{15}$ = £6,000.

The balance of £15,000 − £6,000 = £9,000 will be treated as capital on which you may be liable to pay capital gains tax (p 121).

The income tax charge is raised under Schedule D Case VI unless the premises are used in your business, in which case your taxable trading profits are correspondingly increased.

The above rules are applicable to trusts and partnerships. They also apply to companies in which case the corporation tax charge (p 172) may be adjusted.

There are certain rules for treating leases for longer periods than fifteen years as being for periods shorter than that time. This applies if you sell a property and take a new lease under which the rent for the earlier years of the lease is greater than that for the later years. Thus if for example you sell a forty-five year lease for £30,000 and take back one for twenty years at £3,000 annual rent for the first ten years and £1,000 per annum for the remainder, your new lease will be treated as being for ten years and you will be charged to income tax on £30,000 $\times \frac{16-10}{15}$ = £12,000.

Development Gains (FA 1974 Ss38–48 & Schs 3–10)

Where you sold a property between 17 December 1973 and 31 July 1976, part of any profit which you made could be treated as a development gain and subjected to income tax under Schedule D Case VI (p 113). Your development gain was in fact a part of your capital gain on the sale and is described in more detail later (p 140). Note that it also applied in certain cases where a property was let for the first time after development.

Development Land Tax (D.L.T.A. 1976 & F2A 1979 S24 & Sch 4)

For property sales after 31 July 1976, development gains tax no longer normally applies and is superseded by development land tax. Prior to 12 June 1979, the rate was 66⅔% for annual disposals of less than £150,000 chargeable realised development value (p 142), with 80% on the excess. After that date, however, a single rate of 60% applies. Further details are given in Chapter 15 (p 140).

7. Income from Dividends and Interest

How Dividends are Taxed
(S232, FA 1971 Sch 6(27) & FA 1972 S84 & Sch 14)

Prior to 6 April 1973, when a United Kingdom company paid dividends it normally deducted income tax at the standard rate (38.75%) and paid only the net amounts to its shareholders. Dividends paid to you by United Kingdom companies after 5 April 1973 do not have tax deducted. Instead the amount paid to you carries with it a tax credit of currently 3/7ths (p 173). Special rules may apply to any shareholders who live abroad (p 108).

The income tax deducted before 6 April 1973 by the company was accounted for to the Revenue under the rules of Schedule F. Similarly, United Kingdom companies pay Advance Corporation Tax of currently 3/7ths of the dividends paid (p 173). The following are examples of payments by companies to their shareholders (distributions) that are treated in this way:

(a)   Dividends on ordinary shares.
(b)   Dividends on shares with special rights such as preference and deferred shares.
(c)   Capital distributions made in cash, such as dividends paid out of the capital profits of a company.
(d)   Scrip dividend options after 5 April 1975 (p 54).

The gross amounts of your dividends including tax credits (and taxed interest) receivable in the tax year are included with your investment income for total income purposes (p 22).

Dividends, etc. and Your Return

You must enter the amounts of your dividends in your income tax return (p 150). You show, in the separate section provided, details of your dividends from each of your shareholdings with a full description of each holding, as well as the actual payments and relevant tax credits. If there is no room on the form you should prepare a separate list and submit it with your return.

As well as dividends, etc. from companies you must include in this section of your return the gross amounts of any payments due to you for taxed interest on government securities, trust income, the income proportion of annuities, etc. All of these will have been taxed by deduction at the source before you receive them. Also include in this section any loan interest that has been taxed before you receive it and all unit trust dividends including those converted into new units instead of being paid direct to you.

Income Tax Deduction Vouchers

Prior to 6 April 1973, the gross amount of each dividend was normally stated on the income tax deduction vouchers that accompanied your actual dividend warrants (cheques). These vouchers certified that the companies had deducted income tax at 38.75% on making the dividend payments to you. Similar certificates are still provided for interest payments under deduction of income tax. In the case of income distributions from trusts, tax deduction certificates are provided by the trustees (form R185E). All of these tax deduction certificates are accepted by the Revenue in connection with income tax repayment claims (p 158).

Since 6 April 1973, the form of dividend vouchers has changed. These now show the actual dividend payment made to you together with the tax credit. The vouchers certify that Advance Corporation Tax of an amount equal to the tax credit will be accounted for to the Collector of Taxes.

Dividends from Overseas Companies

Any dividends that you receive from overseas companies are normally net of both overseas tax deducted at source and United Kingdom basic rate income tax. The United Kingdom income tax is sometimes at a lower rate than 30%. This is because you have been given some measure of relief from double taxation by the paying agents and collecting agents who are concerned with transmitting to you your overseas dividends. (For a fuller treatment of double tax relief see page 98.)

You should enter on your tax return the gross amounts of your overseas dividends and also show the amounts of foreign and United Kingdom tax deducted at source.

The gross amounts of your overseas dividends are included in your total income (p 22) but you may get some double tax relief in respect of the overseas taxes against your tax liability.

Interest Paid on Government Securities, etc. (Ss93–107)

The normal basis of charge to income tax is by deduction at source under Schedule C. This applies to interest payable on certain 'gilt edged securities' of the United Kingdom and overseas governments where the interest is paid here. The tax is assessed on the Bank of England or other paying authority concerned who deduct it from the interest paid to you resulting in your receiving only the net amount. The gross amounts however must be entered in your income tax return.

Certain United Kingdom government securities may be held for you on the National Savings Stock Register or Trustee Savings Bank Register in which case the interest will be paid to you gross without any tax deduction. Interest is also paid gross on $3\frac{1}{2}$% War Loan and on holdings of United Kingdom government securities which produce less than £2.50 gross interest for you half-yearly. Income tax will then be assessed under Case III of Schedule D (p 50).

Provided that a claim is made to the Revenue on behalf of the individual concerned, the interest on certain specified United Kingdom government securities will be paid gross to any owner who is not ordinarily resident in this country (p 96).

Table 7: United Kingdom Securities on which interest may be paid gross to Non-Residents

3%	Treasury Stock, 1979	$5\frac{1}{2}$%	Treasury Bonds, 2008–12
3%	Treasury Stock, 1966 or after	$5\frac{3}{4}$%	Funding Loan, 1987–91
$3\frac{1}{2}$%	War Stock 1952 or after	6%	Funding Loan, 1993
$5\frac{1}{4}$%	Funding Loan, 1978–80	$6\frac{1}{2}$%	Funding Loan, 1985–87
$5\frac{1}{2}$%	Funding Stock, 1982–84	$6\frac{3}{4}$%	Treasury Loan, 1995–98
$7\frac{3}{4}$%	Treasury Loan, 1985–88	$7\frac{3}{4}$%	Treasury Loan, 2012–15
8%	Treasury Loan, 2002–06	$9\frac{3}{4}$%	Treasury Stock, 1981
$8\frac{1}{4}$%	Treasury Loan, 1987–90	$10\frac{1}{2}$%	Treasury Stock, 1979
$8\frac{1}{2}$%	Treasury Loan, 1980–82	$11\frac{1}{2}$%	Treasury Stock, 1979
$8\frac{1}{2}$%	Treasury Loan, 1984–86	$11\frac{1}{2}$%	Treasury Stock, 1981
$8\frac{3}{4}$%	Treasury Loan, 1997	12%	Treasury Loan, 1983
9%	Treasury Loan, 1994	$12\frac{1}{2}$%	Treasury Loan, 1993
9%	Treasury Convertible Stock, 1980	$12\frac{3}{4}$%	Treasury Loan, 1995
		$12\frac{3}{4}$%	Treasury Stock, 1992
9%	Treasury Loan, 1992–96	13%	Exchequer Stock, 1980
$9\frac{1}{2}$%	Treasury Stock, 1980	13%	Treasury Stock, 1990
$9\frac{1}{2}$%	Treasury Loan, 1999	$13\frac{1}{4}$%	Treasury Stock, 1997

Interest not Taxed at Source (Schedule D Case III) (S109)

Tax is charged under Schedule D Case III on the following:

(a) Any interest whether receivable yearly or otherwise.
(b) Any annuity or other annual payment received without the deduction of tax.
(c) Discounts.
(d) Income from securities payable out of the public revenue unless already charged under Schedule C (p 49).
(e) Small maintenance payments (p 38).
(f) Various kinds of investment income as specifically directed.

Table 8: Examples of Schedule D Case III Income

Bank deposit interest.
Discount on Treasury Bills.
Interest on $3\frac{1}{2}$% War Loan.
National or Trustee savings bank interest apart from the tax free portion of £70 (p 5).

Table 8 continued

Income received gross on government securities (p 49) :

(a)   held on post office register
(b)   amount under £2.50 half-yearly.

Gross payment of share and loan interest by a registered industrial and provident society.

Basis of Charge under Schedule D Case III (S119)

You will normally be assessed to income tax on the basis of your Case III income arising during the previous tax year. Special rules must be followed for fresh income and sources that have come to an end (p 52). No deductions are allowed in computing the assessable income.

A company is assessed to corporation tax on its actual Case III income for each of its accounting periods (p 172).

Your income must be included when it becomes due for payment to you whether or not it is actually paid. For example bank deposit interest is often due in June and December and so your 1979–80 assessment would be based on the interest receivable in June 1978 and December 1978. You should not however include your accrued interest from January 1979 to 5 April 1979 because this will not normally be payable to you until June 1979.

Special Rules for Fresh Income (S120)

If you acquire a new source of Case III income your assessments will be as follows :

(1)   For the tax year when the income first arises you are assessed on the income actually arising in that year.
(2)   Where the income first arose on 6 April in the preceding tax year your assessment for the second year will be based on the income of the first tax year (subject to 5 below).
(3)   Where the income first arose on any day other than 6 April in the preceding tax year your assessment for the second tax year will be based on the income actually arising in that year.
(4)   Your assessment for the third tax year will be based on the income arising in the previous tax year (subject to 5 below).
(5)   You have the right to elect that your first assessment to be made on the basis of the income for the previous tax year, should be adjusted to the actual income arising in the year of assessment. This would normally apply to the third year of assessment except in (2) above. The election should be made to your Inspector of Taxes within six years of the end of the year of assessment concerned.
(6)   In theory the Revenue can apply the special assessment rules to all new Schedule D Case III sources of income. In practice

however if you already have a deposit with one bank, the Revenue will not always seek to treat a new deposit with a different bank as being a fresh source.

Example 11: Fresh Schedule D Case III Income

Mr A opened a deposit account with B Bank Ltd on 31 May 1975 when he deposited £1,000. He has varied the amounts held on deposit since that time but has not yet closed the account. He received interest on his deposit account as follows:

June 1975	£3	June 1977	£18
December 1975	£15	December 1977	£15
June 1976	£20	June 1978	£24
December 1976	£30	December 1978	£28

What are his Schedule D Case III assessments based on the above income?

Mr A – Assessments under Schedule D Case III

1975–76: Actual income arising in year to 5 April 1976 (£3+£15)   £18

1976–77: Actual income arising in year to 5 April 1977 (£20+£30) (source not held at 6 April 1975)   £50

1977–78 (a)   Normal basis – income arising in preceding tax year, i.e. year to 5 April 1977   £50

     (b)   Optional basis – Actual income in year to 5 April 1978 (£18+£15)   £33

(Mr A should elect for (b) and his 1977–78 assessment will be the lower amount of £33.)

1978–79: Preceding year, i.e. to 5 April 1978   £33

1979–80: Preceding year, i.e. to 5 April 1979 (£24+£28)   £52

Special Rules where Source of Income Ceases (S121)

(1)   If a source of Case III income ceases during a tax year you will be assessed for that year on the actual income arising from 6 April in that tax year until the closure or disposal of the source.

(2)   Your assessment under Schedule D Case III for the tax year preceding that in which the source ceases will be adjusted if

the actual income for that year is greater than the assessment already made.
(3) Any adjustment required for the preceding year (see 2) will be separately assessed on you.
(4) Strictly speaking the cessation rules should be applied to each source but in practice the Revenue may not apply them to the closure of one bank deposit account if you have others that continue.

Example 12: Cessation of Schedule D Case III Source

Mr C, who has held money on deposit with the D Bank Ltd for many years permanently withdrew his entire funds on 15 January 1980. He has no other bank deposit accounts. He has received interest on his deposit account as follows:

June 1977	£22	June 1979	£46
December 1977	£29	December 1979	£50
June 1978	£37	15 January 1980	£15
December 1978	£33		

What are Mr C's Schedule D Case III assessments on this income?

Mr C – Schedule D Case III Assessments

1978–79: (a) Preceding year, i.e. to 5 April 1978
(£22 + £29)   £51

         (b) Actual income arising in year to 5 April
1979 (£37 + £33)   £70

1979–80: Actual income from 6 April 1979 to 15
January 1980 (£46 + £50 + £15)   £111

Note: For 1978–79 Mr C's assessment is first £51 based on the income for the previous tax year. When the Revenue learn of the cessation they will raise an additional assessment of £70 – £51 = £19 so as to increase the total 1978–79 assessment to the actual interest received (£70).

Building Society Interest (S343 & FA 1971 Sch 6(40))

Any building society interest which you receive is free of basic rate tax (p 5). You are charged to higher tax rates on the grossed up equivalent as if you had suffered basic rate income tax at 30% on your interest (p 22). This notional 30% basic rate tax is however deducted from your tax bill.

The reason that building societies are empowered to pay interest to you in this way is that they are assessed to a special composite tax rate on their own profits. By means of this arrangement the Revenue are able to make good the basic rate income tax not charged on the interest (p 117).

Scrip Dividend Options (F2A 1975 S34 and Sch 8)

Up to 5 April 1975, many companies gave their shareholders the option of receiving extra shares instead of a cash dividend. The effect of taking the shares was that your cost was treated as nil for capital gains tax purposes so that when you sold the shares, you paid capital gains tax on the entire proceeds (subject to pooling – see p. 130). You did however save the excess of your top higher rate tax over the basic rate because the shares which you received were not treated as income for tax purposes.

From 6 April 1975, your taxable dividend income (p 48) includes any shares which you obtain by exercising an option to take a dividend in such a form. In this case, you are treated for tax purposes as if you had received the dividend in cash. If, however, the cash equivalent is substantially less than the market value of the shares, on the day when market dealings commence, the Revenue may substitute that market value for the cash value.

8. Income from Businesses and Professions

The profits from trades, professions and vocations are normally assessed under Schedule D Case I (trades) and Schedule D Case II (professions and vocations). There are certain special rules which apply to partnerships (Chapter 15) and companies (Chapter 18).

Trade includes manufacturing, retailing, wholesaling and all kinds of trading ventures.

A profession is an occupation requiring special intellectual skills sometimes coupled with manual skills (e.g. doctor of medicine, architect, accountant, barrister).

A vocation has been defined as the way that a person passes his life (e.g. composer, author, actor, singer).

What is Trading ?

Your regular business will normally be treated as a trade requiring assessment under Schedule D Case I. There are however certain other activities which might constitute trading depending on the circumstances. The following are some general guidelines:

(1) Regular buying and selling normally constitutes trading although this does not usually apply to purchases and sales of shares by an individual.

(2) An isolated transaction might be held to be trading if it is by its very nature commercial. For example a single purchase and sale of a quantity of unmatured whisky is normally treated as a trading transaction. This is because the ownership of unmatured whisky is mainly for commercial purposes.

(3) Isolated transactions involving the purchase and sale of works of art are not normally trading. Here, the works of art are owned to be admired and not exclusively (if at all) for commercial purposes. Capital gains tax however might be payable on sales of works of art for over £2,000 each (p 136).

(4) Isolated transactions in income producing assets are not usually treated as trading. Capital gains tax would normally apply (p 121).

(5) What you do to something that you purchase before selling it might decide that you are trading. For instance if you buy a ship, convert it and then sell it you will be treated as trading.

(6) Repetition of the same transaction is evidence of trading.

(7) If you deal in property this is likely to be treated as trading (p 45).

(8) In connection with a transaction that you carry out the possession of expert business knowledge will increase your chances of being treated as trading.

What Business Expenses are Allowed ?

In computing the amount of your profits to be charged under Case I or Case II of Schedule D you are allowed to deduct any sums wholly and exclusively incurred for the purposes of the trade, profession or vocation subject to various special rules (see below). Only expenses of a revenue nature are deductible however and these must be distinguished from capital expenditure (p 3).

Table 9: Allowable Business Expenses

To the extent that they are incurred wholly and exclusively for business purposes the following are deductible (the list is not exhaustive) :

(1)　　The cost of goods bought for resale and materials used in manufacturing.

(2)　　Wages and salaries paid to employees.

(3)　　Pensions paid to past employees and their dependants.

(4)　　Redundancy payments made to previous employees.

(5)　　The running costs of any premises used for the business including rent and rates, light and heat, repairs (not capital improvements), insurance, cleaning, etc.

(6)　　Discounts allowed on sales.

(7)　　Carriage, packing and delivery costs.

(8)　　Printing, postage, stationery and telephone.

(9)　　Repairs to your plant and machinery.

(10)　Staff welfare expenses.

(11)　Insurance regarding loss of profits, public liability, goods in transit, burglary, etc.

(12)　Advertising.

(13)　Trade subscriptions.

(14)　Professional charges of a revenue nature – e.g. audit fees.

(15)　Legal charges of a revenue nature, e.g. debt collection, preparing trading contracts and settling trading disputes.

(16)　If you pay a premium for the lease of your business premises and the recipient is taxed under Schedule A you can claim the cost of the premium as a deduction from your business profits spread over the term of the lease.

(17)　Various taxes and national insurance payments.

(18)　Travelling expenses including hotel bills and fares on business trips but excluding the cost of travelling between your home and business (unless you also do business from home).

(19)　The entertaining of overseas customers and your own staff but not entertaining UK customers.

(20)　Gifts which incorporate an advertisement for your business provided that the value for each recipient each year does not exceed £2.

(21)　Bad debts which arose in the course of trading. Also provisions made for specific debtors whom you anticipate may not pay.

Table 9 continued

(22) A trader's expenses of obtaining a patent are normally allowable. The outright purchase of a patent is a capital expense however which normally qualifies for capital allowances.

(23) Interest payments including hire purchase interest.

(24) Running expenses of motor vehicles excluding such proportion as is attributable to private use.

Table 10: Expenses not Deductible from Business Profits
(S130)

(1) Any payments or expenses not wholly and exclusively laid out for the purposes of the business.

(2) Expenses incurred for the private or domestic purposes of yourself or your family.

(3) Where expenses contain some business and some private element the proportion attributable to the latter is not deductible. In the case of a private dwelling house used for business purposes the deductible proportion is not normally allowed to exceed two-thirds of the rent and other costs.

(4) Any capital used for improvements to your business premises.

(5) Any loss not connected with the business.

(6) Any reserves and provisions made for anticipated expenses such as repairs, retirement benefits, etc., including general bad debts reserves but not reserves for specific bad debts.

(7) Any annuity or other annual payment (other than interest) payable out of the profits (p 16).

(8) Payments of income tax, capital gains tax and corporation tax, etc.

(9) Your own drawings as the owner or part owner of the business.

(10) Depreciation and amortisation of plant and machinery, motor vehicles, buildings, etc. Capital allowances are normally available however (p 64).

(11) Any royalty payment from which you deduct income tax.

(12) Entertaining expenses unless in connection with overseas customers and their agents or your own staff.

(13) Professional charges of a capital nature. For example legal fees in connection with a new lease, architects' fees for designing a new building, accountants' fees connected with the purchase of a new business. These expenses can often be added to the cost of the assets for capital gains tax purposes (p 125).

(14) Fines for illegal acts and connected legal expenses.

(15) Charitable and political donations.

(16) The cost of acquiring capital assets such as plant and machinery, motor vehicles, buildings, etc. Capital allowances are frequently available however (p 64).

The Computation of your Assessable Profits for Schedule D Cases I and II (Ss 130–142)

If you conduct a business or profession you will normally have annual accounts prepared on a commercial basis including a profit and loss account or an income and expenditure account. Your annual accounts should normally be drawn up to the same date in each year but need not coincide with the tax year (ended 5 April).

The profit shown by your annual accounts will form the basis of your assessment under Case I or Case II of Schedule D, but it will normally require adjustment in some or all of the following ways:

(a) Add to your profit any non-deductible expenses that had been charged in your accounts (p 57).

(b) Deduct from your profit any items included in your accounts which are not taxed under Cases I and II of Schedule D either because they are non-taxable or because they are liable to tax under another Case or Schedule. Examples are:
Capital profits liable to capital gains tax (p 121).
Interest receivable taxed under Schedule D Case III (p 50).
Rents receivable taxed under Schedule A (p 39).
Interest received net, income tax having been deducted at source (p 49); also dividends (p 48).
Amounts originally set aside as reserves and now recredited in your accounts provided the original amounts were not allowed against your taxable profits.

(c) Deduct from your profit any allowable expenses not already charged in your accounts.

(d) Add to your profit any trading profits not already included.

(e) From your profits adjusted as above, deduct your capital allowances for the year (p 64).

(f) Deduct from your profit any stock relief that you claim (p 60).

(g) Deduct any relief which is due to you in respect of periods worked overseas in your business (p 103).

Example 13: Schedule D Case I Computation

Mr A carries on a manufacturing business. His accounts for the year to 31 December 1977, which show a net profit of £9,000, include the following:

Expenses

Depreciation of motor vehicles	£430	Charitable donations	35
		Entertaining expenses –	
Depreciation of plant and machinery	670	UK customers	250
		Overseas customers	100
Bad debts provision (5% × sales debtors)	650	*Income*	
		Bank deposit interest	£70
Legal expenses re debt collection	60	Profit on sale of motor car	50
Legal expenses re new lease (not a renewal)	70	Bad debts provision no longer required (general)	200

58

Example 13 continued

Ignoring capital allowances compute Mr A's adjusted Case I profit.

Mr A – Schedule D Case I Computation based on Accounts for year ended 31 December 1977

Net profit per accounts		£9,000
Less:		
Bank deposit interest (assessed Schedule D Case III)	£70	
Profit on sale of motor car (capital)	50	
Bad debts provision no longer required	200	
	———	320
		£8,680
Add: Disallowable expenses:		
Depreciation (£430+£670)	£1,100	
General bad debts provision	650	
Legal expenses re new lease	70	
Charitable donations	35	
Entertaining UK customers	250	
	———	2,105
Adjusted profit		£10,785

Stock Valuation

An important·factor in the preparation of business accounts is the valuation of stock and work in progress. This is the amount of unsold raw materials, finished goods and work in progress that was owned at the end of the accounts period. The stock, etc. must be valued at each accounting date and the profits are augmented by the excess of the closing stock over the opening stock or decreased by the deficit. It is clear that if the closing stock is valued on a more generous basis than the opening stock then the profits shown will be higher than the true profits and vice versa.

The Revenue pay careful attention to the manner in which businesses value their stock and they normally insist that for tax purposes the opening and closing stocks are valued on the same basis. The usual basis adopted is that each item in stock is valued at the lower of its cost or net realisable value. The exact cost to be included may or may not contain an addition for expenses depending on the exact basis adopted. The general rule in ascertaining cost is that identical items should be identified on the basis that the earliest purchases were sold or used first (FIFO). In all cases the method chosen must be used consistently. 'Net realisable value' is what it is estimated will be obtained from disposing of the stock in the ordinary course of business at the balance sheet date, after allowing for all expenses in connection with the disposal.

Stock Relief (F2A 1975 Sch 10, FA 1976 S37 & Sch 5 & F2A 1979 S13 & Sch 3)

This was brought into effect for companies by the Finance Act 1975 (p 171) and later extended to the trades and professions of individuals and partnerships. You can claim relief if your trading stock, including professional work in progress, increases during your 'base period'. 'Base periods' are normally accounting years ended in 1975–76, and subsequently. Previously, however, there was a two-year base period which ended with the date when your 1974–75 accounting year ended. There are special rules for new businesses and changes in accounting date.

Different rules apply to base periods ending in 1974–75 and those ending thereafter. For the two year period you obtained relief equal to the excess of your stock valuation at the end of the two years over that at the beginning. From this was deducted 10% of your 'relevant income' for the 'base period'. If you had not previously qualified for stock relief, a special 5% bonus was then added and the resultant relief was deducted from your assessable profits for your accounts year ending in 1974–75. 'Relevant income' was your taxable trading income excluding investment income and before capital allowances. (If your 'base period' was more than 24 months then both your stock increase and 'relevant income' were proportionately reduced.)

For 'base periods' ending after 1974–75 which are normally only 12 months, you again obtain relief for your stock increase over the period less a deduction of part of your 'relevant income'. The percentage is now 10%, (15% for 'base periods' ending before 6 April 1979), and 'relevant income' is after deducting capital allowances (p 64). For companies, the 15% deduction has remained throughout (p 185).

Note that in valuing stock for relief purposes, any payments received on account for goods still held must be deducted. Also, work in progress which has been completed but not yet billed must be excluded. If, as a result of a stock relief claim, a loss is produced, it can be relieved in a broadly similar way to a trading loss (p 71). (The current stock relief is not available for terminal loss claims.)

The time limit for making stock relief claims must be carefully watched. Any claim which you have for this relief must be made within two years after the end of the year of assessment in which the 'base period' ends. Thus a claim for the year to 30 June 1976 must be made by 5 April 1979. If your 'base period' ends after 5 April 1979, but not before, you may claim less than your full entitlement to stock relief for that period. Any unclaimed balance, however, is not available for carry foward. If, however, you claim the maximum possible relief, this may exceed your profits and result in a trading loss which is relievable in the normal ways (p 71), including carrying forward any unused balance.

Recoupment of Previous Stock Relief

If during a base period ending after 5 April 1975 your stock decreases, then you suffer a recoupment of past stock relief. What happens is that there is added to your taxable profits the amount of your stock decrease, limited however to the total previous unrecouped stock relief which you previously had enjoyed.

Thus suppose you make no stock relief claim prior to 1978–79. For your accounts year to 30 June 1978, your stock increases from £100,000 to £180,000 and your taxable profits after capital allowances are £200,000. On 30 June 1979, your stock is say £150,000. Your stock relief for the year to 30 June 1978 is £180,000 – £100,000 – 15% × £200,000 = £50,000. Thus your taxable profits for the year to 30 June 1978 are reduced by £50,000. For the year to 30 June 1979 however, your taxable profits are increased in respect of the stock relief recoupment of £180,000 – £150,000 = £30,000.

On cessation, previous unrecouped stock relief is assessed, subject to a claim for 'top-slicing'. If you had previously traded for between one and two years, your extra tax is reduced broadly to twice the tax on half the recoupment assessment. More than two years previous trading gives a reduction to three times the tax on one third of the recouped stock relief.

Under new rules, stock relief from the first two years of the stock relief scheme (see above) normally becomes safe from recoupment from the first day of the first 'base period' ending after 5 April 1979. Further, an automatic write-off will apply for any period regarding unrecovered past relief originally obtained for a period ending at least six years earlier. In calculating the amount of unrecouped relief to be written off, you must allocate any recoupments which you suffer to the latest periods first, which should prove beneficial.

Basis of Assessment (S115)

The normal basis of assessment under Cases I and II of Schedule D is the profits of the accounts year ending in the preceding tax year. Thus if a business makes up its annual accounts to 30 September its 1979–80 Schedule D Case I assessment will be based on the profits for the year to 30 September 1978 (i.e. ending in the preceding tax year 1978–79). Special rules apply to the opening and closing years (see below) and also where you change your accounting date.

Opening Years (Ss116 & 117)

(1)   In the first tax year of a business, profession or vocation the assessment is based on the profits from the starting date until the following 5 April. If accounts have been prepared for the first full year or other period so as to bridge that date then the profits must be apportioned on a time basis. Thus if a business started on 6 July 1978 and makes up its accounts to 5 July 1979 showing a profit of £2,400 for that year, the assessment for 1978–79 will be based on the period 6 July 1978 to 5 April 1979, i.e. £2,400 × 9/12 = £1,800.

(2) The assessment for the second tax year of a business trade or vocation is normally based on the profits for the first complete twelve months of operations. Thus in the above example the assessment for 1979–80 will be based on the profits for the first complete year, i.e. to 5 July 1979 and will therefore be £2,400.

(3) The third tax year's assessment is normally on the preceding year basis subject to the election option mentioned under (4). In the example above the 1980–81 assessment is thus £2,400 (profits for the accounts year ending in the preceding tax year).

(4) The taxpayer has the option to elect that the assessment for both the second and third tax years (but not only one of them) should be based on the actual profits for those years (see Example 15). The election should be made to the Inspector of Taxes within seven years of the end of the second year of assessment.

**Example 14: Schedule D Cases I and II –
Assessments for Opening Years**

Mr A started in business on his own account on 1 July 1975 and prepared accounts for an eighteen-month period to 31 December 1976 producing an adjusted profit of £2,700. He selected 31 December as his regular accounting date and his adjusted profit for the year to 31 December 1977 was £360 and for 1978 it was £720. What are Mr A's Schedule D Case I assessments based on those profits?

Mr A – Schedule D Case I Assessments

Tax Year	Basis	Base Period	Calculation	Assessment
1975–76	Actual	1.7.75–5.4.76	£2,700 × 9$\frac{1}{6}$/18	£1,375
1976–77	First year	1.7.75–30.6.76	£2,700 × 12/18	£1,800
1977–78	Preceding year	1.1.76–31.12.76	£2,700 × 12/18	£1,800
1978–79	Preceding year	1.1.77–31.12.77		£360
1979–80	Preceding year	1.1.78–31.12.78		£720

The assessments for Mr A's second and third tax years total £3,600 (£1,800 + £1,800). Mr A can effect a saving by electing that his assessments for those years should be on the actual profits made in 1976–77 and 1977–78 as follows:

Example 14 continued

1976–77	6.4.76–31.12.76	$£2,700 \times 8\frac{5}{6}/18$	£1,325	
	1.1.77–5.4.77	$£360 \times 3\frac{1}{6}/12$	95	
				£1,420
1977–78	6.4.77–31.12.77	$£360 \times 8\frac{5}{6}/12$	£265	
	1.1.78–5.4.78	$£720 \times 3\frac{1}{6}/12$	190	
				£455

The reduction in the aggregate assessments for 1976–77 and 1977–78 is £1,725 (£3,600 – (£1,420 + £455)).

Closing Years (S118)

(1) For the tax year in which a trade, profession or vocation is permanently stopped the assessment under Schedule D Case I or II is based on the actual profits from the previous 6 April until the date of cessation.

(2) Regarding the two years prior to the tax year in which the cessation takes place, assessments will have normally been made on a preceding year basis. The Revenue has the right however to make additional assessments so as to cover any excess of the actual profits for those two tax years. This adjustment only works in favour of the Revenue and if your profits for the two tax years preceding that in which your business ceases are less than the original assessments for those years, you will not be able to obtain any reduction.

Example 15: Schedule D Cases I and II – Assessments for Closing Years

Mr E ceases to trade on 31 July 1979 having made adjusted profits as follows:

Year ended 31 July 1976	£2,500
Year ended 31 July 1977	£2,400
Year ended 31 July 1978	£3,600
Year ended 31 July 1979	£3,000

What are Mr E's final assessments on these profits?

Before it was known that Mr E was ceasing to trade, his assessments would be as follows:

Tax Year	Basis	Base period	Schedule D Case 1 assessment
1977–78	Preceding year	Year to 31.7.76	£2,500
1978–79	Preceding year	Year to 31.7.77	2,400
Total for 1977–78 and 1978–79			£4,900

Example 15 continued

When cessation on 31.7.79 is notified to the Revenue they will adjust the assessments for 1977–78 and 1978–79 as follows:

1977–78:

Actual	6.4.77–31.7.77	£2,400 × $3\frac{5}{6}$/12	767	
	1.8.77–5.4.78	£3,600 × $8\frac{1}{6}$/12	2,450	
			———	3,217

1978–79:

Actual	6.4.78–31.7.78	£3,600 × $3\frac{5}{6}$/12	1,150	
	1.8.78–5.4.79	£3,000 × $8\frac{1}{6}$/12	2,042	
			———	3,192

Revised total for 1977–78 and 1978–79	£6,409
Less: Already assessed	4,900
Additional assessments 1977–78 and 1978–79	£1,509

1979–80:

Actual	6.4.79–31.7.79	£3,000 × $3\frac{5}{6}$/12	£958

Capital Allowances (C.A.A., etc.)

You are not normally allowed to deduct from your taxable profits the cost or depreciation of capital assets. You can however deduct capital allowances in respect of the cost of certain assets used in your business or profession including the following:

(1)   Plant and machinery (p 65) – this category includes also furniture, fittings, office equipment and motor vehicles, together with the cost of industrial buildings thermal insulation and of making certain buildings comply with the fire regulations.
(2)   Industrial buildings (p 70) – this includes factories and warehouses, etc.
(3)   Agricultural and forestry buildings, etc. (p 70).
(4)   Hotel buildings, etc. (p 70).
(5)   Scientific research expenditure (p 71).
(6)   Patents and know-how (p 71).
(7)   Mines, oil wells and dredging, etc. (not covered in the text).

Base Period (C.A.A. S72)

For a business, profession or vocation (including partnerships) the capital allowances are computed according to the assets purchased and those used in the annual accounts period (i.e. the base period). A deduction is then made from the Schedule D Case I or Case II assessment in respect of the total capital allowances for that tax year. For example if a business makes up its accounts to 31 December each year then its Schedule D Case I assessment for

1979–80 will be based on its accounts for the year to 31 December 1978 (ending in the preceding tax year). Similarly its 1979–80 capital allowances will be based on the year to 31 December 1978.

In the opening or closing years of a business base periods of less than one year might arise. It is also possible that one base period applies to two tax years in which case the additions during the base period are allocated to the earlier tax year for the purposes of calculating the allowances. If there is a gap between base periods, the gap is added to the second base period unless this marks a cessation of trading – in this case you add the gap to the first period.

Capital Allowances on Plant and Machinery
(FA 1971 Ss 40–50 & Sch 8, FA 1972 S67 & FA 1976 Ss39–43)

The main allowances available on plant purchased new or second-hand at any time after 26 October 1970 are normally a first year allowance for the year of purchase and a writing down allowance for each subsequent year. Special rules apply to motor vehicles (p 68). Balancing charges and allowances can arise when plant is sold (p 66).

First Year Allowances (FA 1971 Ss 41–43 & FA 1972 S67)

For the base year in which you purchase each item of plant or machinery you will obtain a first year allowance of 100% of the cost. You will not get this allowance however if the expenditure is incurred in a year during which you permanently cease to trade. If the plant is sold before you bring it into use your trade will not get any first year allowance.

Any business (including one carried on by a company) may disclaim all or part of the first year allowance on any plant. (This is of value if you wish to spread your capital allowances more evenly and obtain more benefit in future years.) A company must give notice of the disclaimer of the Inspector of Taxes within two years of the end of its accounts period. Any other business is in practice allowed to withdraw all or part of its claim before the assessment becomes final.

The first year allowance rate of 100% applies to expenditure incurred after 21 March 1972. The rate was 60% prior to 20 July 1971 and 80% from 20 July 1971 until 21 March 1972. Prior to 27 October 1970 however there was no first year allowance; instead, what was known as an initial allowance was granted at rates up to 30% depending on the circumstances. Before 27 October 1970 investment grants were given on certain new plant.

If you obtain second-hand plant and machinery from someone 'connected' with you, first year allowance might not be given to you. This is because complicated rules exist to prevent the high rates of first year allowances being claimed as the result of artificial arrangements between connected persons. Anti-avoidance legislation has also been brought in concerning leasing partnerships from which a loss benefit otherwise would be obtained from first year allowances (p 119).

Writing Down Allowance (FA 1971 S44 & FA 1976 S39)

In the second year, each asset is put into a 'pool' at its cost price less the first year allowance obtained and a writing down allowance of 25% is given on the balance. You can take less than 25% in any year except for a company (p 177). The writing down allowance is not given for the first year. Of course if the full 100% first year allowance is claimed, there is no balance to bring into the 'pool'.

In the third and subsequent years a 25% writing down allowance is also given. Various rates of writing down allowance were obtained prior to 27 October 1970. These rates were normally 15%, 20% or 25% depending on the estimated life of the particular assets. For purchases before 5 November 1962 a lower scale applied.

Any unexpired balance of cost incurred up to 27 October 1970, however, which is brought forward to a basis period which ends after 5 April 1976 is normally taken into the 'pool'. Writing down allowance is thus taken on it at 25%. Exceptions to this pooling rule include new ships and cars which originally cost over £2,000.

If the base period is less than a year, the rate of writing down allowance is proportionately reduced. Thus if the base period for a business is only six months for a given year of assessment then any writing down allowances for that period would be at the rate of $25\% \times 6/12 = 12\frac{1}{2}\%$ in respect of expenditure after 26 October 1970. The rate of first year allowance however is not restricted in this way.

Sales of Plant and Machinery – Balancing Allowances and Charges (FA 1971 S44)

If you sell an item of plant from your 'pool' of purchases after 26 October 1970, you simply deduct the sale proceeds from the 'pool' balance. If the proceeds exceed the original cost of the plant however, you only deduct the cost from the pool and the excess is a capital gain (p 121). Should the sale proceeds exceed your 'pool' balance the excess is treated as a balancing charge and it is added to your assessment for the relevant year. By means of the balancing charge, the Revenue recoup the excess of capital allowances that would otherwise have been given to you.

If you sold any plant, etc., that had been purchased prior to 27 October 1970 you compared its remaining balance after capital allowances with the sale proceeds. Then any excess of the proceeds was a balancing charge (see above) and any deficit was a balancing allowance which was added to your capital allowances for the year. Strictly speaking you were required to consider each such item of plant separately in order to calculate the balance of its unexpired cost after capital allowances. Most items are brought into the 'pool', however, for the first base period ending after 5 April 1976 (p 64), and so this complication no longer normally applies.

Regarding plant, etc. (apart from some motor cars) purchased after 26 October 1970, balancing allowances normally only occur in the event of a cessation. If you permanently cease to trade during a period then you receive for that period a 'balancing allowance' equal to the remainder of your 'pool' (of expenditure on assets after 26 October 1970 less allowances already obtained).

Example 16: Capital Allowance on Plant and Machinery

Mr A has been carrying on a manufacturing business for many years and makes up his accounts to 31 December each year. At 31 December 1976 the capital allowances written down value of his plant, etc., was £4,800.

Mr A purchased the following new plant:

Date	Description	Cost
on 3 February 1977	Machines	£1,000 (sold 5.12.78 for £450)
on 5 September 1977	Office furniture	650
on 2 March 1978	Typewriters	100
on 1 April 1978	Machines	500

No other additions were made before 31 December 1978.

Compute Mr A's capital allowances for 1978–79 and 1979–80 assuming that he disclaims his first year allowances for 1978–79 but not for 1979–80.

	'Pool'	Total allowances
Balance brought forward *1978–79* (base period year to 31.12.77)	£4,800	
Additions:		
3.2.77	£1,000	
5.9.77	650	
	1,650	
Writing down allowance 25% × £4,800	(1,200)	£1,200
Balance forward	5,250	
1979–80 (base period year to 31.12.78) Additions:		
2.3.78	100	
1.4.78	500	
First year allowance	600	
		600

Example 16 continued

Sale proceeds	450	
Writing down allowance 25% × £4,800	4,800 (1,200)	1,200
Balance forward	£3,600	£1,800

Motor Vehicles (FA 1971 Sch 8, FA 1976 S43 & F2A 1979 S14)

First year allowances are not given on motor vehicles unless they are designed to carry goods ; or are of a type unsuitable for use as private vehicles ; or are vehicles for hire to the public such as taxis or hire cars. To qualify for first year allowance as a hire car, a vehicle purchased after 12 June 1979 must not be leased to any one person for more than 30 consecutive days, nor more than 90 days in total in any 12 months. Previously this restriction did not apply.

This is important if your *car is leased* through your business (or company) because if it does not qualify for first year allowance and its equivalent retail cost price exceeds a given limit, the rental deduction from the taxable business profits is correspondingly restricted. The limit is £8,000 retail cost equivalent if the car is first rented after 12 June 1979. Previously, this figure was £5,000 (£4,000 before 7 April 1976).

The actual deductible rental is found by multiplying the actual rental by $(8,000 + \dfrac{RP - 8,000}{2})$ and divided by RP. (RP is the retail price of the car, when new.)

If you buy a car for use in your business you will obtain the 25% writing down allowance for every year including the first. Special rules apply however to cars costing over £8,000 in which case your allowance for any year is restricted to 25% × £8,000 i.e. £2,000. Each car that costs over £8,000 must be treated as a separate 'pool' which when sold, gives rise to its own balancing allowance or balancing charge. Cars costing £8,000 or less are not treated in this way and must be added to your 'pool' of plant and machinery. For cars purchased before 13 July 1979, the limits were £5,000 and £1,250 and for those purchased before 7 April 1976, £4,000 and £1,000 respectively.

Example 17: Higher Priced Motor Cars

On 1 April 1977 Mr C purchased for use in his business two cars costing respectively £5,000 and £6,000. The first of these is sold on 30 June 1978 for £4,800 and another is bought on 21 June 1979 for £9,000. The Revenue direct that 20% of the use of each car should be treated as being for private purposes. Mr C prepares his annual accounts to 31 July each year. Compute the capital allowances available on the cars, up to 1980-81.

Example 17 continued

	(1)	(2)	Total allow-ances	Allowances available to business (80%)
Cost 1 April 1977 (year to 31.7.77)	£5,000	£6,000		
1978–79 Writing down allowance (restricted)	1,250	1,250	£2,500	£2,000
	3,750	4,750		
1979–80 Writing down allowance		1,187	£1,187	£950
		3,563		
Proceeds 30.6.78	4,800			
Balancing charge	£1,050			£(840)
1980–81 Addition 21 June 1979	9,000			
Writing down allowance (restricted)	2,000	891	£2,891	£2,313
Balances forward	£7,000	£2,672		

Note: Because the business use is restricted to 80% the balancing charge is restricted in this way.

Hire Purchase (FA 1971 S45)

If you buy plant or machinery on hire purchase you are entitled to full capital allowances as soon as you bring it into use in your business. You receive allowances on the capital proportion of the total instalments – the interest proportion is allowed against your business profits in the year that the respective instalments are paid. Thus if you buy under hire purchase a machine whose cash cost would be £1,000 and you are paying a total of £1,600 over three years you get capital allowances on £1,000 as soon as you start to use the machine (i.e. first year allowances of 100% or such lesser amount as you choose). You would also deduct the interest of £600 from your profits for the three years during which you are paying off the instalments (i.e. about £200 each year).

Industrial Buildings
(C.A.A. Ss1–17, FA 1972 S67 & FA 1975 S13)

The costs of new industrial buildings that are used in your business (i.e. factories, warehouses, etc.) qualify for an initial allowance of 50%. The initial allowance rate for expenditure from 6 April 1970 to 21 March 1972 was 30% (increased to 40% in a development area) and 40% from 22 March 1972 to 12 November 1974. Additions and improvements to industrial buildings qualify for industrial buildings allowances.

Each year (including the first) a writing down allowance of 4% of the original cost is obtained. (The allowance is 2% if the expenditure was incurred before 6 November 1962.)

If a building is sold on which industrial buildings allowances have been obtained then the sale proceeds must be compared with the balance of original cost less initial allowances and writing down allowances obtained. Any excess proceeds will be assessed as a balancing charge and any deficit will be allowed as a balancing allowance. Any excess of the proceeds compared with the original cost must be disregarded for this purpose but may give rise to a capital gain (p 121).

Agricultural Buildings Allowance (C.A.A. Ss68–69 & FA 1978 S39)

If you are the owner or tenant of any farm or forestry land, you will obtain allowance for your expenditure on certain constructions on that land. These include farmhouses, farm or foresty buildings, cottages and fences, etc.

The allowance is given in the form of a writing down allowance of one-tenth of your original expenditure for each of the first ten years of your ownership. For expenditure after 11 April 1978, an initial allowance of up to 20% may be claimed. The balance is eligible for writing down allowance at 10% of the original cost for each year including the first.

If your expenditure is on a farmhouse then your allowance will normally be based on only one-third (maximum) of the total cost to take account of the personal benefit.

Hotel Buildings (FA 1978 S38 & Sch 6)

Expenditure incurred on the construction or improvement of certain hotel buildings after 11 April 1978 qualifies for an initial allowance of 20% in the first year. Also, in the first year and then annually, a writing down allowance of 4% of the original cost is obtained.

To qualify for the allowance, the hotel must have at least 10 bedrooms for letting to the public and provide breakfast, and an evening meal. Also, it must be open for at least 4 months in the season from April to October inclusive.

Scientific Research Allowance (C.A.A. Ss90–95)

Capital expenditure incurred on scientific research for the purposes of your trade is wholly allowed in the year that the expenditure arises. Any revenue expenditure will be allowed as a charge against your taxable profits provided that it is related to your trade or it is medical research related to the welfare of your employees.

Patent Rights and 'Know How' (Ss 378–388)

If you purchase a patent to use in your business then you will obtain a writing down allowance of one-seventeenth of the expenditure for each of the seventeen years starting with that in which you made the purchase. If you sell the patent then the excess or deficit of the proceeds compared with the unexpired balance of cost (after writing down allowances), is treated as a balancing charge or allowance (p 66). If however the proceeds exceed the original cost, then you are assessed to income tax under Schedule D Case VI on this excess (normally spread over six years or the remainder of the patent if less). Note that costs in connection with creating and registering your own patents are treated as deductible revenue expenses (S132).

Any payments that you make to obtain 'know how' for your business or profession entitle you to a writing down allowance of one-sixth of such expenditure for each of the first six consecutive years. If you sell 'know how' that had been used in your business, the proceeds are taxed as trading receipts. If however you cease to trade within the six years, you are allowed to charge the balance of your 'know how' expenditure against the taxable profits of your final trading period.

Relief for Losses (Ss168–175)

If the adjusted results (after stock relief p 60) for your business, profession or vocation show a deficit of income compared with expenditure for a particular year then your assessment under Case I or Case II of Schedule D will be nil for the related tax year. Thus if your accounts run to 31 December and you make an adjusted loss of £1,000 for 1978 your 1979–80 assessment will be nil. The loss of £1,000 for the year to 31 December 1978 should be augmented by your 1979–80 capital allowances (say £600) and the resultant total loss of £1,600 is available for relief. This is first given against (a) your other income for the tax year in which you suffer the loss and (b) that for the following tax year.

((a) includes your business assessment on the profits for the year prior to the loss.)

Strictly speaking you should apportion your loss to the actual tax years that span your accounts year: thus if your loss for the year to 31 December 1978 is £1,600 this is allocated as to £1,600 × 3/12 = £400 to 1977–78 and £1,600 × 9/12 = £1,200 to 1978–79. Except in the first years of trading however, the Revenue normally allow you to allocate the loss for a given accounts year to the tax year in which it ends. Thus the £1,600 loss for the year to 31 December 1978 is allocated to 1978–79 and your relief is set against other income for 1978–79 and 1979–80.

A strict order of set-off must be followed – the loss is first set against your other earned income for the year, then against your unearned income; then against your wife's earned income and then her unearned income.

The above loss relief is given under Section 168 of the 1970 Taxes Act and you must claim it by making the required election to your Inspector of Taxes within two years of the end of the tax year to which it relates. If your loss is not entirely relieved as above then you can claim that the balance should be carried forward and set off against future profits from the same trade, profession or vocation (Section 171 Taxes Act 1970).

Loss in New Business (FA 1978 S30)

If you carry on a business or profession personally or in partnership, a special new relief is available. This applies to any loss which you make in your first year of assessment, or in any of the next three years, but the relief applies to no year earlier than 1978–79. A written claim is required within two years of the end of the year of assessment.

The losses, which include capital allowances and stock relief, are offset against your income for the three years of assessment prior to the year in which the losses are made, taking the earliest first.

Terminal Losses

If you cease to carry on a trade, profession or vocation and make an adjusted loss in your last complete year of trading, you get relief for this so-called 'terminal loss'. The relief is augmented by your capital allowances apportionable to your last twelve months of trading. The terminal losses are allowed against your business assessments for the three years prior to that in which you cease to trade.

Example 18: Relief for Losses

Dr D made a loss of £2,000 in his practice for the year to 31 December 1977 having made a profit of £600 for 1976. In 1978 his profit is £2,000. His only other income is taxed dividends amounting to £500 for 1977–78, £550 for 1978–79 and £600 for 1979–80. What loss relief can Dr D obtain?

Dr D's loss of £2,000 for the year to 31 December 1977 will be allocated to the tax year 1977–78 (p 67).

Example 18 continued

1977–78 loss relief (S168)

(1) Against 1977–78 Schedule D Case II assessment	£600
(2) Against 1977–78 Dividends	500
	£1,100

1978–79 loss relief (S168)
Against 1978–79 Dividends £550

1979–80 loss relief (S171)
Against 1979–80 Schedule D Case II assessment £350

(Case II assessment for 1979–80 becomes £2,000 − £350 = £1,650)

Earnings Basis and Cash Basis

If you are carrying on a trade, you will normally be taxed on an 'earnings basis'. This means that your sales for each accounts period are included as they arise and not when you receive the money. Sales normally arise when they are invoiced. In a retail shop the sales usually arise as the customers pay over the counter. Your expenses are also deductible on an arising basis and the actual date of payment is not relevant.

If you are carrying on a profession or vocation however, the Revenue may tax you on a 'cash basis', which means by reference to the actual cash received, taking no account of uncollected fees at the end of each accounts period.

This basis is usually used for barristers. Other professions must prepare their opening accounts on an earnings basis but have the option of later switching to a cash basis. Normally the expenses are calculated on an arising basis but in some small cases the actual expense payments are used ignoring accruals.

Post-cessation Receipts (Ss143–151)

If, after you permanently cease your trade, profession or vocation, you receive amounts relating to those activities, such amounts are known as 'post-cessation receipts'. An example is a late fee payment that had not been included in your accounts because either they are prepared on a cash basis or the fee was not included in your outstandings.

Post-cessation receipts are usually taxed under Schedule D Case VI (p 113). They are normally treated as earned income and you can set off unrelieved losses and capital allowances from before the cessation. You can however elect that any post-cessation receipts for the first six years after cessation should be added to your income from the business, etc. on its last day of trading.

Relief is available for those born before 6 April 1917 and in business on 18 March 1968, who are taxed on a fraction of their post-cessation receipts varying between 19/20ths and 5/20ths. The latter fraction applies if you were born before 6 April 1903; if you were born before 6 April 1904 the fraction is 6/20ths and so on.

Class 4 National Insurance Contributions

Since national insurance contributions are not, strictly speaking, a form of taxation, the subject is not covered in this book. Self-employed persons and others liable to Schedule D income tax under Cases I and II may be charged, in addition to their normal flat-rate Class 2 contributions, an earnings related amount under Class 4. Since the latter is very much, in effect, an additional form of income tax, the following points are mentioned concerning Class 4:

(1) For 1979–80 you pay Class 4 contributions on 5% of your income under Cases I and II of Schedule D between £2,250 and £7,000. The maximum is thus 5% × £4,750 = £237.50. For 1978–79, 5% was charged on your income between £2,000 and £6,250.

(2) For 1977–78 the limits were £1,750 and £5,500, for 1976–77 they were £1,600 and £4,900, whilst for 1975–76, they were £1,600 and £3,600. For all of those years the rate was 8%. Prior to 6.4.75, the charge did not apply.

(3) Class 4 is payable on your Schedule D assessments under Cases I and II for the tax year; after capital allowances, but with no deduction of personal allowances, pension contributions etc. Your share of partnership income is also included.

(4) If your wife has self-employed earnings, these are also charged to Class 4 as if her earnings were separate from yours.

(5) Class 4 does not apply to men over 65 at the end of the previous year of assessment, and women then over 60.

(6) Your contributions for each year of assessment are normally collected through your income tax assessment on your self-employed earnings. Thus it is payable in two equal instalments (p 154).

(7) If you are not resident in the UK (p 89) Class 4 will not apply.

9. Income from Employments and PAYE

Your income from employments or from any office that you hold is normally taxed under Schedule E which is divided into three cases as follows (S181 and FA 1974 S21 and Sch 2, and FA 1977 Sch 7) :

(1) **Schedule E Case I** applies if you are both resident and ordinarily resident (p 96) in the United Kingdom. Your income tax assessment under this case is usually based on the actual income earned here during the tax year. For 1974–75 and subsequent years, however, you are charged on half your United Kingdom earnings (whether remitted here or not) from an employer who is not resident in this country if you yourself are not domiciled here. (Prior to 6 April 1974 UK tax on these so-called 'foreign emoluments' was only payable if you brought the money here.)

For 1974–75 and subsequent years of assessment this case also applies to any work which you do wholly abroad (unless you work for a non-resident employer and are yourself non UK domiciled). You are normally charged to tax on 75% of the earnings from your overseas employment but if however you are absent from this country for a continuous period of 365 days or more, you are not charged to UK tax on overseas earnings during that period. (You are allowed to spend up to 1/6th of your time in the UK without losing this relief.)

From 1977–78, to obtain the 25% deduction mentioned above, you must either have 30 'qualifying days' overseas in the year of assessment, or work for a non UK resident employer (p 97).

(2) **Schedule E Case II** applies if you are either not resident in the UK or are resident but not ordinarily resident here. Then you will normally be assessed to tax under this case on your earnings for duties performed here. In the case of 'foreign emoluments' (see above), however, only half your earnings for 1974–75 and subsequent years for duties performed here is chargeable to income tax in this country. (Prior to 1974–75 you then paid no tax unless you brought the money into the UK.)

(3) **Schedule E Case III** applies if you are UK resident and do work wholly abroad but remit salary here during the course of your overseas employment. The assessment is based on the actual amounts remitted to this country in the tax year (p 99) but (after 5 April 1974) if one of the other cases (see above) applies to the income, then Case III does not operate. This case now normally only applies to non UK domiciled people.

The Distinction between Schedule D Case I or II and Schedule E

This distinction is sometimes very fine as for instance in the case where you have a number of part-time employments and do some of the work at home. If you can show that you are in fact working on your own account and are self-employed (not an employee) then you will be assessed under Schedule D which normally results in your being able to deduct more of your expenses from your taxable income than if you were assessed under Schedule E. From 1978–79, divers and diving instructors are normally assessable under Schedule D (FA 1978 S29).

Employment Outside the United Kingdom

If your United Kingdom employment involves you in work abroad this is normally taxed as being derived from your employment in this country and is included in your taxable income. However, in respect of any work that you do abroad, special rules apply which may result in your paying less tax (p 104).

Amounts included in your Income

Any amount that you derive from your office or employment is normally included in your taxable income. This applies to the value of any payments in kind as well as cash.

Typical Items

Normal salary or wage.
Overtime pay.
Salary in lieu of notice (but see p 88).
Holiday pay.
Sick pay.
The value of luncheon vouchers in excess of 15p per day.
Cost-of-living allowance.
Christmas or other gifts in cash excluding personal gifts such as wedding presents.
Annual or occasional bonus.
Commission.
Director's fees.
Director's other remuneration.
Remuneration for any part-time employment.
Salary paid in advance.
Payment for entering into a contract of employment.
Tips from employer or from customers or clients of employer.
Settlement by employer of debts incurred by employee.
Payment by employer of employee's National Insurance contributions.
Value of goods supplied free of cost to employee by employer.
Value of shares or other assets received from employer for no charge, or amount by which their market value exceeds any payment made for them.

Fringe benefits (see below).
Travelling allowances in excess of expenditure incurred for business use (p 78).
Share options (p 84).

Fringe Benefits
(FA 1976 Ss60–72 & Schs 7–9 & FA 1977 S35 & Sch 8)

This is a wide term used to describe any tangible benefit which you obtain from your employment that is not actually included in your salary cheque. Fringe benefits are taxable according to the rules outlined below.

If you are an employee earning less than £8,500 each year, including the value of any benefits, then the taxation of your fringe benefits is on a comparatively favourable basis. If however you earn over £8,500 or are a director, then you are normally taxed more strictly on the actual value of the benefits obtained. If you fall into this latter class then your employers must submit to the Revenue a form P11D for you every year. This form covers your expenses and benefits (p 82).

You are not caught by the rules as being a *director*, if you own no more than 5% of the company's shares and work full time for it. (In the case of charities, etc., you do not need to work full time.) If you work for several companies which are connected, your earnings including benefits must be taken together for the purposes of the rules.

The taxation of certain fringe benefits is summarised in the following table according to whether or not you are a P11D employee (i.e. a director or earning over £8,500). Note that for 1978–79 the earnings threshold, for what are now known as *'higher paid employments'*, was £7,500 and for 1977–78 the figure was £5,000.

Table 11: Fringe Benefits – Taxation 1979–80

	Details	Non-P11D employee	P11D employee or director
(1)	Free private use of motor vehicle supplied by your employers.	Tax free (provided some business use is made).	Taxable (p 79).
(2)	Company house occupied rent free.	Taxed on annual value of benefit (i.e. open market rental and expenses paid) unless you need to occupy house to do your job properly.	Taxed on annual value unless you must live there to perform your duties (p 81).

Table 11 continued

(3)	Board and lodging.	If you receive cash you are taxed on it. Otherwise tax free.	Taxed on cost to employer of board and lodging subject to a limit (p 81).
(4)	Working clothing – e.g. overalls.	Tax free.	Tax free.
(5)	Suits and coats, etc.	Taxed on estimated second-hand value.	Taxed on full cost to employer.
(6)	Private sickness insurance cover.	Taxable (tax free before 6 April 1976).	Taxed on premiums paid by your employers (p 81).
(7)	Interest free loan.	Tax free.	Taxable subject to certain exemptions (p 80) – to participator, etc., of close company (p 180) – employee shareholdings (p 85).
(8)	Share options.	Taxable (p 84).	Taxable (p 84).
(9)	Employee's outings.	Tax free.	Normally tax free.
(10)	Luncheon vouchers.	Tax free up to 15p per day – excess taxable.	Tax free up to 15p per day – excess taxable.
(11)	Subsidised staff canteen.	Tax free.	Tax free provided facilities available to all staff.
(12)	Pension and death in service cover.	Normally tax tree (p 86).	Normally tax free (p 86).
(13)	Cash vouchers.	Taxable (p 81).	Taxable (p 81).
(14)	Assets at employee's disposal.	Normally tax free.	Taxable (p 81).

Travelling and Entertainment Allowances (S189)

An allowance or advance that you derive from your employer to meet the costs of travelling, entertaining or other services you perform on his behalf is not taxable provided that you actually incur expenditure for these purposes. (Your employer is able to deduct the payments from his taxable profits. Entertaining expenses however are not normally deductible, unless in connection with overseas customers and their agents (p 57).) Should you incur expenditure of less than the full allowance or advance and are not required to pay back the unexpended portion to your employer, this excess must be included in your taxable income.

If you are a P11D employee (p 82) any allowance made to you by your employers for travelling, etc., is normally included in your taxable income in full. If you incur travelling expenses, etc., in the course of your employment you must make a claim to that effect and you will be allowed to deduct from your taxable income the amount of your expenses. If you are not a P11D employee (or director) any expense allowances or payments on your behalf are not normally included in your taxable income.

You are not in general allowed any deduction for your travelling expenses between your home and your employer's place of business. Thus if your employer makes you any allowance for this expense it is wholly taxable in your hands.

For 1976–77 and subsequently, no tax is payable on travel facilities provided for *servicemen* and *women* going on and returning from *leave* (FA 1977 S37).

If you *travel abroad* in connection with your employer's business, the cost is allowable. If you also have a holiday abroad during the same trip you will be taxed on an appropriate proportion of the cost of your trip as a personal benefit. If your employers pay for your wife to accompany you (and she is not an employee herself) her own trip would normally be taxed as a personal benefit although some allowance could be obtained if for example she acted as your secretary during the trip or it was necessary for her to go for reasons of your health.

After 5 April 1977 no benefit is assessed on you if your employer pays for the actual journeys of your family in visiting you, provided you *work abroad* for at least 60 continuous days. This applies to your wife (or husband) and any of your children who are under 18 on the outward journey. Also covered are journeys by your family in accompanying you at the beginning of your overseas period or by you in visiting them at the end. Two return trips for each are covered by the rule, in any tax year (FA 1977 S32).

Motor Cars (FA 1976 Ss63–65 & Schs 7 & 9)

The following rules apply to you if yours is a director's or higher paid employment (p 77):

(a) If a car is provided for you by your employer and your business use is 'insubstantial' compared with your private use, you will be taxed on the running expenses for your private use paid for by your employers. You will also be taxed on the car's capital value assessed as 20% of the cost of the car reducing to 10% if its age at the end of the year of assessment is 4 years or more. For these purposes, 'insubstantial' is taken by the Revenue to mean 10% of your total use, or less.

(b) The above treatment does not apply if you make more substantial business use of your company car. In this case you will be taxed on a benefit derived from a scale which is to cover both the capital value and all running costs of your company car. This includes petrol and oil costs borne by your employer, but if you are reimbursed for any money which you lay out, you are assessed on the amount and must make an expenses claim for business use. The scales are as follows for (i) *1977–78* and (ii) *1978–79* and *1979–80*.

Cars with original market value up to (i) £6,000 and (ii) £8,000	Scale benefits assessed			
	Cars under 4 years old		Cars over 4 years old	
	(i)	(ii)	(i)	(ii)
Cylinder capacity –				
1300cc or less (x)	£175	£190	£120	£130
1301cc–1800cc (y)	225	250	150	165
over 1800cc (z)	350	380	235	255
Original market value –				
£6,001–10,000	500	—	335	—
8,001–12,000	—	550	—	365
over £10,000	800	—	535	—
over £12,000	—	880	—	585

Note: Cars without cylinder capacities are assigned the same scale charges according to their values when new as follows:

	(i)	(ii)
(x)	under £2,000	£2,500
(y)	£2,000–2,999	£2,500–3,499
(z)	£3,000–6,000	£3,500–8,000

(c) Provided you do not have the use of a particular car but simply take one from a car pool and do not garage it at home overnight, you will not normally be assessed to any benefit. This is subject, however, to the further condition that any private use of the car is merely incidental to your business use thereof.

Use of Assets (FA 1976 S63)

If your employer places an asset at your disposal for your personal use (e.g. a television set) your annual taxable benefit is 10% of its market value when you first began to use it. This rule does not apply to cars (see above) nor to land for which 'annual value' is used (S531) and only relates to those in director's or higher paid employment (p 77).

Beneficial Loan Arrangements (FA 1976 S66 & Sch 8)

(a) For 1978–79 and subsequent years, if you or a 'relative' have a loan by reason of your director's or higher paid employment at no interest or at a lower rate than the 'official' one then you will be taxed on the benefit of your interest saving compared with the official rate, subject to the following rules.

(b) The 'official rate' is 9% for 1978–79 and 1979–80.

(c) 'Relative' means parent, grandparent, child, grandchild, etc., brother, sister or spouse of yourself or any of the relatives aforementioned.

(d) No charge to tax will be made if the cash value of the benefit does not exceed £50.

(e) No charge to tax will be made if tax relief would have been available for any interest paid on the loan.

(f) For 1978–79 and 1979–80 the charge on loans taken out after 26 March 1974 is half the normal rate. (Loans taken out before that date will not give rise to any taxable benefit because any interest paid would qualify for tax relief.)

Medical Insurance (FA 1976 S68)

For 1976–77 and subsequent years, all directors and employees are taxed on any medical insurance premiums borne by their employer. This does not apply however to medical insurance covering overseas service.

Cash Vouchers (FA 1976 S71)

For 1977–78 and subsequent years, all employees (and directors) are normally taxed on the value of cash vouchers received as a result of their employment. That value is the money for which the vouchers are capable of being exchanged.

Living Accommodation provided for Employees
(FA 1977 Ss33 & 34)

From 1977–78 modified rules apply. In general, living accommodation provided to you because of your employment results in a taxable benefit. You are taxed on the open market rental value of the property, or the actual rent paid by your employer, if this is more. Amounts which you pay towards the cost are deducted.

You are exempted from the charge, however, if any of the following circumstances apply:

(a) You have to live in the accommodation in order to perform your duties properly.

(b) It is customary in your type of employment to have accommodation provided and it helps you to do your job better.

(c) Your employment involves you in a security risk and special accommodation is provided with a view to your safety.

The above exemption also covers rates paid for you, but does not apply in circumstances (a) and (b), if you are a director, unless you have broadly no more than a 5% shareholding and work full time or work for a charity, etc.

If your employment is 'director's or higher paid' (p 77), you will still be assessed on payments by your employer for your heating, lighting, cleaning, repairs, maintenance and decoration, etc., as well as on the value (10% – p 80) of domestic furniture and equipment provided. A limit applies, however, which is 10% of your net emoluments from your job which is after deducting capital allowances, pension contributions and expenses claims, and excludes the expenditure for your benefit.

Income from Employment and Your Return

You must enter in your return your occupation and your employer's name and address. Show your total gross earnings before any deductions unless this is not required by the type of return that you are sent by the Revenue. If your duties are performed wholly abroad, this must be indicated.

Include separate details of any director's fees voted by each company before deductions. Also show any part-time or casual earnings. Full details must also be shown in a special column provided on your return, of your wife's earnings from employments including directorships and casual employment.

You must give details of your benefits in kind including goods and vouchers received as well as living accommodation. Also show details of any share options granted by your employer (p 84).

If you are a P11D employee (p 77) you must enter the total amount of any expenses payments made to you and the total cost to your employer of any benefits provided for you. If the Inspector has granted a dispensation to your employer however, you may leave the relevant expenses payments out of your return. (A dispensation will be granted if the Inspector is satisfied that all of the expenses payments are covered by allowance expenses.)

Any leaving payments and compensation must be separately shown (p 88).

A separate section in your return is provided for details of your expenses in employment (p 83) including fees or subscriptions to professional bodies and superannuation contributions.

Expense Payments for Directors and Others (Form P11D) (Ss195–203 & FA 1976 S72)

If you have a director's or higher paid employment (p 77), your employers must complete a form P11D for each tax year in respect of all benefits in kind and expense payments made to you or on your behalf.

For 1978–79, the following particulars must be entered by your employer on your form P11D regarding any expenses payments made and benefits, etc., provided by him.

(1) Entertainment – all payments made exclusively for entertaining including the amount of any round sum allowance, specific allowances, sums reimbursed and sums paid to third persons (entertaining disallowable to your employer must still be included).

(2) General round sum expense allowances not exclusively for entertaining.

(3) Travelling and subsistence – fares, hotels, meals, etc., and payments from your employer for travel between your home and work from which no PAYE has been deducted.

(4) Cars.

    (a) Owned or hired by employer –
        (i)   Make, model and registration date.
        (ii) Value when new and engine capacity.
        (iii) Period for which car available to you in year.
        (iv) Payment by you towards running costs.
        (v) Wages of any driver provided for you.

    (b) Owned by you –
        (i)   Allowances from employer towards your running expenses.
        (ii) Contribution from employer towards purchase price, depreciation or hire.

(5) House, flat, etc., provided by employer – address of property – gross rating value – if rented by employer the rent, repairs and insurance borne by him – payments by the employer of your home expenses – annual value of the use of furniture and fittings owned by your employer.

(6) Subscriptions.

(7) Private medical and dental attention and treatment.

(8) Educational assistance for self or family.

(9) Goods and services supplied free or below market value – equivalent cash benefit.

(10) Work done to your own home or other assets by your employer.

(11) Wages and upkeep of personal or domestic staff provided by your employer.

(12) The market value of any cars or other assets given to you by your employer (other than personal gifts outside the business).

(13) Cost of vouchers given to you by your employer.

(14) Beneficial loans – particulars of loans giving rise to benefit assessment (p 80).

(15) Other expenses and benefits including your own national insurance contributions (if paid by your employer), holidays, home telephone, etc.

The total of the above items is extended on your P11D and then your employer deducts the following:

(a) The amounts of any of the above expenses that you have repaid to your employer (unless already deducted from the items shown).

(b) Amounts included above from which tax has been deducted under PAYE.

Deductions You May Claim (Ss189–194)

You may claim any expenses which you have to incur wholly, exclusively and necessarily in performing the duties of your employment. These do not include:

(a) The cost of travel between home and work.
(b) The cost of business entertainment except where the expense is disallowed in computing your employer's tax assessment or is reasonable entertainment of an overseas trading customer.

If you are a director or a P11D employee (p 77) you should make a claim to the Revenue in respect of any allowable expenses that have been included by your employer in your form P11D. The claim should certify that the expenses covered were incurred 'wholly, exclusively and necessarily' in performing the duties of your employment. You will not then be taxed on payments for such expenses made by your employer whether made to you or third parties.

Any expenses that you personally incur in connection with your employment should be included on your return and these include:

Overalls, clothing and tools.
Travelling.
Business use of your own car including capital allowances (p 68).
Home telephone and other expenses.
Professional fees and subscriptions relating to your work.
Your own contributions to any superannuation (pension) scheme operated by your employers (p 86).
In certain employments (e.g. entertainment industry) such expenses as hairdressing, make-up, clothes cleaning, etc.

Share Option and Share Incentive Schemes
(S186, FA 1972 S77 & FA 1973 Sch 8)

As a director or an employee of a company, you may be granted an option to take up shares in the company. When you exercise your option, the notional 'gain' will be included in your Schedule E assessment for the tax year in which you exercise the option. You thus pay income tax on the 'gain' (as earned income) calculated thus:

Market value of shares on day you exercise
option (i.e. when you take up the shares)   £A

Less: Price paid by you for the shares   £B
Price paid by you for the option (if any)   C
                                                        ——   D
                                                                  ——
Assessable 'gain'   £E
                                                                  ══

If you subsequently sell the shares themselves at a profit this will be liable to capital gains tax (p 121) calculated as follows:

Net proceeds obtained on the sale of the shares   £F

Less: Price paid by you for the shares   £B
       Price paid by you for the option (if any)   C
       Gain already assessed under Schedule E   E

                                            ———   A

Capital gain   £G

Share Incentive Schemes

(FA 1972 S79 & Sch 12, FA 1973 Sch 8 & FA 1974 S20)

These are schemes under which you are allowed to purchase shares in the company where you work because of your employment or directorship and not simply because of a general offer to the public. Prior to 27 March 1974, such a scheme could be approved by the Revenue if it satisfied similar rules to those appertaining to approved share option schemes (see above). Also, the shares could not be subject to any restriction which might artificially distort their value after you got them. Another rule was that the scheme had to be open to all those who had been full-time employees continuously for at least five years and were over 25. In this case you would normally only pay capital gains tax on any profit that you made from the future sales of the shares.

If you now obtain shares under certain incentive schemes, you are assessed to income tax under Schedule E on the increase in the market value of your shares between their acquisition date and the earliest of the following:

(a)   seven years from when you bought the shares;
(b)   the time when you cease to be a director or an employee of the company;
(c)   the time when you sell the shares; and
(d)   the time when your shares cease to be subject to any special restrictions.

Your Schedule E assessment is made for the tax year during which the earliest of the above times arises. The above rules apply to shares from non-approved share incentive schemes obtained after 5 April 1972 and in any incentive schemes obtained after 25 March 1974, but certain *profit sharing schemes* are excluded provided various conditions are satisfied, including the following:

(a)   the shares are publicly quoted or are not in one company which is controlled by another;
(b)   the shares are not subject to any special restrictions;
(c)   the scheme is open to all employees of the company aged 25 and over with at least 5 years continuous service; and
(d)   you receive your shares as part of your (taxable) emoluments according to a prearranged basis, geared to the profits of the company.

Employee Shareholdings (FA 1976 S67)

New rules apply if you are a director or higher paid employee (p 77) and after 6 April 1976 you acquire shares at an under value by reason of your employment. The shares need not be in the company which employs you.

You are treated as obtaining shares at an under value if you pay less than the market value of fully paid shares of the same class at that time. This applies whether or not you are under any obligation to pay more at a future time. You are taxed on the shortfall of what you pay for the shares compared with market value when you bought them. This shortfall is treated as an interest free loan (p 80) and you are treated as if your taxable earnings were increased by the benefit of such a loan. This continues until the shortfall is ended or the shares are sold, even if you cease your employment.

Profit Sharing Schemes (FA 1978 Ss53–61 & Sch 9)

Starting from 6 April 1979 tax relief is available for employees participating in a company share scheme which has been approved by the Revenue. Under such a scheme, trustees are allowed to acquire shares in the company to the value of up to £500 for any employee in any year.

A participant must agree to his shares remaining with the trustees for at least 5 years unless he dies, retires or becomes redundant. The scheme must be open to all employees with 5 years service or more. The employers may allow those with shorter service to join, however.

Any dividends on the shares are paid over to the participants. When any participant sells his shares after 5 years, the original value, or proceeds if more, will be charged to income tax according to the following scale:

Period held – years	% of original value (or proceeds if less) charged to income tax
Over 5 but less than 7 (or earlier redundancy, etc.)	50%
7–9	25%
10 or over	Nil

Retirement Pension Schemes (Ss208 & 220–225 & FA 1970 Ss19–26 & Sch 5)

Any National Insurance contributions that you pay are not deductible from your taxable income. Your employer however deducts his share of such contributions from his taxable profits. On your retirement your state pension is taxable as earned income and any widow's pension payable to your wife is also taxable in this way. Up to 5 April 1975 you also paid graduated contributions securing a higher state pension unless you were 'contracted out'. You could 'contract out' if you belonged to a pension scheme operated by your employer. There is now a new government 'Reserve Pension Scheme' with similar rules, operating from April 1978.

Any pension paid to you out of your employer's own staff superannuation scheme is taxable as earned income. The same applies to any retirement pension paid by your employer that has not been provided for under any scheme.

Retirement schemes are either 'contributory' or 'non-contributory'. In the latter case the employer bears the entire cost and in the former case the employee makes his own regular contributions to the scheme. If you work for a big company it may run its own pension scheme which will put aside funds to provide pensions for its employees. A separate pension trust is set up and investments are made on which no taxation is payable either on income or capital gains. The employees' contributions (if any) are deductible from their taxable earnings and amounts set aside by the company are deductible from its taxable profits. To qualify for this taxation treatment Revenue approval must be obtained (see below).

Instead of managing their own pension scheme many employers arrange for it to be operated by an insurance company. In return for annual premiums paid to it based on the salaries of the employees covered, the insurance company provides retirement pensions and also sometimes lump sum payments in the event of the death in service of any employee. Subject to Revenue approval (see below) the company deducts the contributions that it pays from its taxable profits and the employees deduct their contributions (if any) from their taxable earnings.

Conditions for Revenue Approval of Occupational Pension Schemes (FA 1970 Ss19 & 20)

If a new scheme is to obtain Revenue approval it must satisfy various conditions which are outlined below. Existing schemes may have been approved under different conditions but by 6 April 1980 they must be re-examined by the Revenue and approved under the current rules. If an old scheme is varied it must also be re-approved under the current rules.

(1) The following rules *must* be satisfied to obtain Revenue approval:

(a) The scheme only provides pensions, lump sum benefits, etc., for employees on their retirement or death : payable to themselves or their widows or dependants, etc.

(b) The employer must recognise the scheme, provide written details to all the employees and contribute to the scheme.

(c) The employer must be trading in this country and the scheme must be administered by someone here.

(2) If the following conditions are satisfied the Revenue are normally bound to approve the scheme:

(a) Any retirement pension is payable at an age between 60 and 70 (or 55 and 70 if a woman). The amount of the pension must not exceed one-sixtieth of final remuneration for each year of service (maximum 40 years). Thus if on your retirement you are earning £4,000 per annum and you have worked for 30 years your maximum pension is $£4,000 \times 30/60 = £2,000$.

(b) After the death of an employee after his retirement the pension payable to his widow must not exceed two-thirds of his own pension.

(c) No other benefits are payable under the scheme.

(d) The only way in which an employee can obtain a lump sum is that on his retirement he can give up part of his pension and receive not more than three-eighteths of final remuneration for each year of service (maximum 40 years). Thus if you retire after 30 years of service when you are earning £4,000 per annum you can take in cash up to $3/80 \times 30 \times £4,000 = £4,500$.

(3) At the discretion of the Revenue they may approve a scheme which:

(a) Exceeds the limits in (2) above for benefits for less than forty years service;

(b) Provides pensions for the widow, children or dependants following the death in service of an employee;

(c) Provides a lump sum death in service payment of up to four times final salary;

(d) Allows retirement at not earlier than 50 (45 for a woman) or on earlier incapacity;

(e) Provides for the return of employee's contributions;

(f) Relates to a trade conducted only partly in this country by a non-resident employer.

Compensation for Loss of Office
(Ss187–188 & Sch 8 & FA 1978 S24)

If a 'golden handshake' payment is made to you on your retirement, resignation, redundancy or removal from that office, etc., at least the first £10,000 will normally be tax free. Prior to 6 April 1978 this figure was £5,000.

The excess (if any) over £10,000 will be taxed as your earned income subject to certain reliefs (see below).

The employer is usually able to deduct 'golden handshake' payments from his taxable profits unless for example they are abnormally high payments to controlling directors or are made in connection with a sale of the actual business or made just before its cessation.

If you have a service contract that provides for a lump sum payment to be made to you when you leave your employer this payment will not be tax free because it is treated as arising out of your employment. This point should be borne in mind when service contracts are drawn up.

The tax treatment of any 'golden handshake' payment made to you will depend on whether it is *ex gratia* (i.e. made by your employer beyond any possible legal liability) or a 'compensation' payment. The latter term refers to an amount that you could have obtained by suing your employer for compensation for loss of office and the amount is estimated to be what the court would have awarded you. Many 'golden handshake' payments combine these two factors and so they must be apportioned between the 'compensation' part and the *ex gratia* part.

If you receive a 'compensation' payment you deduct £10,000 and pay tax on the balance subject to 'top-slicing' relief (see below). If you receive an *ex gratia* payment you pay tax on it (subject to top-slicing relief), after deducting the higher of £10,000 or the amount of your 'standard capital superannuation payment'. The latter is calculated as follows:

(1) Take your average annual emoluments for the three years up to your ceasing your employment.
(2) Divide this average by twenty and multiply by your total years of service.
(3) Deduct from the above result any tax free sum received under a retirement scheme operated by your employer.

For example if your earnings for the last three years were £10,000, £12,000 and £14,000 and you worked for 24 years in all with your employer then your average remuneration for the final three years would be £12,000 and your standard superannuation benefit is thus £12,000 × 24/20 = £14,400. Supposing that you receive an *ex gratia* payment of £20,000 you will pay tax on £20,000 − £14,400 = £5,600 subject to 'top-slicing relief'.

If your 'golden handshake' payment is entirely a 'compensation' payment then the 'top-slicing' calculation will consist of taking the amount received less £10,000 and dividing it by the remaining unexpired years of your contract.

The amount obtained is then charged to income tax (at basic and higher rates) on the basis that ignoring other earnings from your contract, it is your 'top slice' of earned income for the year in which it is regarded as received. You then multiply this tax by the number of unexpired years of the contract in order to obtain the total income tax payable. You are normally taxed on the payment on the basis that it is regarded as received when your employment terminates.

The same principle is used in the case of an *ex gratia* golden handshake payment except that you always use six years instead of the unexpired years of the contract. For example, suppose you receive an *ex gratia* payment of £12,000 net of your standard superannuation benefit. Divide by six giving £2,000 and calculate income tax on this at your top rates for earned income (ignoring other earnings from your contract) for the relevant year (say £1,200). Then you multiply by six giving 6 × £1,200 = £7,200 which is the income tax payable on your *ex gratia* payment after top-slicing relief.

Any payments received by a former employee in the following circumstances are normally tax free:

(1) *Ex gratia* payments on the death or permanent disability of the employee.
(2) Terminal grants to members of HM Forces.

(3) *Ex gratia* payments on the termination of a job where the employee worked abroad either:
    (a) for three-quarters of his entire term of service or
    (b) for the whole of the last ten years or
    (c) where the total service is more than 20 years, for half the total service period including any ten of the last 20 years.

The PAYE System (S204)

Most of the Schedule E income tax payable on earnings from employments in this country is collected under the 'pay as you earn' system (PAYE), which covers both basic rate and higher rate income tax.

Your employer is responsible for administering the PAYE on your own wages and that of your fellow employees. From each wages payment that you receive, whether it be weekly or monthly your employer must deduct the relevant income tax and pay to you the net amount. (If income tax had been previously over-deducted by your employer or if you suddenly become entitled to higher relief you may be due to receive a repayment of income tax which your employer will make to you.) Your employer then has to pay over to the Collector of Taxes the total PAYE income tax deductions (less refunds) in respect of the previous month.

Your employer must keep a separate tax deduction card for each of his employees (including directors but not partners). If the employee is paid weekly then the card has spaces for each week during the tax year ended 5 April – in the case of employees who are paid on a monthly basis, monthly tax deduction cards are used with a line for each month of the tax year. On the weekly tax deduction cards the following particulars are entered and calculated:

(1) National insurance contributions.
(2) Gross pay for the week.
(3) Cumulative pay for the tax year to date.
(4) Total 'free pay' to date (see below).
(5) Total taxable pay to date (3–4).
(6) Total tax due to date (see below).
(7) Tax to be paid or repaid for the week (see below).

(Similar details for each month are entered on the monthly tax deduction cards.) The total 'free pay' to date is obtained from 'Table A' in the tax tables provided by the Revenue. This table shows for each week the 'free pay' applicable to each code number (see below). If your total pay is less than your 'free pay' to date then you pay no more tax for that week and would normally get a refund.

The tax to be paid or repaid for the week (see 7 above) is calculated by subtracting the total tax due to date for the previous week from that for the current week (see 6 above). The total tax due to date is found each week from the tax deduction tables. These show the tax attributable to the relevant total taxable pay to date.

The tax deduction tables in use are designated tables B, C and D. Table B shows tax due at the lower and basic rate. Table C shows for each week or month (see below) the amounts to be taxed at each of the higher rates. Successive columns in table C cover all of the higher rates of tax from 40% to 60% (p 22).

If you have only one employment your tax is calculated from table B if your earnings are below the higher rates level. Should your earnings make you liable for income tax at the higher rates however, your PAYE tax payable is calculated from table C which is in fact supplementary to table B.

Where your earnings are substantial and you have more than one employment the Revenue will normally direct that tables B and C are used for your main employment. For your other employments however they might issue you with code D1 or D2, etc. The tax payable under these codings is shown in table D. This lists the tax payable at the various higher rates from 40% (code D0) up to 60%. Thus if you receive a salary of £5,000 from a directorship for which your code is D3, you have PAYE deducted at 55% on your entire salary from this directorship. At the end of the year, when your assessment is issued by the Revenue (p 28) your tax is adjusted to its correct level. The 'D' codings merely provide the Revenue with a very approximate method of taxing at source your salaries from employments other than your main one.

The Revenue provide monthly tax deduction tables for use where salary payments are made on a monthly basis. The tax deduction cards (whether weekly or monthly) have a column in which to enter the amount deductible for earnings-related national insurance contributions, which are collected through the PAYE system.

Your Code Number

Your code number is calculated from your income tax allowances and reliefs. It is allocated to you each tax year by the Inspector of Taxes and takes into account all the reliefs to which you are entitled against which some of your other income may be set off. Account may also be taken of any Schedule E income tax underpaid or overpaid for the previous year.

Normally a notice of coding is sent to you by the Inspector of Taxes each year. This itemises the various allowances and reliefs to which you are entitled (p 6). Any other necessary adjustments are also shown on your coding notice which shows at the bottom the adjusted balance of your allowances and also the code number which corresponds to that figure.

In order to convert your total allowances and adjustments into your code number, you simply divide by ten and round down to the nearest whole number. Thus if your allowances, etc., for 1979—80 total £1,915, your code number is 191. For administrative purposes, your code number will normally end in the letter L, H, P or V depending on whether it respectively includes single or wife's earnings allowance; married allowance or single allowance plus additional personal allowance; full single age allowance; or full married age allowance.

The above remarks normally apply to your coding in respect of your main employment. If you have other employments and the Revenue consider that your taxable earnings after deductions for the year will not exceed £10,000, you will be coded 'BR' in respect of each of your other employments. This means that table B (p 91) is applied to your total earnings from each employment except your main one. No deductions are normally made for your allowances, etc., because these are included in your coding for your main employment. If however your earnings are likely to exceed £10,000 then the Inspector of Taxes is likely to allocate you with 'D' codings (p 91) in respect of your supplementary employments.

In order to prepare your notice of coding accurately the Inspector of Taxes will refer to your Income Tax Return which you should submit in good time each year (p 150). If he does not have your Income Tax Return in time, the Inspector may provisionally base your code number on your allowances for the previous years or he may only allow in your coding the single man's personal allowance.

Employers' PAYE Returns

At the end of each tax year your employer must complete a form P35 and send this to the Revenue together with all of the tax deduction cards for his employees for that year. Also any forms P11D required for the year (p 82) should be sent to the Revenue with the form P35. The latter is a summary of the total tax due to be deducted for the tax year in respect of all of the employees. The earnings-related National Insurance contributions are also entered for each employee. The details are obtained from the tax deduction cards. The total income tax due to be paid over for the year by the employer is then found by adding up all of the tax entries on the form P35 and from this is deducted the total of the actual payments made. A similar procedure is followed regarding the earnings-related National Insurance contributions except that the amount to be paid over also includes the employer's contributions.

The balances shown by the form P35 represent underpayments or overpayments of PAYE income tax and earnings-related contributions: if the employer has underpaid he should send a cheque with the form and if he has overpaid a repayment will subsequently be received.

At the end of each tax year the employer should issue to each of his employees a form P60 which is a certificate of gross earnings for the year and of income tax deducted under PAYE.

Change of Employer

If you leave your employment your old employer should complete for you a form P45 in triplicate showing your name, district reference, code number, week or month number of the last entries on your tax deduction card, total gross pay to date and total tax due to date. Your old employer sends Part 1 of the form P45 to his Inspector of Taxes and hands to you Parts 2 and 3 which you must give to your new employer. The latter enters your address and date of starting on Part 3 and sends it to his Inspector.

Your new employer should prepare for you a tax deduction card in accordance with your form P45 and deduct PAYE tax from your wages in the normal way.

If you are not able to give a form P45 to your new employer, he must deduct tax under the 'emergency' system which assumes you are single and gives you no other allowances. If this happens you should make an income tax return to the Inspector of Taxes or supply the necessary details to him so that he can issue you with your correct code number which your employer will then use, making any necessary tax repayment to you.

10. Domicile and Residence

The Importance of Domicile and Residence

The domicile and residence of a tax payer has a considerable effect on his liability to United Kingdom income tax, capital gains tax and capital transfer tax. The position is summarised in the following table and dealt with in more detail in Chapters 11 and 12. (Domicile is defined on p 95 and residence on p 96.)

Table 12: The Tax Effects of Domicile and Residence

Tax	Situation of assets or where income arises	Tax treatment depending on taxpayers' residence and domicile		
		Taxed on arising basis	Taxed on remittance basis (p 99)	Tax free
Income Tax Schedule D Cases I & II	UK	All Classes		
	Abroad	Not normally applicable		
Case III	UK	All Classes		
	Abroad	Not normally applicable		
Cases IV & V other than trades, professions, pensions, etc.	UK	Not applicable		
	Abroad	UK domiciled resident and ordinarily resident	Non-domiciled, UK domiciled resident but not ordinarily resident	Non-resident
Case V relating to trades, professions, pensions, etc.	UK	Not applicable		
	Abroad	UK domiciled resident and ordinarily resident 75% of income (90% pensions)	Non-domiciled, UK domiciled, resident but not ordinarily resident	Non-resident
Case VI	UK	All classes		
	Abroad	Not normally applicable apart from anti-avoidance rules (p 118)		
Schedule E		(p 75)		
Capital Gains Tax	UK or Abroad	UK domiciled and resident or ordinarily resident	Non-domiciled but resident or ordinarily resident	Neither resident nor ordinarily resident
Capital Transfer Tax (residence is immaterial)	UK	UK domiciled or non-domiciled		
	Abroad	UK domiciled or deemed domiciled (p 187)		Non-domiciled

What is Domicile?

Your domicile is the country which you regard as your natural home. It is your place of abode to which you intend to return in the event of your going abroad. For most people it is their country of birth. Everyone has one domicile only. Unlike dual nationality, it is not possible to have two domiciles under English law. There are three main categories of domicile:

(a) Domicile of origin.
(b) Domicile of choice.
(c) Domicile of dependency.

Domicile of Origin

You receive a domicile of origin at birth; it is normally that of your father at the date of your birth. In the case however of an illegitimate child or one born after the death of his father his domicile of origin is that of his mother.

Your domicile of origin can be abandoned and you can take on a domicile of choice (see below). You will quickly revert to your domicile of origin however if you take up permanent residence again in that country.

Domicile of Choice

If you abandon your domicile of origin and go and live in another country with the intention of permanently living there, the new country will become your domicile of choice. You will normally have to abandon most of your links with your original country of domicile (p 98).

If you lose or abandon your domicile of choice, your domicile of origin automatically applies once again, unless you establish a new one.

Domicile of Dependency

Certain dependent individuals are deemed incapable of choosing a new domicile and the latter is always fixed by the operation of the law. Dependants for this purpose include infants, married women before 1 January 1974 and mental patients.

An infant (under 16 years of age) automatically has the domicile of his father if he is legitimate, and otherwise that of his mother. If however a girl of under 16 marries then she takes on her husband's domicile. (Prior to 1 January 1974 the relevant age was 18.)

Prior to 1 January 1974, a wife assumed the domicile of her husband while they were married. After the end of the marriage (by death or divorce) the woman kept her former husband's domicile unless she took on a fresh domicile of choice. Since 1 January 1974, however, a wife's domicile is independent of that of her husband. If married before that date, the husband's domicile remains as the wife's domicile of choice in the first instance.

95

What is Residence?

Your residence for tax purposes is something which is fixed by your circumstances from year to year and you may sometimes be treated as being resident in more than one country at the same time.

Residence depends on the facts of each case and is determined by the individual's presence in a country, his objects in being there and his future intentions regarding his length of stay. The main criterion is the length of time spent in the country during each tax year. Another important point is whether a 'place of abode' is kept in the country (p 97).

What is Ordinary Residence?

If you have always lived in this country you are treated as being ordinarily resident here. Ordinary residence means that the residence is not casual and uncertain but that the individual who resides in a particular country does so in the ordinary course of his life. It implies residence with some degree of continuity, according to the way a man's life is usually ordered.

If you come to this country with the intention of taking up permanent residence here, it is Revenue practice to regard you as being both resident and ordinarily resident in the United Kingdom from your date of arrival. If however you originally did not intend to take up permanent residence here, you would not be considered ordinarily resident unless you stay here for two complete tax years and keep a place to live in this country.

The Residence of an Individual (Ss49–51)

If a person visits this country for some temporary purpose only and not with the intention of establishing his residence here he is not normally treated as being a UK resident unless he spends at least six months here during the tax year.

An overseas visitor however might be treated as acquiring UK residence if he pays habitual substantial visits to this country. The normal requirement would be to come here for at least four consecutive years and stay for an average of at least three months each year. If you wish to remain non-resident you must avoid such habitual visits.

If you pay only short casual visits abroad you will not lose your United Kingdom residence, but if an entire tax year is included in any continuous period spent abroad you will normally be treated as being non-resident for at least the intervening tax year (p 98).

The Residence of a Company (S482)

A company is deemed to be resident where its central control and management are carried out. This is not necessarily where the company is registered although normally the central control and management would be exercised in the country in which the company is registered. If however a company simply has its registered office here but carries on all its business from offices abroad and holds its board meetings abroad, it is non-resident.

If a company registered abroad transacts some of its business in this country, it will not normally be treated as being UK resident provided its management and control are exercised abroad, which includes all board meetings being held abroad.

S482 contains penal provisions to prevent a UK company from becoming non-resident without Treasury consent being obtained. Such consent is also required to transfer part or all of its business to a non-resident.

The Residence of a Partnership (S153)

Where any trade or business is carried on by a partnership and the control and management of the trade is situated abroad, the partnership is deemed to be resident abroad. This applies even if some of the partners are resident in this country and some of the trade is carried on here (p 149).

The Residence of a Trust

A trust is generally treated for capital gains tax purposes as being resident and ordinarily resident in the United Kingdom unless its general administration is ordinarily carried on outside this country and a majority of the trustees are neither resident nor ordinarily resident here.

Place of Abode in the United Kingdom (S50)

If you maintain a house or flat in this country available for your occupation this will usually be a factor towards deciding that you are resident here. Your residence position will however be decided without regard to any place of abode maintained for your use in the United Kingdom in the following circumstances.

(a) You work full-time in a trade, profession or vocation no part of which is carried on in this country.
(b) You work full-time in an office or employment, all the duties of which (ignoring merely incidental duties) are performed outside the United Kingdom.

The Effect of Visits Abroad (S49)

If you are a British subject or a citizen of the Republic of Ireland and your ordinary residence has been in the United Kingdom you are still charged to income tax if you have left this country if it is for the purpose of only occasional residence abroad.

In order to obtain non-residence for UK tax purposes your overseas residence must be more than merely occasional – it must have a strong element of permanency. The normal Revenue requirements are as follows:

(a) A definite intention to establish a permanent residence abroad.
(b) The actual fulfilment of such intention.
(c) Normally a full tax year should be spent outside this country

before you are considered non-resident. Thus if you leave the country permanently on 30 September 1978 you will only be confirmed as non-resident after 5 April 1980. If you went abroad for the purposes of an employment or to carry on a trade, once you are accepted by the Revenue as being no longer resident here, your non-residence is made retrospective to your date of departure; in other cases it will run from the next 6 April.

How to Change your Domicile and Residence

As has been already indicated, domicile and residence normally run together but domicile is much more difficult to change.

The way in which to change your residence is summarised above. You simply establish a permanent residence abroad and remain out of this country for a complete tax year. After that you must avoid returning to this country for as much as six months in any one tax year, averaging less than three months here every year. If however you have a place of abode available for you in the United Kingdom you are regarded as being resident here for any tax year during which you pay a visit (no matter how short); unless your residence abroad is for the purpose of an overseas trade or employment (p 97).

In order to change your domicile to a new domicile of choice, you should take as many steps as possible to show that you regard your new country as your permanent home.

The following points are relevant to establishing a particular country as your new domicile:

(1) Develop a long period of residence in the new country.
(2) Purchase or lease a home.
(3) Marry a native of that country.
(4) Develop business interests there.
(5) Make arrangements to be buried there.
(6) Draw up your will according to the law of the country.
(7) Exercise political rights in your new country of domicile.
(8) Arrange to be naturalised (not vital).
(9) Have your children educated in the new country.
(10) Resign from all clubs and associations in your former country of domicile and join clubs, etc., in your new country.
(11) Any religious affiliations that you have with your old domicile should be terminated and new ones established in your new domicile.
(12) Arrange for your family to be with you in your new country.

The above are some of the factors to be considered and the more of these circumstances that can be shown to prevail, the sooner you will be accepted as having changed your domicile.

11. Tax on Foreign Income

Overseas Income from Investments and Businesses (Ss109 & 122–124 & FA 1974 Ss22 & 23)

If you obtain any income from investments and businesses situated overseas, you will normally be charged to income tax under Case IV or Case V of Schedule D. Case IV applies to income from 'securities' unless the income has already been charged under Schedule C (p 46). Case V applies to income from 'possessions' outside the United Kingdom. This includes businesses but does not cover emoluments from any overseas employment (p 104).

Your income assessed under Case IV and V of Schedule D will be included in your total income for tax purposes (p 22).

Frequently your overseas income will have already suffered tax in its country of origin. If you also have to pay United Kingdom income tax on this income you will normally be entitled to some relief so as to limit the extent that you are doubly taxed on the same income (p 106).

The normal basis of assessment under Cases IV and V of Schedule D is the amount of income arising in the tax year preceding the year of assessment. In the opening and closing years of a source of income however, special rules apply (p 102).

In certain special circumstances the 'arising basis' is not used and the normally more favourable 'remittance basis' applies. If you are UK domiciled and ordinarily resident, however, your assessments on overseas businesses and pensions for 1974–75 and subsequent tax years are based on only 90% of the income arising from pensions and 75% from businesses.

What is the Remittance Basis?

Under the remittance basis you are only taxed on the amount of income actually brought into this country in the tax year preceding the year of assessment (whilst you still possess the source of overseas income). If you are assessed on the remittance basis and bring income into the United Kingdom in a tax year after the source has come to an end you are not liable to United Kingdom tax on it at all (p 102). Remittances can be made in cash or kind (p 100).

If you make no remittances you will have no liability to United Kingdom tax on your overseas income that is taxable on the remittance basis, no matter how high your income is in any year, although you might well suffer foreign tax.

When Does the Remittance Basis Apply? (S122)

Your Case IV and V assessments will be based not on the 'arising' basis but on the remittance basis:

(a)   if you are resident in this country but not domiciled here (p 96); or

(b) if you are a British subject or a citizen of the Republic of Ireland and are resident in this country but not ordinarily resident here.

For years of assessment up to and including 1973–74, even if (a) or (b) did not apply, you were taxed on a remittance basis;

(1) if the income was derived by you from personally carrying on any trade, profession or vocation abroad in partnership, or in certain cases on your own; or

(2) if the income arose to you from any pension abroad.

Any remittances of this pre-1973–74 income after 5 April 1974 are not taxed here, even if no tax was payable when it arose.

You may have some overseas income that is taxed on a remittance basis and some that is taxed on an arising basis. In this case you should clearly segregate the two sources of income by using separate bank accounts since income from the latter can be brought into this country without paying any additional tax here because it has already been charged to United Kingdom tax.

Note that if you are not resident in this country (p 96) you will not normally be charged to tax in respect of your Case IV and Case V income, even if it is remitted here.

What are Classed as Remittances? (S122)

Whilst you have any continuing sources of overseas income in respect of which income arising abroad has not been fully transmitted to this country, any sums brought into the United Kingdom will normally be first considered to be remittances of overseas income.

The above will not apply if you keep separate bank accounts for income and capital, bringing in funds from the latter only.

As well as cash and cheques, any property imported or value arising here from property not imported will be classed as remittances. Thus if you buy a car abroad out of your overseas profits and bring it into this country this is a remittance (although strictly speaking the second-hand value of the car at the time of importation should be used instead of the cost of the car). Similarly if you hire an asset abroad out of unremitted overseas income, any use that you get from the asset in this country should be valued and treated as a remittance.

If you borrow money against sums owing to you for overseas income and bring the former into this country, this is a remittance. Similarly if you borrow money here and repay it abroad out of overseas profits this is known as a 'constructive remittance' and is taxable. Other forms of 'constructive remittances' include the payment out of overseas income of interest owing in this country, and the repayment out of such income of money borrowed overseas which was made available to you in this country.

If you use non-remitted overseas income to buy shares in United Kingdom companies this is normally treated as a remittance unless you do so through a third party abroad who actually acts as the principal in the transaction.

You are able to use non-remitted overseas income to cover the cost of overseas visits (including holidays) and provided you bring none of the money back to this country there is no taxable remittance. For this purpose the Revenue allow you to receive traveller's cheques in this country provided they are not cashed here.

If overseas profits are remitted to the Channel Islands or the Isle of Man this is not treated as a taxable remittance since those countries are not regarded as part of the United Kingdom for taxation purposes. They are however treated as being part of the United Kingdom for the purposes of exchange control. This is most important since it is a United Kingdom exchange control rule that income earned abroad should be remitted to the United Kingdom. This rule is satisfied by sending the money to, say, Jersey or Guernsey without in turn incurring any United Kingdom income tax liability.

The Basis of Assessment under Schedule D Cases IV and V (S122 & FA 1974 S23)

As previously mentioned the normal basis of assessment is the amount of income arising in the tax year preceding the year of assessment. In certain cases however the assessment is based on the remittances in the previous tax year (p 99).

A few deductions are allowed in computing the income arising including the following:

(a) Any annuity paid out of the income to a non-resident of this country.

(b) Any other annual payment out of the income to a non-resident.

(c) Normal trading expenses against any trade, etc., which you have abroad.

(d) Normal maintenance costs against rental income arising abroad.

(e) 10% of any pensions and 25% of any business profits assessable after 1973–74.

(f) If you pay any overseas taxes for which you get no form of double tax relief then you can deduct such payments in computing your overseas income arising.

(g) If your overseas pension (or part of it) arises under the German or Austrian law relating to victims of Nazi persecution, the deduction is 50%. This includes cases where refugees from Germany were later credited with unpaid social security contributions thereby getting higher pensions.

Special Rules for Fresh Income (S123)

If you have a new source of Schedule D Case IV or V income your assessments will be as follows:

TAX ON FOREIGN INCOME

(a) For the tax year in which the income first arises on the income for that year.

(b) Unless the income first arose on 6 April, the assessment for the second tax year will also be on the actual income arising in that year.

(c) Your assessment for the third tax year will be based on the income arising in the preceding tax year. Also if income first arose on 6 April your assessment for the second tax year will be based on the income arising in the previous year.

(d) You have the option of electing that your first assessments falling to be made on a preceding year basis as in (c) above should instead be on the income actually arising in the respective tax year.

(e) In the case of income assessable on a remittance basis (p 99) the above rules are applied by substituting the remittances during the tax year for the income arising during the tax year.

Special Rules where Source of Income Ceases (S124)

(a) If an overseas source of income ceases in a given tax year then your assessment for that year is on the income arising in it.

(b) Your assessment for the tax year preceding that in which the source ceases is increased to the actual income arising if this is greater than the original 'preceding year' assessment.

(c) If you obtained no income from the terminated source during its last two years then if you so elect within two years after the end of the tax year in which the source ceased, your assessment for the last tax year in which any income arose is adjusted to the actual income for that year. Also the assessment for the following year is cancelled – this would otherwise have been on the preceding year's income.

The assessment for the tax year prior to the one in which income last arose will be increased to the actual income arising if this is greater than the original 'preceding year' assessment.

(d) If you have obtained no income from an overseas source for six years, you can elect that it should be treated as having ceased in the last tax year in which income arose. Your assessment for that year is then adjusted to 'actual' and the following year's assessment is cancelled. The previous year's assessment may require to be increased to the actual income arising as in (b) above.

(e) The above rules apply to income assessed on a remittance basis – you simply consider the remittances during the tax year instead of the income arising. Rules (c) and (d) above are of particular application to situations where the assessments are on a remittance basis since you may choose to make no remittances for a number of years so that you incur no United Kingdom tax on the relevant overseas income for those years.

(f) Where you are assessed on the remittance basis (p 99) you

102

will not be liable to United Kingdom tax on any income that you bring into this country during a tax year later than the one in which your overseas source ceases.

Example 19: Assessments under Schedule D Cases IV and V

Mr A is resident in the United Kingdom but not domiciled here. On 1 July 1972 he opened a bank deposit account in Jersey and made the following remittances of his Jersey bank deposit interest to this country:

31 December 1972	£50
31 December 1973	£100
31 December 1974	£75
31 December 1975	£110
31 December 1976	£90

No further income remittances were made after 31 December 1976. On 31 January 1980 the Jersey bank deposit account is closed. What will Mr A's income tax assessments be on his Jersey deposit interest?

Because Mr A is not domiciled in this country his assessments under Cases IV and V of Schedule D will be on a remittance basis as follows:

1972–73	First year – actual			£50
1973–74	Second year – actual			£100
1974–75	Third year – preceding year basis	£100		
	Reduced on claim by Mr A to actual			£75
1975–76	Preceding year basis	£75	adjusted to actual on claim by Mr A	£110
1976–77	Preceding year basis	£110		£90
1977–78	Preceding year basis	£90		NIL

Note: Since the source is closed during 1979–80 and no interest is remitted during 1979–80 or 1978–79 the assessments for the last years in which remittances were made are adjusted as shown on election by Mr A which results in £75 dropping out of assessment.

Professions Conducted Partly Abroad

If you are engaged in any profession or vocation that is conducted partly within this country and partly overseas, you will normally be assessed on your entire 'global' profits under Case II of Schedule D (p 55). It is only if you conduct a separate profession or vocation entirely abroad that Schedule D Case V will apply.

This rule is particularly applicable to actors and entertainers, etc., who travel widely in the conduct of their professions. The rule does not apply however to income from an office or employment the duties of which are conducted entirely abroad.

Relief for Overseas Trading by Individuals
(FA 1978 S27 & Sch 4)

For 1978–79 and subsequent years a new relief applies against assessments under Schedule D Cases I–II on trades, professions or vocations including partnerships. If you carry on such a trade, etc., reside in the UK and are absent from it for at least 30 'qualifying days' in a year of assessment, you will be able to claim the relief. Your claim must be within two years of the end of the year of assessment, however.

The relief consists of a deduction from your assessment of 25% of the proportion relating to your total 'qualifying days'. Thus if you have 'qualifying days' of say 4 months in a year of assessment when your assessable profit is £15,000, this will be reduced by relief of £15,000 × 25% × 4/12 = £1,250.

A 'qualifying day' is broadly one spent abroad on business and is defined in terms almost exactly similar to those used in the case of earnings from overseas employments (see below).

Earnings from Overseas Employments
(Ss181 & 184 & FA 1974 S21 & Sch 2 & FA 1977 S31 & Sch 7)

The 25% Deduction

Prior to 6 April 1974, if you were a United Kingdom resident, you were assessed to income tax under Case III of Schedule E in respect of any remittances to this country during the tax year, derived from any *overseas employment* that you had at that time. After 5 April 1974 however, you are normally assessed to tax under Case I of Schedule E, on 75% of such earnings.

An overseas employment is one the duties of which are performed outside this country. If an employment is performed partly here and partly abroad, you will normally be taxed on the income arising under Case I of Schedule E (p 75). Special rules apply however if you are not domiciled here (p 95). Any duties that you perform in this country which are purely incidental to the performance of your overseas employment are normally disregarded and so the special treatment would apply.

Before 6 April 1977 a separate contract with a UK employer concerning overseas duties sufficed as an overseas employment. After that date however, the requirement is that you have a 'foreign employment', which needs to be with an employer who is not resident in the UK. Otherwise, you must work abroad for at least 30 'qualifying days', in order to obtain the 25% deduction from your overseas earnings in computing the taxable amount.

A *'qualifying day'* is one away from the UK which you devote substantially to overseas employment including related travelling. (Not included is any day on which you return to the UK before midnight.) Concerning continuous periods abroad of at least seven days, however, these can be considered as a whole so that intervening rest days would be permitted.

If you work both abroad and in the UK for the same or associated employers, there are rules to split your earnings fairly between your UK and overseas activities. This is done broadly on a time basis, note also being taken of the nature of your respective duties.

The 100% Deduction

After 5 April 1974 you are not normally liable to UK tax on any income from overseas employments which you earn during a 'qualifying period' of absence from this country of at least a year. This does not need to be a tax year and you are allowed to spend here up to one-sixth of the period, but no more than 63 days in any one visit. After 5 April 1977 the maximum time allowed back in the UK is normally 62 days, otherwise the required continuous 'qualifying period' is broken. This means that you must start reckoning your qualifying period from when you return overseas again.

Also, the one-sixth test is applied to all periods cumulatively from the start of your 'qualifying period' until the end of each overseas visit. Thus if you start your overseas service by being away for 20 days, come back for 20 days and return for 20 days, your 'chain' is broken because you have spent one-third of the 60 days in the UK instead of the maximum of one-sixth.

Remittances

The rules concerning the remittance of Schedule E Case III income are exactly the same as for income assessable under Cases IV and V of Schedule D (p 101). The remittance basis now broadly only applies for overseas employments if you are UK resident and not domiciled here and/or not ordinarily resident.

Remittances of income from overseas employments are not taxable here in any of the following circumstances:

(1) If made later than the tax year in which the employment ceases.
(2) If made during a tax year in which you are not resident here (whether or not you are ordinarily resident in this country).
(3) If made after 5 April 1974, and you are UK domiciled and ordinarily resident.

Expenses concerning work overseas (FA 1977 S32)

Provided your employer ultimately bears the cost, normally you are not taxed as a benefit on any of the following expenses concerning overseas employments:

(a) Travelling to take up your overseas employment or returning

on its termination. (Expense relief is available if you bear the cost yourself.)
(b) Board and lodging overseas.
(c) Certain visits by your family (p 79).

Double Taxation Relief (Ss497–518)

The United Kingdom government has entered into agreements with the governments of other countries for the purpose of preventing double taxation under the United Kingdom tax law and under the tax law of such other countries in respect of the same income. A further object of certain of those agreements is to render reciprocal assistance in the prevention of tax evasion.

Under particular double taxation conventions certain classes of income are made taxable only in one of the countries who are party to the agreement, for example that in which the taxpayer resides. Certain other income is taxable in both of the countries concerned but in the case of United Kingdom residents, the overseas tax is allowed as a credit against the United Kingdom tax.

If there is no double tax convention between this country and another one then 'unilateral relief' may be available. This means that if you are a United Kingdom resident and obtain income from the other country you are normally allowed to set off any overseas tax suffered against your United Kingdom tax liability on the same income. If you are not allowed to do so then you can deduct the overseas tax in computing the overseas income taxable in this country.

Table 13: Double Taxation Relief – List of Countries which have General Agreements with the United Kingdom

Country	Year of main agreement	Country	Year of main agreement
Antigua	1968	Fiji	1975
Australia	1967	Finland	1969
Austria	1969	France	1968
Barbados	1970	Gambia	1947
Belgium	1967	German Federal	
Belize	1947	Republic	1964
Botswana	1977	Ghana	1977
Brunei	1950	Gilbert & Ellice Is	1950
Burma	1950	Greece	1953
Canada	1966	Grenada	1949
Cyprus	1974	Guernsey	1952
Denmark	1950	Indonesia	1974
Dominica	1949	Irish Republic	1976
Egypt	1977	Israel	1962
Falkland Islands	1949	Italy	1960
Faroe Islands	1950	Jamaica	1973

Table 13 continued

Country	Year of main agreement	Country	Year of main agreement
Japan	1969	St Christopher &	
Jersey	1952	Nevis	1947
Kenya	1973	St Lucia	1949
Korea	1977	St Vincent	1949
Lesotho	1949	Seychelles	1947
Luxembourg	1967	Sierra Leone	1947
Malawi	1955	Singapore	1966
Malaysia	1973	Solomon Islands	1950
Malta	1962	South Africa	1979
Isle of Man	1955	South West Africa	
Mauritius	1947	(Namibia)	1962
Montserrat	1947	Spain	1975
Netherlands	1967	Sudan	1975
Netherlands Antilles	1970	Swaziland	1968
New Zealand	1966	Sweden	1960
Nigeria (terminated)	1947	Switzerland	1977
Norway	1969	Tanzania	1952
Pakistan	1961	Trinidad & Tobago	1966
Philippines	1976	Uganda	1952
Poland	1976	USA	1976
Portugal	1968	Zambia	1972
Rhodesia	1955	Zanzibar (Tanzania)	1952
Romania	1975		

Note: In addition to the above general agreements, arrangements of a more restricted kind have been entered into with Argentina, Brazil, Jordan, Lebanon, Venezuela and Zaire covering the double taxation of profits from shipping and air transport. There is an agreement with Iceland covering shipping profits only and agreements with Ethiopia, Hungary, Iran and USSR cover only air transport.

12. Non-residents, Visitors and Immigrants

On what Income are Non-residents Liable to United Kingdom Tax?

If for a given tax year you are not a United Kingdom resident (p 96) you will normally be liable to United Kingdom income tax only on income arising in this country. If your income arising here is also taxed in your country of residence you will in many cases be entitled to double taxation relief (p 106). Should there be a double taxation agreement between your country of residence and the United Kingdom (p 106) this agreement may provide that certain categories of income arising in this country should only be taxed in your own country and not here. The following paragraphs cover the position if no double tax relief is obtained.

Business Profits in the United Kingdom (S109, etc.)

If you are non-resident but carry on a business in this country you will be charged to tax here on your profits. You will be assessed to income tax under Schedule D Case I (p 55) at the lower, basic rate (30%) and higher rates if your total income liable to United Kingdom tax is sufficiently high (p 22).

If your United Kingdom business is operated by a manager, etc., he is charged to the tax on your behalf but if your only business in this country consists of selling through a broker or agent, you will not be chargeable.

Income from Property and Land in the United Kingdom (S67, etc.)

Income tax under Schedule A (or Schedule D Case VI) is charged on this income (p 39). If you are non-resident you will nevertheless have to pay United Kingdom income tax on this income – the basic rate normally should be deducted at source. Furthermore such income is frequently not covered by the respective double taxation agreement.

Interest received from Sources in the United Kingdom (Ss 109 & 119–121)

You are liable to income tax under Schedule D Case III on this income (p 51).

Interest on United Kingdom Securities (Ss93–107)

Income tax at the basic rate (30%) will be withheld from interest payments made to you unless some lower rate (or nil rate) is specified in any double taxation agreement (p 106).

Dividend Payments to Non-Residents
(S232 & FA 1972 Ss87 & 98, etc.)

If you are non-resident, your dividends from UK companies normally carry no basic rate tax credits unless you get relief under S27 (p 111), or under certain double taxation arrangements (see below). Thus if you receive a dividend of £70, you will normally pay overseas tax on this amount with no deduction for the £30 tax credit which you would have got, if you were a UK resident. You may be liable however to the excess of the higher rate income tax and investment income surcharge over the basic rate (p 22) on the actual dividend payments. Such tax would qualify for relief against your overseas tax subject to the relevant double tax arrangements (p 106).

Provided the relevant double tax agreements have been revised to permit it, special arrangements can be made between UK companies and the Board of Inland Revenue. These enable a UK company, when paying a dividend to an overseas resident, also to pay him an amount representing the excess over his UK tax liability on the dividend, of the UK tax credit to which he is entitled under the relevant double tax agreement (p 106).

Income from Employments in the United Kingdom
(S181, etc., & FA 1974 S21 & Sch 2)

If you are not resident in this country (or if resident if you are not ordinarily resident) you are assessed to United Kingdom tax under Case II of Schedule E in respect of any emoluments during the relevant tax year regarding duties performed here.

The above does not apply however to 'foreign emoluments' which before 6/4/74 were exempted from charge under Schedule E Cases I and II. 'Foreign emoluments' are those of a person not domiciled in this country from an office or employment with an employer who is not resident here. For 1974–75 and subsequent tax years 50% of your 'foreign emoluments' are charged to Schedule E income tax.

For 1976–77 and later years of assessment, 75% of your 'foreign emoluments' are taxed here if you are then United Kingdom resident and have been so for at least nine of the last ten years.

Higher Rate Income Tax

If you are not resident in this country but are liable to United Kingdom income tax on part or all of your income, this may be taxed at the lower, basic and higher rates. This will depend on the amount of your income liable to United Kingdom income tax. Thus if for 1979–80 this comes to £12,000 after allowable deductions, including £6,000 of investment income you will pay income tax at 25% on £750, 30% on £9,250, 40% on £2,000 and investment income surcharge on £1,000. Thus your total UK income tax will be £3,762.50 + £150 = £3,912.50 (subject to possible double tax relief).

Interest Paid to Non-Residents in respect of Certain United Kingdom Government Securities (S99)

The interest on certain specified United Kingdom government securities (p 49) can be paid to you gross without the deduction of any United Kingdom income tax provided the following conditions are satisfied:

(1) You are not ordinarily resident in this country (p 96).
(2) A claim has been made on your behalf to the Revenue requesting that payment is made to you without the deduction of any United Kingdom income tax.

If the above conditions are satisfied then the Bank of England will be instructed to remit to you overseas the gross amounts of interest as they become payable, without the deduction of any United Kingdom income tax at the source.

Rules for Taxation of Visitors' Income (S51)

If you come to this country as a visitor only and you do not intend to establish your residence here, you will not normally be charged to United Kingdom income tax on income arising elsewhere. This applies provided you have not actually been in this country for more than six months during the relevant tax year.

As a general rule you are not subject to United Kingdom income tax unless you are chargeable as a person resident here (p 96).

Even if you are not resident in this country during a given tax year you will normally be chargeable to United Kingdom income tax on your income arising from sources within the United Kingdom. However interest on certain government bonds is exempted if you make the required application to the Revenue (p 50). You may also be entitled to double taxation relief in respect of your income arising in this country (p 106).

When Does an Habitual Visitor become a UK Resident?

If you are a visitor to the United Kingdom you are treated as resident here for tax purposes in any year of assessment in which you spend more than six months in this country.

Even if you do not stay for six months in any tax year, you will be regarded as becoming resident if you come here year after year (so that your visits become in effect part of your habit of life) and those visits are for a substantial period or periods of time. The Revenue normally regard an average of three months as being substantial and the visits as having become habitual after four years. Further, if your arrangement indicated from the start that regular visits for substantial periods were to be made the Revenue would regard you as being resident here in and from the first tax year.

If however a place of abode is maintained for you in this country, subject to certain specified exceptions, you will be regarded by the Revenue as being resident here for any year in which you pay a visit to the United Kingdom (p 97).

The Position of Visiting Diplomats (Ss372–374)

Special tax exemptions are given to visiting diplomats including Agents-General, High Commissioners, consuls and official agents. Consular officers and employees of foreign states who visit this country are afforded certain tax exemptions here, even if they stay in the United Kingdom for sufficiently long normally to be treated as resident here. The conditions for the exemptions to apply are that:

(a) The individual is not a citizen of the United Kingdom or colonies.
(b) He is not engaged in any trade, profession or employment in this country (apart from his diplomatic duties), and
(c) he is either a permanent employee of the foreign state or was not ordinarily resident in the United Kingdom immediately before he became a consular officer or employee here.

The tax concessions which apply when appropriate arrangements have been made with the foreign state concerned include the following:

(a) Any income of the individual which falls under Cases IV and V of Schedule D (p 101) is not subject to income tax here.
(b) Certain overseas dividends and interest on securities are not taxed in this country.
(c) Emoluments of the individual from his consular office or employment are not taxed here.
(d) No capital gains tax (p 121) is payable on disposals of assets situated outside the United Kingdom.

The Entitlement of Certain Non-residents to UK Tax Reliefs (S27)

Unless you are resident here or fall within the categories listed below, you will not obtain any United Kingdom personal reliefs and allowances (p 6) against your income tax liability in this country.

If you fall within the undermentioned categories however, you will normally obtain against your income taxable in this country a proportion (A/B) of the income tax reliefs that you would have got if resident here. (A is your total income subject to UK tax and B is your total income throughout the world. Any income on which you obtain double tax relief must be excluded from both A and B.) The specified categories are as follows:

(a) Subjects of Great Britain or the Republic of Ireland.
(b) Employees of the Crown or Crown protectorates or missionary societies.

(c)   Residents of the Isle of Man or the Channel Islands.
(d)   Previous residents of the United Kingdom who have gone abroad for reasons of their own health or that of a member of their families.
(e)   Widows of Crown servants.

Note to get this relief, you must submit a claim to the Revenue giving details of your United Kingdom and world income.

Immigrants

If you come from abroad to this country with the intention of taking up permanent residence here the following tax consequences will result:

(1)   You will normally get full United Kingdom personal reliefs and allowances for income tax for the entire tax year during which you arrive.

(2)   If you have any British government securities on which you had been receiving interest gross as a non-resident (p 50) as soon as you arrive here you will normally be treated as resident and so you will be liable to tax on this interest.

(3)   You will not be taxed here on any lump sum payment that you receive from a former employer or overseas provident fund in respect of the termination of an overseas employment.

(4)   If you have any income assessable under Case IV or V of Schedule D on a remittance basis (p 99) and the source ceases before you arrive here, you will have no liability on any sums remitted. If the source ceases in your year of arrival but after you take up permanent residence here, your liability is on the lower of your total remittances in the tax year and the income arising from your date of arrival until the date that the source closed.

(5)   If you had a source of income outside this country before coming here, this source is not treated as being a fresh one on your arrival. Thus if you had possessed the source for some years the preceding year basis will normally apply.

13. Miscellaneous Aspects

Miscellaneous Profits – Schedule D Case VI
(Ss109, 125 & 176)

Miscellaneous profits not falling within any of the other cases of Schedule D are charged to income tax under Case VI. Such income includes:

(a)   Profits from furnished lettings (p 42).
(b)   Income from underwriting (if not a business). Lloyds underwriting profits, however, are assessed under Schedule D Case I (p 55).
(c)   Income from guaranteeing loans.
(d)   Income from dealing in futures.
(e)   Certain capital sums received from the sale of United Kingdom patent rights.
(f)   Post cessation receipts (p 73).
(g)   Certain 'anti-avoidance' assessments (p 117).
(h)   Development gains (p 140).

The basis of assessment under Schedule D Case VI is the actual income arising in the tax year. Expenses incurred in earning the income can be deducted in ascertaining the assessable profits.

Losses sustained in any Case VI transaction (including furnished lettings) can be set off against Case VI profits of the same or any subsequent year; they cannot however be set off against income assessable under any other Case or Schedule (S176).

Tax Free Organisations (S360, etc.)

Approved charities are exempt from tax on any income that is used only for charitable purposes from:

(a)   land and buildings;
(b)   interest dividends and annual payments; and
(c)   trades carried on by the beneficiaries of the charity or trades exercised in the course of executing the actual purposes of the charity.

Approved charities are also exempt from capital gains tax.

Other organisations whose income in certain circumstances may be free of tax include registered and unregistered friendly societies, trade unions, mutual associations and pension funds.

Depending on the exact circumstances, tax exemption may apply to government bodies, foreign diplomats and United Nations Organisation officials in this country and the salaries of the members of visiting forces.

Patent Holders (Ss378–385)

If you own a patent and you grant the right to use it to somebody else he will normally pay you a periodical royalty in respect of the patent user. This royalty is normally subject to tax by deduction at source at the basic rate (30%). If however the payer does not deduct tax then you would normally be assessed to income tax under Case VI of Schedule D.

The gross equivalent of any patent royalties that you receive must be included in your total income for income tax purposes (p 22), but you get a credit for the basic rate tax already suffered by deduction at source. Where you receive a lump sum payment, in respect of royalties for the past user of your patent, you can spread the payment backwards over the period of use in order to calculate your income tax liability.

If you sell any patent rights for a capital sum, this will be chargeable under Case VI of Schedule D provided you are resident in this country. You can however spread the payment forward over a period of six years in computing your income tax liability. If however you are non-resident, the payer should deduct income tax at 30% in paying you (subject to possible double tax reliefs and exemptions).

Authors' Copyright Sales and Royalties
(Ss389 & 390)

Unlike patent royalties, copyright royalties paid to authors, etc., are made gross without the deduction of any income tax. If you have such receipts and you are an author or composer, etc., by profession, then your royalties will be taxed under Schedule D Case II as part of your professional earnings (p 55). If however you are not an author by profession, then any royalties that you receive may be assessed under Schedule D Case VI.

If you assign the copyright in the whole or a part of a work, any sum that you receive is taxable by reference to the tax year or accounting period in which it is received. If you make the required claim to the Revenue however, you can normally obtain relief by spreading the payment as follows:

(1) If it took you more than twelve but less than twenty-four months to prepare the work of art, one-half of your proceeds is taxed as if received when paid to you and the other half of the proceeds is taxed as if received one year earlier. If you took more than twenty-four months on the writing, composing, etc., of the work, then you are taxed on one-third of the proceeds as if received when paid to you, another third is taxed as if received one year earlier and the remaining third is taxed one year earlier still. Thus a three-year spread is obtained.

(2) If you are the author of an established work and not less than ten years after the first publication you wholly or partially assign your copyright or grant an interest therein, for a period of at least two years, you can spread any lump sum received. The period over which the sum is spread is the lesser of six years or the duration of the grant or licence.

Sub-Contractors
(FA 1971 Ss29–31 & Sch 5, FA 1974 S25 & F2A 1975 Ss39 & 68–71 & Sch 12 & F2A 1979 S15)

If you are an independent or self-employed contractor and are not engaged under a contract of employment, you will be taxed under Schedule D Case I and not under Schedule E. This will normally be advantageous to you because you will be able to deduct various expenses such as travelling from your home or other base of operations to the site, etc., where you are working for the time being.

Special rules apply to payments made by a building contractor or similar organisation in the building trade to a sub-contractor after 5 April 1972 in connection with building and construction work. The contractor must deduct tax at the rate of 30% from each payment made to the sub-contractors who work for him excepting those with exemption certificates (see below). Before 6 November 1979 the rate was 33%, and before 6 November 1978 it was 34%. The tax deducted must be paid over to the Revenue. Each sub-contractor then prepares accounts under Schedule D Case I which include the gross equivalents of the payments made to him. Income tax is computed on the basis of the accounts (p 58) and from the amount payable is deducted the tax already suffered by deduction at source. If the income tax liability is less than the tax deducted, a repayment is obtained.

If you are a sub-contractor in the building trade you will normally be able to obtain an exemption certificate from your Inspector of Taxes if you complete the necessary application form and can show that you have a regular place of business in this country and make regular returns of your business profits having done so for a period ending within the last three years. If you obtain an exemption certificate and show it to a building contractor for whom you do work, then he will be permitted to pay you gross without the tax deduction described above.

From 6 April 1977 all existing certificates have been withdrawn and new ones issued subject to stricter tests. Also, the scheme now applies to certain companies.

Farming

If you carry on a farming or market gardening business in this country you will be treated as carrying on a trade. You will be assessed to income tax under Schedule D Case I (p 55).

In addition to the normal Schedule D Case I rules, some special ones apply, including the following:

(a) If you have more than one farm they will all be assessed as one business (S110).

(b) You may receive *deficiency payments* from the government in respect of certain crops, etc. These are by concession included in your taxable profits for the year when they are received rather than when the crop is sold.

(c) If you have a farm of between twenty and one hundred acres you may be eligible to benefit under the National Farmers' Union *Small Farmers' Scheme*. Grants received under this scheme are treated as either capital receipts or revenue receipts for tax purposes according to their nature. For example, field husbandry grants are revenue and grants to cover the reclamation of waste land are capital.

(d) Normally all your livestock will be treated for tax purposes as stock-in-trade. If you have any 'production herds' however, you can elect within two years from the end of your first year of assessment that the *herd basis* should apply. 'Production herds' are those kept for the purpose of obtaining products from the living animal (e.g. wool, milk, etc.). Where a herd basis election has been made the initial cost of the herd is not charged against your profits but is capitalised together with the cost of any additional animals. The cost of rearing the animals to maturity is also capitalised. Any sales proceeds are taxable and the costs of replacement animals are deductible from your taxable profits. If you sell your entire herd you are not charged to tax on the proceeds (S139 & Sch 6). The time limit was extended by the 1973 Finance Act (S35), so as to allow any election made between then and 5 April 1976. Any such election made outside the two year limit, however, is only valid for the chargeable period in which it is made and subsequent periods.

(e) A special *agricultural buildings allowance* is available (p 70).

(f) If you carry on any farming or market gardening activities without any reasonable expectation of profit and on a non-commercial basis you will normally be treated as conducting merely *hobby farming*. The effect of this will be that you will not be granted tax relief for any losses from your farming against your other income. You will however be permitted to carry forward any losses from your hobby farming to be set off against future taxable profits from the same source (S180).

(g) Relief is now available regarding *fluctuating profits* of individual farmers or partnerships. You are able to claim to average the profits of any pair of consecutive years of assessment, provided you do so within 2 years of the end of the second year. If the taxable profits for either or both years are later adjusted, the original claim is set aside but a new one can be made by the end of the year of assessment following that in which the adjustment is made. Another condition is that the profits in the lower year must be no more than 70% of the profits of the better year. If the lower profits are 70% to 75% of the higher, however, limited spreading is allowed.

Another point to note is that if a loss is made in any year, for the purposes of the spreading rules, the profits are treated as nil and the loss is relieved in the usual ways (p 71). The first year which may be included in a claim is 1977–78 (FA 1978 S28).

Building Society Arrangements (S343)

Under special arrangements made with the Revenue, building societies are allowed to pay interest to their depositors and share-holders, etc., without the deduction of income tax.

If you receive any building society interest you are not assessed to basic rate income tax on it but you must include the grossed up equivalent in your total income for tax purposes (p 22) as if income tax at the basic rate (30%) had been deducted on payment of the interest to you. This 'notional' tax deduction cannot be reclaimed by you however under any circumstances since the building societies do not actually pay it to the Revenue.

Building societies pay a special composite tax rate on their income which partially compensates the Revenue for the income tax not charged on the interest paid to the investors.

Insolvents

When a person becomes bankrupt a receiving order is made on a certain date and all income tax, surtax and capital gains assessments that have been made by that date for previous years are treated as debts in the bankruptcy. Also any assessments made for the tax year ending on the following 5 April will rank as debts in the bankruptcy provided the assessments were made before the date of the receiving order. The Revenue can select one tax year for which there are outstanding taxation assessments and those assessments will rank as preferential debts. This means that they will be paid in full before any payment is made on the non-preferential debts. The remaining assessments will rank as non-preferential debts.

In the case of VAT (p 224) tax payable for the 12 months prior to the date of the receiving order, etc., ranks as a preferential debt.

Any future income of the bankrupt individual will be charged to tax in the normal way. Thus any salary would be subjected to PAYE (p 90) – also income tax would be payable on other income.

Anti-Avoidance Provisions (Ss460–496)

There is an important distinction between *tax evasion* and *tax avoidance*. Tax evasion refers to all those activities deliberately undertaken by a taxpayer to free himself from tax which the law charges upon his income, e.g. the falsification of his returns, books and accounts. This is illegal and subject to very heavy penalties (p 162). Tax avoidance, on the other hand, denotes that the tax-payer has arranged his affairs in such a way as to reduce his tax liability legally – for example by investing in tax free securities such as national savings certificates.

Tax avoidance is also effected in more complicated and devious ways with particular use being made of overseas trusts and companies. In order to prevent abuse of the United Kingdom tax rules in this way, a number of anti-avoidance provisions have been introduced.

Unfortunately, some of the rules introduced to counter sophisticated avoidance schemes penalise quite innocent commercial activities, not carried out with a view to tax saving. It is thus important to consider the anti-avoidance provisions, particularly when involved in overseas operations and company reorganisations or takeovers. The following are some of the more important provisions to consider.

Transactions in Securities (Ss460–468 & FA 1973 Sch 11)

These provisions charge you to income tax under Schedule D Case VI in respect of any 'tax advantage' that you obtain as a result of one or more 'transactions in securities'. For these purposes a 'tax advantage' is a saving of income tax, or corporation tax but it does not apply to capital gains tax. 'Transactions in securities' include the formation and liquidation of companies as well as purchases and sales of shares, etc. A frequent application of this legislation is to prevent tax savings effected by obtaining the use of the undistributed profits of companies by means of schemes involving 'transactions in securities'.

You can avoid being assessed under these provisions if you can show that the transactions concerned were carried out for commercial purposes and one of your main objects was not tax saving. If you are planning to carry out certain transactions which you fear may be covered by these provisions you have the right to apply for clearance to the Revenue giving all relevant facts and they must let you know within one month whether such clearance is granted.

Transfer of Assets Abroad (Ss478–481)

The object of these provisions is to prevent you from avoiding tax by transferring some of your assets abroad. The provisions normally, but not exclusively, apply to transfers of assets made by persons ordinarily resident in this country (p 96). If as a result of such transfer of assets income is payable to persons resident or domiciled abroad (so as to avoid United Kingdom income tax) then if anyone ordinarily resident in the United Kingdom has the 'power to enjoy' any of the income, he can be assessed to income tax under Schedule D Case VI on all or part of the income. 'Power to enjoy' the income is very widely defined and catches for example beneficiaries of trusts, those who can control the application of the income and those who may get some future benefit from it.

There are no provisions under which clearance can be obtained and this particular legislation must be most carefully considered regarding all overseas schemes.

Sales at Undervalue or Overvalue (S485 & FA 1975 S17)

It is laid down that where any sale takes place between people who are connected with each other (this can include partnerships and companies) if the price is less than the open market value of the goods, then in calculating the tax liability on the trading income of the seller, the sales proceeds must be adjusted to the true value of the goods if the Revenue so direct. This does not apply if the purchase is made by a taxable business in this country as a part of its trading stock. If the purchaser is an overseas trader however the sale is not exempted from these provisions.

A similar adjustment must be made for the buyer if the price is more than the open market value of the goods.

Other provisions cover capital gains on sales between connected persons.

Sale of Income derived from Personal Activities (Ss487, 489 & 490)

The object of these provisions is to prevent you from saving tax by contriving to sell your present or future earnings for a capital sum thereby paying no tax or only capital gains tax instead of income tax at basic and higher rates. Subject to the precise rules, any such capital sum is to be treated as earned income arising when it is receivable and is chargeable under Case VI of Schedule D subject to the benefit of not attracting investment income surcharge.

These provisions might apply if you receive a capital sum from the sale of a business which derives part of its value from your personal services.

Artificial Transactions in Land (Ss488–490) and 'Sale and Leaseback' (FA 1972 S80)

These provisions are considered in detail in the chapter which deals with income from land and property (p 45). Note that tax advantages from sales of land with the right to repurchase are countered as from 2 December 1976 (FA 1978 S32).

Capital Allowances (FA 1973 Ss30–32 & FA 1976 S41)

Complicated anti-avoidance provisions now operate concerning the claiming of relief for capital allowances in certain contrived situations. These provisions were designed to counter certain tax saving schemes involving leasing arrangements in group situations and consortiums ; also leasing partnerships between individuals and companies.

Group Relief Restrictions (FA 1973 Ss28 & 29)

These provisions can act to restrict, or prevent group loss relief being available for one group company (p 178) in respect of the trading losses of another. A particular point to watch is that if a group of companies has arranged to sell a loss-making company, relief for the losses of that company may not be available to the other group members for periods prior to the accounting period in which the sale actually takes place.

Interest Schemes (FA 1976 S38)

Complicated tax avoidance schemes have been developed concerning 'manufactured' interest relief. Anti-avoidance rules operate broadly regarding interest payments after 8 June 1976.

Capital Gains Tax (FA 1977 Ss40, 41 & 43)

The 1977 Finance Act brought into effect various rules for countering the avoidance of capital gains tax in certain situations. The latter include 'value-shifting' schemes, where an allowable loss has been created artificially by moving value out of one asset and possibly into another.

There are also anti-avoidance rules concerning capital gains tax resulting from company reconstructions, takeovers and amalgamations (p 131). A clearance procedure applies, however, which is similar to that applying for transactions in securities (p 118). Also, the rules do not apply if you can show that the arrangements were carried out for commercial, rather than tax-saving purposes.

Commodity Futures (FA 1978 S31)

As from 6 April 1976, losses created by means of certain artificial dealing partnerships may no longer be relieved against general income.

14. Capital Gains Tax

Subject to the specific rules that are summarised in the following pages, you will be charged to capital gains tax in respect of any chargeable gains that accrue to you on the disposal of assets during a given tax year. You deduct from your capital gains any allowable capital losses (p 127). The basic rate of capital gains tax is 30% (maximum) but for individuals and trusts a lower rate of 15% is applicable in certain circumstances (see below). Companies pay corporation tax at 52% on 15/26ths of their capital gains (p 178), subject to a special rate of 10% for authorised Investment Trusts and Unit Trusts (p 132).

The references throughout this chapter are to the Capital Gains Tax Act 1979 which consolidates the relevant legislation from Finance Act 1965 onwards.

What is a Chargeable Gain? (CGTA S28)

A chargeable gain is a gain which accrues after 6 April 1965 to a taxpayer (including a company, trust, partnership, individual, etc.) such gain being computed in accordance with the provisions of the relevant legislation. There must however be a disposal of assets in order that there should be a chargeable gain (p 124).

Who is Liable? (CGTA Ss2, 12 & 14)

Any taxpayer (including a company, trust, partnership, individual, etc.) is chargeable to capital gains tax on any chargeable gains accruing to him in a year of assessment during any part of which he is: (a) resident in this country (p 96), or (b) ordinarily resident here (p 96).

Also even if neither resident nor ordinarily resident here, a taxpayer who carries on a trade in the United Kingdom through a branch or agency, is generally liable to capital gains tax accruing on the disposal of: (a) assets in this country used in his trade, or (b) assets held here and used for the branch or agency.

If you are resident or ordinarily resident here during a tax year you will be liable to capital gains tax on realisations of assets throughout the world. An exception is made however if you are not domiciled in this country (p 95) ; in that case you are only charged to capital gains tax on your overseas realisations of assets to the extent that such gains are remitted here (p 99).

Alternative Basis of Charge Before 6 April 1978 (FA 1965 S21 & FA 1976 S52)

In calculating your capital gains tax liability for *1977–78 or any earlier tax year*, instead of paying the basic maximum 30% rate you paid a lower amount in the following circumstances :

CAPITAL GAINS TAX

(a)   If your capital gains were not more than £5,000 then your tax was restricted to the amount payable if you applied your top income tax rates to one-half of your capital gains (less capital losses) for the tax year. (Your top tax rate was that on your income including one-half of your capital gains.)

(b)   If your capital gains exceeded £5,000 then your tax was restricted to the amount payable if you applied your top income tax rates to £2,500 plus the amount by which your net capital gains for the tax year exceeded £5,000. Thus if your net gains were £6,000 you applied your top tax rates to £3,500 (i.e. £2,500 + £6,000 − £5,000).

(c)   For the above purposes you deducted from one-half of your capital gains (or £2,500 plus the excess over £5,000) any personal reliefs and allowances (apart from life assurance relief) that had not already been relieved against your income for income tax purposes (p 6).

(d)   No charges on income could be deducted from the capital gains.

(e)   For 1977–78 if your investment income plus half of your capital gains exceeded £1,500 you paid investment surcharge (p 25) on the excess. (If you or your wife were over 65, this figure was £2,000.)

(f)   Except in the tax year of your marriage, if this was after 6 April 1976, the capital gains of your wife and yourself were considered together, for the above purposes. Any capital gains of your children, however, were treated separately (even if they were minors).

(g)   The above rules only applied until 1977–78, in which year new relief for gains totalling not more than £9,500 came into force. For 1977–78 the most favourable of the two methods was applied to your gains, but subsequently only the new rules are effective (see below).

Relief for Gains Totalling under £9,500
(CGTA S5 & Sch 1)

For 1977–78 and subsequent years, your net capital gains (including those of your wife unless you are separated) are taxed at less than 30% as follows:

(a)   If your chargeable gains are no more than £1,000, no tax is charged.

(b)   The excess over £1,000 is taxed at 15%, provided your total net gains are no more than £5,000.

(c)   Should your total net gains be in the band from £5,000 to £9,500, your tax is £600 (£4,000 at 15%) plus half of the excess over £5,000. Thus on total gains of £8,000 you would pay £600 + (8,000 − 5,000)/2 = £2,100.

(d)   The old alternative basis (p 121) applied for 1977–78 only, provided it produced a lower charge.

(e)   Any set-off for losses from previous years (p 127) is restricted so as to leave £1,000 of gains to be taxed at the nil rate.

In this way your nil rate band is protected. All losses for the year must be deducted, however, in arriving at the net gains.

(f) These rules apply to personal representatives for the tax year of death and the following two years.

(g) The rules also apply to trusts for the mentally disabled and for those receiving attendance allowance. For any other trusts set up before 7 June 1978 a lower limit of £500 applies for complete capital gains tax exemption, with marginal relief limiting the tax to one-half of the excess over £500 (p 168). Thus if a trust has net gains of £900 for 1978–79, its capital gains tax is limited to (£900 − £500) × $\frac{1}{2}$ = £200.

What Assets are Liable? (CGTA Ss19-21)

Subject to various exemptions (see below) all forms of property are treated as 'assets' for capital gains tax purposes including:

(a) Investments, land and buildings, jewellery, antiques, etc.
(b) Options and debts, etc.
(c) Any currency other than sterling.
(d) Any form of property created by the person disposing of it or otherwise coming to be owned without being acquired. (This would cover any article which you made or work of art created by you.)

What Assets are Exempted? (CGTA – see below)

The following classes of assets are exempted from charge to capital gains tax subject to the relevant rules:

Table 14: Assets Exempted from Capital Gains Tax

(1) Private motor vehicles (S130).
(2) If you make gifts to an individual of no more than £100 total value during the tax year any gain is exempted from charge (S6).
(3) Your own home – this is known as your 'main private residence' (p 135).
(4) National Savings Certificates, Defence Bonds, Development Bonds, Save-as-you-earn, etc. (S71).
(5) Any foreign currency which you obtained for personal expenditure abroad (S133).
(6) Any decoration for gallantry (unless purchased) (S131).
(7) Betting winnings including pools, lotteries and premium bonds (S19(4)).
(8) Compensation or damages for any wrong or injury suffered to your person or in connection with your profession or vocation (S19(5)).
(9) British government securities which you have held for one year or more or which passed to you on somebody's death (S67).

Table 14 continued

(10) Life assurance policies and deferred annuities provided that you are the original owner or they were given to you. If you bought the rights to a policy from its original owner you may be liable to capital gains tax on surrender, maturity or sale of the policy, or death of the life assured (S143).

(11) Chattels sold for £2,000 or less (p 136).

(12) The gift to the nation of any assets (e.g. paintings) deemed to be of national, scientific or historic interest; also land, etc., given to the National Trust (S147).

(13) The gift after 12 March 1975 of historic houses and certain other property of interest to the public, provided they are given access – also funds settled after 2 May 1976 for its upkeep (Ss 147–148).

(14) Tangible movable property which is a wasting asset (i.e. with a predictable life of 50 years or less). This includes boats animals, etc., but not land and buildings (S127).

(15) Disposals after 6 April 1976 by a close company (p 180) of assets on trust for the benefit of its employees (S149).

(16) If you sell a debt this is not liable to capital gains tax provided you are the original creditor and the debt is not a 'debt on security' (a debenture, etc.). Otherwise capital gains tax applies. The 'debt on security' requirement no longer applies, however, to certain business loans (excluding those from associated companies) made after 11 April 1978. Loss relief may be available on such debts and also on certain business guarantees made after that date (S134).

(17) For 1975–76 and 1976–77, if your total disposal proceeds in the tax year were less than £1,000 you were exempted from capital gains tax for that year. For 1974–75 and earlier tax years this limit was £500.

(18) For 1977–78 and subsequent years, if your net gains are no more than £5,000, the first £1,000 is exempt (p 122).

What Constitutes a Disposal (CGTA Ss19–26)

The following are examples of circumstances in which you will be treated as making a disposal or a part disposal of an asset:

(a) The outright sale of the whole asset or part of it.

(b) The gift of the asset or a part of it – the asset must be valued at the date of gift and this valuation is treated as the proceeds. Gifts to charities however are not liable to capital gains tax (p 138).

(c) If an asset is destroyed, e.g. by fire, it is a disposal.

(d) If you sell any right in an asset, for example by granting a lease, this is a part disposal although if you obtain a fair rent there is normally no capital gains tax liability.

(e) If any capital sum is received in return for the surrender or forfeiture of any rights, this is a disposal. For example, you may receive a sum of money for not renewing a lease in accordance with a renewal option which you possessed.

(f) If you die, you are deemed to dispose of all of your assets at your date of death but no capital gains tax is payable. Whoever inherits your assets does so at their market value at your death.

(g) The first business letting of certain property between 17 December 1973 and (normally) 1 August 1976 (p 141).

The following are not treated as disposals of assets for capital gains tax purposes.

(a) If you give or sell an asset to your wife this is not treated as a capital gains tax disposal, provided she is living with you during the relevant tax year. In that case your wife is charged to capital gains tax on any subsequent disposal that she makes of the asset as if she had bought it when you originally acquired it at the actual cost to yourself.

(b) If you transfer an asset merely as security for a debt but retain the ownership this is not a capital gains tax disposal. This would apply for example if you mortgage your house.

(c) If you transfer an asset to somebody else to hold it as your nominee, this is not a disposal provided that you remain the beneficial owner.

(d) Gifts of assets to charities (p 138).

How Your Chargeable Gains are Computed
(CGTA Ss28–36)

The following general rules should be followed:

(1) If the asset sold has been originally acquired before 7 April 1965, special rules apply (p 129).

(2) Special rules also apply in the case of leases and other wasting assets (p 138).

(3) Ascertain the consideration for each of your disposals during the tax year – this will normally be the sale proceeds but in the following cases it will be the open market value of the assets (p 128):

(a) Gifts of assets during the tax year exeeding £100 in value to any individual.

(b) Transfers of assets (by gift or sale) to persons connected with you including close relations other than your wife and your business partner. This also applies to other disposals of assets not at arm's length.

(c) Transactions in which the sale proceeds cannot be valued, or where an asset is given as compensation for loss of office, etc., to an employee. If for example you give your friend a picture from your collection, on condition that he paints your house each year for the next ten years, then since this service cannot be accurately valued, you are treated as disposing of your picture for its market value.

(4) Deduct from the disposal consideration in respect of each

asset its original cost (or value at acquisition) together with any incidental expenses in connection with your original acquisition and your disposal of each asset. Also deduct any 'enhancement' expenditure, i.e. the cost of any capital improvements to the assets not including any expenses of a 'revenue nature' (p 3).

(5) Your incidental costs of acquisition and disposal (see (4) above) include surveyors', valuers' and solicitors' fees, stamp duty, and commission in connection with the purchase and sale. Also the cost of advertising to find a buyer and accountancy charges in connection with the acquisition or disposal. No expenses are deductible however if they have already been allowed in computing your taxable revenue profits (p 3).

Example 20: Computation of Chargeable Gain

Mr A sells a block of flats during 1979–80 for £200,000. The flats were bought during 1970–71 for £100,000 and subsequent capital expenditure amounted to £20,000. Also £10,000 had been spent on decorations and maintenance. The legal costs on purchase were £1,500 and stamp duty was £1,000. Surveyors' fees prior to purchase amounted to £500. £100 was spent in advertising the sale and agents' commission amounted to £6,000. Legal costs on sale were £900. Assuming that Mr A's profit will be taxed as a capital gain, what tax will he pay on it?

Cost of block of flats		£100,000
Add:		
Enhancement expenditure		20,000
(decorations and maintenance not relevant)		
Legal costs on purchase		1,500
Stamp duty on purchase		1,000
Surveyors' fees on purchase		500
Total cost		£123,000
Proceeds		£200,000
Less:		
Cost as above	£123,000	
Advertising	100	
Agents' commission	6,000	
Legal fees on sale	900	
		130,000
Chargeable gain		£70,000
Capital gains tax at 30%		£21,000

Capital Losses (CGTA S29)

If your capital gains tax computation in respect of any disposal during the tax year produces a loss, such loss is deductible from any chargeable gains arising during the year. If after relieving any gains for the tax year there remains a surplus of losses these should be offset against any net capital gains of your spouse. Any remaining surplus of losses is then available to be carried forward and set off against future capital gains of your spouse and yourself.

For 1977–78 and subsequent years your net capital gains are reduced by losses brought forward to the tax free amount of £1,000 and any balance of the losses is carried forward (S5(4)).

Assessment and Payment of Capital Gains Tax (T.M.A. S29 & CGTA Ss7-9 & 40)

Assessments to capital gains tax are raised on the taxpayer concerned in respect of each tax year as soon thereafter as the Revenue obtain the necessary information. In the case of a company however its gains are included in its corporation tax assessment which is due for payment according to the special company rules (p 173).

Your capital gains tax assessment is due for payment three months after the end of the tax year in which the gains arise; or thirty days after the assessment is issued if this is later.

The date on which a capital gain arises is the actual date of sale or gift, etc. In the case of a transaction in which a sales contract is used such as the sale of shares or property it is the date of the contract which applies. It is not the completion date if this is different. Similar considerations apply to fixing the date of acquisition for capital gains tax purposes.

Regarding certain disposals by gift, etc., on or after 11 April 1972 of land and buildings, non-quoted shares, or assets used exclusively in your business, you have the option of paying capital gains tax in 8 yearly or 16 half-yearly instalments. If you pay by instalments you must pay interest at 9% on the overdue tax (6% before 1 July 1974).

After 26 March 1974, controlling interests in companies are included (even if quoted) and disposals of any of the specified assets (except for land and investment companies, etc.) qualify for a new relief. Under the new relief no interest is paid on the instalments unless they are overdue or the total market value of the assets exceeds £250,000.

Prior to 11 April 1972, if the consideration for any disposal was payable by instalments over a period exceeding eighteen months then the gain was treated as accruing over the period during which the proceeds were payable. If any instalments remained outstanding at 11 April 1972 they were treated as being received then and were thus assessable for 1972–73. Concerning sales after 11 April 1972 however, regardless of the period over which the consideration is payable, the gain is assessed for the tax year in which the sale arises. If however you can satisfy the Revenue that you would otherwise suffer undue hardship, payment of the tax can be spread over the period of the instalments (maximum 8 years).

Valuations (CGTA S150 and Sch 6)

It is necessary to value assets in various circumstances for capital gains tax purposes including gifts, transactions between connected persons, acquisitions on death and valuations at 6 April 1965.

The general rule for valuing assets for capital gains tax purposes is that you must take the 'market value' of the assets at the relevant time. 'Market value' means the price which the assets might reasonably be expected to fetch on a sale in the open market.

It is necessary to value only the assets actually being disposed of even though they form part of a larger whole. This is particularly important regarding the shares in a non-quoted company. Suppose you hold 90% of the shares in such a company which are together worth £90,000. If you gift 10% of the company's shares to your son you might assume that their value is £10,000. This would however probably not be true since your 90% holding carried with it full control of the company whereas 10% company's shares is a minority holding which would be normally worth considerably less than £10,000 in the circumstances mentioned. The true market valuation of the gifted 10% holding might only be £1,000 depending on the profit of the company and dividends paid. Note that different valuation rules apply for capital transfer tax purposes (p 189).

Unquoted share valuations at dates after 5 July 1973, and in certain cases earlier, must take account of all information which a prudent arm's-length purchaser would obtain (CGTA S152).

Particular rules relate to the valuation of quoted securities such as shares and debenture stocks. In this case you must normally take the lower of:

(a) the lower of the two prices shown in the Stock Exchange Official Daily List plus one-quarter of the difference between them, or

(b) halfway between the highest and lowest prices at which bargains (other than at special prices) were recorded in the shares or securities for the relevant day.

In valuing quoted shares at 6 April 1965, however, you must take the *higher* of:

(a) midway between the two prices shown in the Stock Exchange Official Daily List (i.e. the middle market price), and

(b) halfway between the highest and lowest prices at which bargains (other than at special prices) were recorded in the shares or securities for 6 April 1965.

Apart from quoted shares other valuations will normally require to be agreed with the Revenue valuation officers such as the district valuers who are concerned with valuing land and buildings.

The valuation of agricultural property gifted after 26 March 1974 is effectively subject to the same reduction as applies for capital transfer tax (p 197).

Relief on Sales of Assets owned on 6 April 1965 (CGTA Sch 5)

Although a short term capital gains tax operated from April 1962 until April 1971 when it was repealed, the present-day system of capital gains tax only operates regarding sales after 6 April 1965. Rules were therefore introduced with the purpose of relieving such part of your capital gains as can be related to the period before 7 April 1965.

The general rule is that you assume that your asset increased in value at a uniform rate and you are relieved from capital gains tax on such proportion of the gain as arose on a time basis prior to 7 April 1965. This is known as the 'time apportionment' method. Thus if your total gain is G and you held an asset for A months prior to 6 April 1965 and B months after that date until the date of sale your taxable chargeable gain is $G \times B/(A+B)$. Your time apportionment benefit is limited to twenty years prior to 6 April 1965. Thus if you acquired an asset before 6 April 1945 you are treated as having acquired it on that date.

Instead of using 'time apportionment' you have the option of substituting for the cost of the asset its market value at 6 April 1965 [Sch 5 (11)]. In order to do this you must make an election to this effect to the Revenue within two years of the end of the tax year in which you make the disposal. (In the case of a company the election must be made within two years of the end of the accounting period in which the disposal is made.) Once you make an election it is irrevocable, even if it results in your paying more tax than on a 'time apportionment' basis.

The 'time apportionment' basis *does not* apply to quoted shares and securities (p 130) ; nor to land with development value when sold (or which has been materially developed after 17 December 1973) which is normally automatically dealt with on the 6 April 1965 valuation basis.

In the same way that your gain is reduced by 'time apportionment' so any loss that you make on a disposal of an asset that you owned at 6 April 1965 is also reduced in this way. Thus if you bought an asset for £5,000 on 6 April 1955 and sold it for £1,000 on 6 April 1975 your total loss is £4,000 of which only £2,000 (£4,000 × 10/20) is an allowable capital loss.

Example 21 : Relief on Sales of Assets owned on 6 April 1965

Mr A bought a picture for £5,000 on 6 April 1952 and sold it for £20,000 (net of expenses) on 6 April 1978. He considers that at

Example 21 continued

6 April 1965 the market value of the picture was £16,000. What is Mr A's chargeable gain?

Proceeds 6 April 1978	£20,000
Less cost 6 April 1948	5,000
Profit	£15,000
Period 6.4.52 to 6.4.65	13 years
Period 6.4.65 to 6.4.78	13 years
Total period of ownership	26 years

Chargeable gain on 'time apportionment' basis

$$\frac{13}{26} \times £15,000 = \quad £7,500$$

Proceeds 6 April 1978	£20,000
Less market value 6 April 1965	16,000
Chargeable gain on election for valuation at 6 April 1965	£4,000

Note: Provided that Mr A is reasonably certain that he can substantiate a valuation of the picture of £16,000 at 6 April 1965 he should make the required election and his chargeable gain will be less. If however as a result of negotiations with the Revenue the valuation is agreed at a figure below £12,500, or failing agreement fixed by the Commissioners below this figure, then Mr A will pay more capital gains tax by making the irrevocable election.

Quoted Shares and Securities (CGTA Ss64–76)

The following rules do not apply to United Kingdom government securities which are exempt from capital gains tax if sold more than a year after purchase. If you sell any such 'gilt edged' securities within a year of purchase you are liable to capital gains tax on your chargeable gain. Also, any compensation stock received on a nationalisation after 6 April 1976 will give rise to a gain or loss when sold. This consists of the gain or loss on your original shares up to the date of issue of the compensation stock, together with the gain or loss on this stock if it is held for less than 12 months before sale (CGTA S84).

'Pooling'

All shares of the same class that you hold must be put into a 'pool'.

The 'pool' is considered indistinguishable regarding the various numbers of shares that it comprises. Thus if you buy 100 ordinary shares in A Limited on 1 May 1966 for £200 and another 200 ordinary shares in A Limited on 30 September 1970 for £1,000 your total pool cost is £1,200 (i.e. £4 per share). If you now sell 100 shares they are not treated as being the original ones which you bought for £200; they are treated as coming from your 'pool' at the average pool cost of £4 per share giving a cost of £400.

You have a separate 'pool' in respect of each class of shares that you hold in each separate company.

'Pooling' does not apply to shares purchased on or before 6 April 1965 unless you elect for all your shares to be valued as at that date (p 133). In the absence of this election, you must allocate any sales first against your holdings at 6 April 1965 on a 'first in first out' basis. After these shares are eliminated you then go to the 'pool'. Thus if you bought 100 shares in A Limited for £100 on 1 October 1960 and a further 100 shares for £200 on 1 February 1963 followed by 100 shares for £300 on 1 June 1969; if you sell 150 shares in June 1978 and 150 shares in June 1979 your disposals in 1978–79 are allocated as follows:

	No.	Cost
Purchased 1 October 1960	100	£100
Purchased 1 February 1963	50	100
	150	£200

Your disposals in 1979–80 are allocated as follows:

	No.	Cost
Purchased 1 February 1963	50	£100
Purchased 1 June 1969	100	300
	150	£400

The above assumes that you had not elected for the application of 6 April 1965 valuation to your shares. If you had made such election and supposing the value of the shares was £1.50 each at 6 April 1965 then the 'pool' becomes 200 at £1.50 (= £300) + £300 = £600, i.e. £2 per share.

Each separate purchase or sale of shares of the same company and class will result in adjustments to the 'pool' except that if you buy and sell shares on the same day the respective sale and purchase are first matched against each other. Any surplus or deficit must then be added to or deducted from your 'pool'.

Bonus Issues, Take-overs and Company Reorganisations
(CGTA Ss77–91)

If you receive a free scrip (or bonus) issue of shares of the same class as those that you already hold, you must treat the additional shares as having been bought when your original shares were bought. Thus if you bought 100 shares in A Limited for £2 each in 1960 and you now receive a bonus issue of 100 shares you will have 200 shares at a cost of £1 each which are all treated as having been brought in 1960. Note however the special rules for scrip dividend options (p 54).

Your company may have a capital reorganisation, in the course of which you receive shares of a different class either instead of or in addition to your original shares. You are not normally charged to capital gains tax on any old shares in your company which you exchange for new ones. Any capital gains tax is only payable when you sell your new holding.

If you take up 'rights' to subscribe for additional shares in a company of which you are a shareholder, your rights shares are treated as having been acquired when your original shares were purchased and the cost of the rights shares is added to the original cost of your holding. If you sell your 'rights' on the market without taking up the shares this is considered to be a 'part disposal' of your holding which is charged to capital gains tax accordingly (p 135). If the proceeds are small in relation to your holding however, you may elect not to pay tax now but set off the proceeds against the original cost of your holding.

In the case of a take-over you may receive cash for your shares in which case this is taxed as an ordinary disposal. If however you receive shares or loan stock, etc., in the acquiring company, you will not normally be liable to pay capital gains tax until you actually sell your new shares or loan stock, subject to certain conditions. One of the conditions was that the acquiring company already held, or obtains as a result of the take-over over 50% of the ordinary share capital of the other company. For shares or debentures issued after 19 April 1977, this percentage is reduced to 25%. At the same time, new anti-avoidance laws have been introduced (p 120). Note that all of the above rules concerning bonus issues, take-overs and company reorganisations apply equally to unquoted shares (p 134).

Investment Trusts and Unit Trusts (CGTA Ss 92–98)

Special rules apply regarding all disposals both of shares owned *by* the trusts and of shares and units *in* the trusts by their share-holders and unit holders after 1 April 1977, and 5 April 1977, respectively. Authorised unit trusts and investment trusts now pay capital gains tax at 10% (previously 17%) on their investment gains instead of the normal tax rate of 52% that other companies pay on 15/26ths of their gains. When the ordinary shareholders of invest-ment trusts sell their shares they are allowed to deduct 10% from the capital gains tax rate that they pay on their investment trust ordinary shares. (For 1978–79 the deduction was 17%.) Thus if you pay the maximum 30% rate on your gains for a given tax year your rate will be only 20% on capital gains arising on the sale of ordinary shares in investment trusts. The same applies to any unit trust units that you dispose of during the tax year.

Note that it is the rate of capital gains tax on your units, etc., which is reduced, not the actual amount of the gain or loss. This means that any capital loss (p 127) which you have from selling other assets is less valuable, if used against gains on unit trusts, since the latter would otherwise only bear a low rate of tax. As a general rule, it is better to realise profits on unit trusts and investment trust shares in years when your gains from other assets exceed your losses.

Holdings at 6 April 1965 (CGTA Sch 5)

'Time apportionment' (p 129) does not apply to quoted shares. Instead you must consider the mid-market price at 6 April 1965 (p 129). Unless you make the election described below, your gain on any sales after 6 April 1965 of shares held at that date is the difference between the proceeds and the higher of the cost of the shares and their value at 6 April 1965. Similarly any allowable capital loss on such share sales is the difference between the proceeds and the lower of the cost of the shares and their value at 6 April 1965. If the price at which you sell shares held at 6 April 1965 is between their value at that date and their cost then you are treated as having no gain and no loss for capital gains tax purposes (subject to the election described below).

As regards disposals after 19 March 1968 of quoted shares and securities which you held at 6 April 1965 you have the right to elect that any capital gains or losses on such disposals shall be calculated by substituting the 6 April 1965 values for the original costs in all cases. The following rules apply:

(1)　Separate elections must be made for you and your wife — your respective holdings are separately considered for these purposes.
(2)　Separate elections are required for ordinary shares and fixed interest securities (such as loan stock and preference shares).
(3)　You and your wife have the option of electing or not in respect of each category (fixed interest securities and ordinary shares).
(4)　The election for each category must be made within two years of the end of the tax year in which the first sale after 19 March 1968 is made. (In the case of a company read accounting year for tax year.)
(5)　Companies, trusts, estates, etc., must make separate elections.
(6)　Once made, the elections are irrevocable.

Making the election will prove particularly beneficial regarding shares whose cost was lower than their value at 6 April 1965 but which have now dropped below the latter value. On a sale of such shares if the election is made a larger allowable capital loss is available.

A further advantage arises if the original costs cannot be ascertained in which case, on election, the 6 April 1965 values are used. Otherwise the Revenue would not normally allow any capital losses on the disposal of these shares.

Example 22: Quoted Shares held on 6 April 1965

Mr A sold no shares from 1967–68 to 1978–79. In 1979–80 he sold all of the ordinary shares that he had held at 6 April 1965 as follows:

Shares held	Company	Cost	Market values 6.4.65	Proceeds
1,000	B Ltd	£2,000	£5,000	£3,000
2,000	C Ltd	£1,000	£2,000	£8,000
4,000	D Ltd	£5,000	£4,000	£3,000

What is Mr A's capital gains tax assessment for 1979–80 (1) on the basis of no election and (2) on the basis that he elects for valuation at 6 April 1965?

(1) No election

	(a) Cost	(b) Market value 6.4.65	(c) Proceeds	(d) Gain (Loss)	Basis
1,000 Shares B Ltd	£2,000	£5,000	£3,000	NIL	No gain No loss
2,000 Shares C Ltd	£1,000	£2,000	£8,000	6,000	(c)–(b)
4,000 Shares D Ltd	£5,000	£4,000	£3,000	(1,000)	(b)–(c)

Capital gains tax assessment 1979–80 £5,000

(2) Election (cost ignored)

	Market value 6.4.65	Proceeds	Gain (Loss)
1,000 Shares B Ltd	£5,000	£3,000	(2,000)
2,000 Shares C Ltd	£2,000	£8,000	6,000
4,000 Shares D Ltd	£4,000	£3,000	(1,000)

Capital gains tax assessment 1979–80 £3,000

Note: The election must be made to the Revenue before 5 April 1982 and will result in a reduction of £2,000 in the 1979–80 capital gains tax assessment.

Unquoted Shares (CGTA S152 & Sch 5)

Many of the above points regarding quoted shares and securities apply also to unquoted shares but the following special rules should be noted:

(1) Regarding holdings of shares at 6 April 1965 the 'time apportionment' rule normally applies to sales after that date

subject to the right of election for valuation at 6 April 196d (p 129). This is not a 'blanket' election for all your non-quoted shares as is the case for quoted shares.

(2) If after 6 April 1965 there is a capital reorganisation or take-over regarding a non-quoted company in which you have shares 'time apportionment' normally stops at that time and on any future sales you have a time apportioned gain or loss to the date of reorganisation or take-over and the full gain or loss after that time. This does not apply however in the case of a bonus issue (p 131); nor, in the view of the Revenue, where in a take-over, shares in one company are exchanged for shares of the same kind in another.

(3) If a reorganisation or take-over as in (2) above occurred before 6 April 1965 any shares still held at that date must automatically be valued at 6 April 1965 and time apportionment does not apply. You still consider, however, the cost of your original holding when computing any capital gain or loss on a future sale.

(4) The 'pooling' rules (p 130) apply to shares acquired after 6 April 1965 but not to acquisitions before that time which must be separately considered on a 'first in first out' basis.

Part Disposals (CGTA S35)

Where part of an asset is disposed of (including part of a 'pool' holding of shares in a particular company) it is necessary to compute the cost applicable to the part sold. This is done by multiplying the original cost by the fraction $A/(A+B)$ where A is the consideration for the part disposed of and B is the market value of the remaining property at the date of the part disposal.

Private Residences (CGTA Ss101-105)

The house or flat where you live is normally exempt from capital gains tax when you sell it, subject to the following rules:

(1) The house must have been your only or main residence during the time that you owned it subject to various allowable periods of absence (see below). You ignore all periods before 6 April 1965 for these purposes.

(2) You are allowed to be absent from the house for the following maximum periods without losing your exemption:

    (a) The last twelve months of ownership (extended by concession to two years if you intended to sell throughout the period).

    (b) Periods of absence totalling three years.

    (c) Any period throughout which you work abroad.

    (d) Any periods up to four years in aggregate when you are prevented from living in your house due to your employment being elsewhere.

    (e) Any period during which you live in job-related accommodation from 31 July 1978.

Provided you have no other residence which you claim to be exempt during the above periods they are taken cumulatively and so you could have a long period of absence and still not lose your exemption. You must however return to your house at the end of such absence (excepting the last twelve months) or else you will lose part of your relief.

(3) Any periods of absence subsequent to 6 April 1965 in excess of the periods allowed (see above) result in the relevant proportion of your sale profit being charged to capital gains tax. For example if you bought your house in June 1969 and sell it in June 1976 at a profit of £7,000 having lived elsewhere for reasons unconnected with your employment for the middle five years, your chargeable gain is £7,000 × 2/7 = £2,000. (You are only allowed three years of absence and so the other two are taxable.)

(4) If a specific part of your house is set aside for business purposes then that proportion of your profits on sale of the house will be taxable. Thus if you have eight rooms of which two are wholly used for business purposes you would normally claim 25% of your house expenses against your business profits and when you sell your house you will pay capital gains tax on 25% of your total gain (arising after 6 April 1965). If however you use no rooms exclusively for business purposes you will not normally be liable for any capital gains tax if you sell your house even though you claim part of your house expenses against your business profits.

(5) If you have two residences you can give written notice to the Revenue within two years of acquiring your second residence so as to elect which of the two should be treated as your main private residence and thereby be exempted from capital gains tax. If you do not elect then the Revenue will decide in the light of the time that you spend at each of your residences which of these is your main private residence.

You also obtain capital gains tax exemption on no more than one residence owned by you and occupied by a dependent relative (p 11).

Chattels Sold for £2,000 or Less (CGTA S128)

A chattel is an asset which is tangible movable property such as a chair, a picture, or a pair of candlesticks. For these purposes a set is treated as one chattel. If you dispose of a chattel for no more than £2,000 you pay no capital gains tax and if your proceeds exceed £2,000 your capital gain is restricted to five-thirds of the excess. Thus if you sell a set of antique chairs for £2,300 (original cost £500) your capital gain is restricted to 5/3 × (£2,300 − £2,000) = £500.

If you bought a chattel for more than £2,000, and sold it for less than £2,000, your allowable loss is restricted to the excess of the cost over £2,000.

The £2,000 exemption limit applies from 1978–79, prior to which it was £1,000. For 1976–77 and earlier years a different marginal relief system applied under which the capital gains tax was limited to half the excess over £1,000.

Replacement of Business Assets (CGTA Ss115-121)

You are liable for capital gains tax in respect of any sales of assets used in your business. Similarly a company is liable on any sales of its business assets. If further business assets are purchased within one year preceding and three years after the sale, 'roll-over' relief is obtained as a result of which the gain on the disposal is deducted from the cost of the new business assets. Thus, the gain is 'rolled over' and no tax is paid until the new business assets are sold, unless the latter are in turn replaced.

To get the relief you must use the old and new assets in the same business. After 11 April 1978, however, if you carry on several trades, they are treated as one for this purpose. Also from that date, roll-over relief applies regarding purchases and sales by you of personally owned assets used in your 'family company' (p 137). Note that to obtain total relief, the entire proceeds must be invested, otherwise you pay tax on your capital gain up to the extent of the shortfall.

If the new business asset is a wasting asset (p 138) it must be replaced by a non-wasting asset within ten years. Otherwise, the rolled-over gain becomes chargeable. This also applies to assets which will become 'wasting' within ten years, such as a lease with 59 years to run.

'Roll-over' relief is applicable to companies (p 178). Also a special extension of the rules covers 'gilts' obtained by companies in exchange for group companies in the aircraft and shipping industries on compulsory acquisition through nationalisation. An election is required within four years of the exchange and then the normal new compensation stock rules do not apply.

Gifts of Business Assets (CGTA S126 & Sch 4)

A new form of roll-over relief applies to certain transfers of assets, other than bargains at arm's length, made after 11 April 1978. In particular, the relief includes gifts of business assets to your relatives. The assets covered are any used in your trade or 'family company' (below) ; also shares in such a company.

A claim is required by the recipient and yourself. Your gain on the disposal is then reduced to nil and the recipient must deduct your original capital gain from his acquisition value for the asset.

Business Retirement Relief (CGTA Ss124 & 125)

If you are over sixty-five and dispose by gift or sale of the whole or part of a business which you have owned for the past ten years, you are exempted from capital gains tax on the first £50,000 of any gain arising in respect of the 'chargeable business assets' of the business. If you have several businesses your total relief is restricted to £50,000. (For disposals before 12.4.78 this figure was £20,000 and £10,000 before 3.7.74.)

'Chargeable business assets' include assets used for the trade, etc., of the business, and also goodwill but not assets held as investments.

The above relief also covers any disposal of shares in a trading company which has been your 'family company' for at least the last ten years during which time you have been a full-time director of the company. A 'family company' is one in which you have 25% of the voting rights or your immediate family has at least 51% including 5% held by yourself. (Before 12 April 1978 the last two percentages were 75% and 10%.) Only the proportion of the gain on the shares attributable to the 'chargeable business assets' of the company compared with its total chargeable assets qualifies for the relief.

If your age is between 60 and 65 your relief as above is limited to £10,000 (£4,000 before 12.4.78 and £2,000 before 3.7.74) for each year by which your age exceeds sixty plus a corresponding fraction of £10,000 for the odd months. Thus if you are $63\frac{1}{2}$ your relief is restricted to £10,000 $\times$ ($63\frac{1}{2} - 60$) = £35,000. If your wife complies with the above requirements, she too will be eligible for the relief if she sells her business or shares in a 'family company'.

Concerning disposals after 11 April 1978, of the whole or part of a business which you have owned for less than 10 years, you obtain 10% of the full relief if you owned the assets for at least one year prior to disposal, 20% relief for at least two years of ownership and so on.

Charities (CGTA Ss145 & 146)

Charities are exempted from capital gains tax in respect of any gains on the disposal of assets provided that such gains are applied to charitable purposes.

If you make a gift of an asset to a charity you pay no capital gains tax on this disposal.

Leases and Other Wasting Assets
(CGTA Ss127, 129 & Sch 3)

A 'wasting asset' is defined as an asset with a predictable life not exceeding 50 years, not including freehold land and buildings, etc. Leases with no more than 50 years still to run are a special kind of wasting asset and are separately treated for capital gains tax (see following).

'Wasting assets' which are also movable property (chattels) are normally exempted from capital gains tax. In the case of other wasting assets apart from leases, you must reduce their original costs on a straight line time basis over the respective lives of the assets. Thus if you buy a wasting asset for £10,000 with an unexpired life of 40 years and sell it after 20 years for £20,000 assuming the residual value after 40 years would have been nil your allowable cost is £10,000 × 20/40 = £5,000; thus your chargeable gain is £20,000 − £5,000 = £15,000.

In the case of a lease with no more than 50 years of its original term unexpired (including leases for shorter terms) the original cost must be written off according to a special formula under which the rate of wastage accelerates as the end of the term of the lease is reached. If you sell such an interest in a property and lease back the premises at a lower rent for less than 15 years, you may be taxed on all or part of the proceeds either as a trading receipt or under Schedule D Case VI (p 113).

15. Capital Taxes on Land

As well as the complicated taxes on income from land and property which are outlined in Chapter 6 (p 39), a very severe system of taxation on capital profits has evolved. Capital gains tax applies to such capital profits, subject to development gains tax applying broadly before 1 August 1976 to any part which is a development gain (see below).

Any realised development value after 31 July 1976 will normally suffer development land tax (p 142) instead of development gains tax. As a further complication, the Revenue have powers to tax the profits from so called 'artificial transactions in land' (p 45), as if they were income.

Development Gains Tax
(FA 1974 Ss38–48 & Schs 3–10)

If you disposed of any land (including buildings) in the United Kingdom between 17 December 1973 and 31 July 1976, part of your gain might have been taxed as income. You were taxed under Case VI of Schedule D (p 113) on any amount of development gain which arose to you but no investment income surcharge was levied on it. Brief details are given below and further particulars are contained in the 1977–78 and two previous editions of this book.

Disposals after 31 July 1976, however, are not normally charged to development gains tax. Instead, development land tax (p 142) applies. An exemption to this rule is where a property was transferred from one spouse to the other before 1 August 1976; a disposal to a third party after that date is still liable to development gains tax.

If a development gain was made by a company, corporation tax was payable on the full amount at 52% or a lower rate if the Company's profits, including the gain, were sufficiently small (p 175). Trusts were charged to tax at 50% on development gains (48% prior to 6 April 1975). Life assurance companies were charged at 37.5% on their development gains in as far as they are attributable to the funds of the policy holders. But pension funds, etc., which are exempted from capital gains tax, were also free from development gains tax.

You were exempted from development gains tax on the sale of your main private residence, as for capital gains tax (p 135).

Computation of Development Gains (FA 1974 S38)
Subject to relief for small disposals (p 141), your development gain was the least of the following:

(a)   the proceeds less 120% of the total cost and expenses.
(b)   the proceeds less 110% of the 'current use value' (see below) at the date of disposal (ignored if the material development had been carried out since 17 December 1973).

(c)   the capital gain on the disposal of the land less the increase in 'current use value' during ownership or since 6 April 1965 if then owned.

What is Current Use Value? (FA 1974 Sch3 & DLTA S7)

This term also applies for *development land tax*, and is the value of your property on the assumption that only development which is not 'material' can be carried out; that is to say it is considered unlawful to carry out any 'material development'. If however at the date of the valuation you already possess planning permission for any development on which work has started, this is included in the current use value of the property. *'Material development'* is defined as the making of any change in the state, nature or use of the land; but there are various exclusions including the following:

(a)   Alterations, etc., which do not involve an increase of more than one-tenth in the cubic content of a building.
(b)   The use of land and buildings for agriculture and forestry.
(c)   The use of land for advertising purposes.
(d)   The change from a temporary use of land to its original use.
(e)   The change from one use to another when both are within one of the following classes (if a building is empty you consider its previous use):

CLASS A—Dwelling house or activities not carried on for profit.
CLASS B—Office or retail shop.
CLASS C—Hotel, boarding house, public house, etc.
CLASS D—Use for activities carried out for profit except those falling within the other Cases or agriculture or forestry.
CLASS E—Manufacturing, processing and warehousing, etc.

Small Disposals Relief (FA 1974 S39 & FA 1976 S129)

If your development gains from disposals of land and buildings in a year of assessment were no more than £10,000, you were relieved from development gains tax for that year. This applied to disposals by either your wife or yourself. In the case of a partnership the exemption figure of £10,000 also applied. For a company or a trust, development gains were exempted from development gains tax if they did not exceed £1,000.

First Letting after Material Development
(FA 1974 Ss45 & 46)

Subject to certain exemptions, where between 17 December 1973 and normally 31 July 1976, a building in the United Kingdom was let to a material extent for the first time following the commencement of development, any person with an interest in it could be treated as making a disposal for capital gains tax purposes. This deemed disposal was taken to be at the market value of the building at the date when it became let to a material extent, i.e. at least 25% of its floor area.

141

CAPITAL TAXES ON LAND

The effect of the provisions was that you could become liable to capital gains tax on a building which you owned merely because you let it after having developed it. Furthermore, your capital gain could be partly taxed as a development gain (p 140) so that you were liable for income tax on that portion.

Development Land Tax (D.L.T.A.)

This tax is charged on real and deemed realisations of development value after 31 July 1976 subject to certain exceptions. The start of a project of material development (p 141) is a deemed realisation for these purposes. The tax applies to both UK residents and non-residents, but relates to land in the UK only.

Development land tax is also charged on part disposals which involve the realisation of development value, including the grant of a lease. In this case the disposal proceeds are the aggregate of the market value of the right to receive the rent together with any premiums or other consideration.

The scope of the tax is wider than development gains tax, which it replaces, since for example charities and pension funds are included. The legislation is very detailed and the following is only a brief outline.

Rate of Development Land Tax
(D.L.T.A. Ss1, 12 & 13, FA 1978 S76 & F2A 1979 S24 & Sch 4)

The rate of the tax is 60% for all taxpayers, whether individuals, partnerships, trusts or companies. The first £50,000 of realised development value is normally free of tax, however, for each year ended 31 March. Note that you and your wife are taxed separately for the purposes of the tax. Thus you each have the £50,000 exemption. If you obtain a property from your spouse however, you must wait a year before disposing of it or else you will not get the exemption when you sell or realise development value.

For the year ended 31 March 1979 and earlier years, the first £10,000 of realised development value was normally free of tax with the next £150,000 being taxed at 66⅔% and the remainder at 80% each year. These two rates were replaced by the single 60% rate for realisations of development value made on or after 12 June 1979.

For the period from 1 April 1979 until 11 June 1979 inclusive, no more than £10,000 of the £50,000 annual exemption is available (leaving the balance for the rest of the year) and the next £150,000 is taxed at 66⅔%.

Computation of Realised Development Value
(D.L.T.A. S4)

The development land tax which you pay is based on your realised development value. This is the surplus of your net proceeds over your incidental costs (stamp duty, legal costs, etc.) and relevant base value (see below).

Relevant Base Value (D.L.T.A. S5)

The relevant base value consists of the highest of three different amounts computed as follows:

A. Cost+
   expenditure on 'relevant improvements'+
   increase in current use value (p 141) since later of 6.4.65 or acquisition date+
   special addition (see below)+
   further addition (see below).
B. 110% of current use value (p 141)+
   expenditure on 'relevant improvements' (see below).
C. 110% of cost+
   110% of expenditure on 'improvements'.

Special Addition, Further Addition and Improvements
(D.L.T.A. S6 & Sch 3 & FA 1977 S55)

These only apply on a disposal of an interest in land which you acquired before 1 May 1977. They do not normally apply to disposals which occur after the start of a project of material development (p 141), unless for example the development value was not fully exploited in the first instance. ('Start' includes digging foundations, etc.)

For land acquired before 13 September 1974, the 'special addition' is 15% of the original cost for every year of ownership up to four. Thus the maximum is 60% of cost.

For land acquired after 12 September 1974, the 'special addition' is 10% of the original cost for every year of ownership up to four. Thus the maximum is 40% of cost. For the above purposes a part of a year counts as a year.

The 'further addition' effectively extends the 'special addition' to 'relevant improvements'. These are amounts spent on enhancing the value of property together with the cost of establishing title to it and preserving and defending this, less the increase in current use value brought about by the improvements. The 'further addition' is found by multiplying the 'special addition' by the amount of the 'relevant improvements' and dividing by the original cost of the property.

'Improvements' includes the cost of prospective works which a landlord agrees to carry out, in connection with a lease which he grants. Such works can be taken into account in computing the development land tax on the part disposal constituted by the grant of the lease, even though the actual work is done later.

Exemptions

The following are some of the exemptions from the tax:

(a) Land outside the United Kingdom. (S1)
(b) Local authorities, etc., are exempt. (S11)
(c) The first £50,000 of realised development value each year per person (husband and wife separate) (p 142).

(d) Gifts are exempt (donor's acquisition, cost, etc., is taken over by recipient). (S10)

(e) Devolution on death is not a chargeable event. (S9)

(f) Principal private residences are exempted (husband and wife can have one each)—also land owned on 12 September 1974 which is developed as a dwelling for your own occupation. (Ss14 & 15)

(g) Land held as trading stock with planning permission on 12 September 1974. (S16)

(h) Deemed disposal of project within three years of acquisition, if you would have obtained no significant amount of realised development value, had you started the development as soon as you obtained the land. (S18)

(i) Industrial development for your own use (tax charge deferred until sale). (S19)

(j) Transfers within a group of companies. (75% holding—S21)

(k) Statutory undertakers (Electricity Board, etc.) if a development is for their own operations (but there is a charge on sale). (S23)

Charities (D.L.T.A. Ss24 & 25)

In general, charities are liable to the tax. If development value is realised from land held at 12 September 1974, however, no development land tax is charged on the charity. This exemption is extended to land held continuously by different charities since before that date.

If a charity develops land acquired after 12.9.74 for its own charitable use, any development land tax is deferred until a subsequent disposal.

Collection (D.L.T.A. S41 & Sch 8)

Subject to an appeal procedure the tax is payable three months after the date of the chargeable occasion, or if later, 30 days after the issue of a notice of assessment.

Spreading the tax is allowed over a period of up to eight years if the consideration for a disposal is rent or in the case of a deemed disposal. If the proceeds consist of instalments of capital, the Revenue allow spreading in cases of hardship. Interest (9%) is normally paid on overdue tax unpaid three months after the chargeable occasion. If the tax is payable by instalments however, the interest will only run from normally the due date of each instalment.

If you sell a property to a local authority, it is empowered to deduct development land tax from the price.

Relief for other Taxes (D.L.T.A. S34 & Sch 6)

The rules concerning the interaction of development land tax with other taxes are complicated but generous. They cover capital gains tax, corporation tax on capital gains, development gains tax, estate duty, capital transfer tax and income tax and corporation tax on trading gains. As a general rule, the part of the gain which is charged to development land tax is not charged to the other taxes.

For example, if you sell a property and make a capital gain of £20,000 and your realised development value is £15,000 you will pay development land tax on £15,000 and capital gains tax on only £5,000 (£20,000 – £15,000).

The relief is not only given when the disposals are at the same time for the purposes of the different taxes, it also normally applies if there are separate disposals to which development land tax and another tax apply. The two disposals must be within a limited period however, which normally is twelve years.

Where you acquire land by way of gift and you later obtain a realised development value from it, you are entitled to a credit against your development land tax based on the capital transfer tax (if any) paid by the donor.

16. Partnerships

What is a Partnership?

Partnership is the relationship which exists between persons in business together with the object of making profits. There does not necessarily have to be a written partnership agreement but the partnership must exist in fact. If no partnership is in fact operating then, even though there may be a written agreement, it would not make the partnership exist.

Since the assessment of a partnership differs from that of an individual in certain respects, the Revenue will seek to establish whether a partnership in fact exists. Points to consider include:

(1)   Is there a written partnership agreement?
(2)   Has a business name been registered for the partnership?
(3)   Can the partners close down the business and are they liable for its debts?
(4)   Do the partners' names appear on business stationery?
(5)   What arrangements exist for dividing the profits (and property on dissolution)?

How Partnership Income is Taxed (S152)

A joint assessment to income tax under Case I or Case II of Schedule D (p 55) is made on the partners in respect of the partnership profits. This includes basic rate (30%) and higher rate income tax (if any) on the profits. The rules for the opening (p 61) and closing years (p 63) are followed as for individuals, as are those for capital allowances (p 64). The 'precedent partner', who is normally the senior partner, must make a joint return of the partnership income each year.

Partnership investment income is split between the partners in their profit-sharing ratios and they personally pay any income tax and investment income surcharge arising.

When the partnership income has been determined for the purposes of Schedule D Case I or Case II, it must be split between the partners according to the proportions in which they share profits during the tax year. These proportions are not necessarily the same as the profit sharing ratios during the year when the profits were actually made. Thus if A and B made £10,000 in the year to 30 April 1978 when they split profits 60:40 their partnership assessment for 1979–80 is on the preceding year basis, i.e. £10,000. This is split in the ratio in which they divide profits for the year to 5 April 1980; suppose this is altered to 50:50 on 1 May 1978 then they will each be assessed on £5,000 for 1979–80. If a partner is remunerated partly by way of a salary and partly by receiving a share of the profits, the salary is normally not assessed under Schedule E but is included in his profit share assessable under Schedule D Case I or Case II.

Interest paid to partners in respect of their capital is also treated as part of the profit share of each partner and is assessed under Schedule D Case I or Case II. Such interest is not an annual payment (p 16), nor is it taxed as investment income (p 48).

Example 23: Partnership Assessments

A, B and C trade in partnership sharing profits equally after the interest and salary allocations shown below. They prepare accounts to 5 April showing the following:

	Profits	Interest		Salary	
		A	B	B	C
5 April 1979	£9,000	£500	£500	£1,000	£2,000
1980	£10,000	£400	£600	£1,500	£1,500

The 1979–80 assessment under *Schedule D Case 1* is as follows:

	TOTAL	A	B	C
Net profit (preceding year) –				
year ended 5 April 1979	£9,000			
Add: Interest A	500			
B	500			
Salary B	1,000			
C	2,000			
	£13,000			
Less: Interest A 400		£400		
B 600			£600	
Salary B 1,500			1,500	
C 1,500				£1,500
	4,000			
Balance split equally	£9,000	3,000	3,000	3,000
Total assessment	£13,000	£3,400	£5,100	£4,500

Notes:

(1) In addition to the above, the normal Schedule D Case I adjustments must be made (p 58).
(2) The interest and salaries for the year to 5 April 1979 are added back to the profits.
(3) The 1979–80 assessments split includes the interest and salaries for the year to 5 April 1980.

Partnership Losses (Ss168–176)

Where a partnership has an adjusted loss for any accounting period, that loss is apportioned between the partners in the same ratio as a profit would have been split. Thus the loss is split according to the profit sharing ratios applying to the year of assessment corresponding to the tax year in which the loss is made. For example if a loss is made in the year to 5 April 1979 this is split between the partners according to their profit sharing ratios for the tax year 1979–80 (assuming that the preceding year basis of assessment applies).

Each partner can use his partnership losses as he chooses according to the various rules for obtaining loss relief (p 71). Thus he can claim for the loss to be relieved against his other income tax assessments for the tax year in which the loss is actually made or the following year. This means that relief can be obtained against the previous year's partnership profits. Also he can carry forward any unused balance of the loss to be set off against future profit shares from the same partnership; this applies even if the partnership had been treated as discontinued because of a partnership change (see below).

Changes of Partners (S154)

If there is any change in the make up of a partnership caused either by a partner leaving or dying or a fresh partner joining, the partnership is treated as ceasing for taxation purposes unless the continuation election described below is made.

The effects of cessation caused by a change of partners are similar to any other Schedule D Case I or Case II cessation (p 63). Thus the assessment for the final tax year is based on the actual profits for that year and the Revenue have the option to increase the assessments for the two previous tax years to the actual profits for those years. Also any unrecouped stock relief (p 60) is brought into charge.

Election for Continuation Basis (S154)

Within two years of the date of a change in the members of a partnership an election can be made to the Revenue that the partnership should be taxed on a continuation basis. This election can be made provided that at least one of the partners in the old partnership remains as a partner in the new partnership. All of the partners in both the old and the new partnership must sign the election.

The effect of the election is that the partnership is not treated as ceasing for taxation purposes at the date of the change. Instead, the Schedule D Case I or Case II assessment for the tax year in which the change takes place is apportioned to the date of the change. Then the old partners are assessed on their share of the assessment apportioned up to the change and the new partners are assessed on the proportion after the change.

For example, suppose that the adjusted profits of a professional partnership for the year to 31 December 1978 are £12,000 and until 5 October 1979 there were three equal partners A, B and C. If with effect from that date B and C sell their partnership shares to D and assuming A, B, C and D all make the necessary election before 5 October 1981, the following Schedule D Case II assessments will arise for *1979–80* (on a preceding year basis):

	6.4.79–5.10.79	6.10.79–5.4.80	*Total*
A	£2,000	£2,000	£4,000
B	2,000	—	2,000
C	2,000	—	2,000
D	—	4,000	4,000
	£6,000	£6,000	£12,000

There are some special rules governing partnerships between individuals and a company (S155). A separate election (FA 1976 Sch 5) to be made within two years of the change, protects previous stock relief.

Partnership Capital Gains (CGTA S60)

When a partnership asset is sold in such circumstances that if owned by an individual, capital gains tax would have been payable, this tax is assessed on the partners according to their shares in the partnership asset. Thus if a capital gain of £1,000 is made from the sale of a partnership asset on 1 January 1980 and A, B, C and D share equally in the partnership assets, a capital gain of £250 each must be added to the capital gains tax assessments for 1979–80 of A, B, C and D respectively (p 121).

Where a share in a partnership changes hands, a share in all of the partnership assets is treated for capital gains tax purposes as changing ownership and this might give rise to capital gains or capital losses regarding the partner who is disposing of his share. Thus if A, B, and C are equal partners and A sells his share to D, A is treated for capital gains tax purposes as disposing of a one-third share in each of the partnership assets to D.

Overseas Partnerships (S153)

If you are in partnership carrying on a trade or business and the control and management of the trade or business is outside the United Kingdom then the partnership is treated for tax purposes as being non-resident. This follows even if you or some of your other partners are resident here (p 96) and some of the business is conducted in this country.

Any profits arising from the partnership trade or business in this country are assessed here under Schedule D Case I. The firm is assessed in the name of any partner resident in the United Kingdom. Regarding the partnership profits earned abroad, these are assessable in respect of any profit shares of the partners resident here under Schedule D Case V according to the special rules outlined in Chapter 11 (p 99).

17. Returns, Assessments and Repayment Claims

Your Income Tax Return (T.M.A. S8)

The Revenue will normally send to you periodically an income tax return for completion. If your income includes Schedule A and/or Schedule D income you will usually have to submit an income tax return each year. If however all your income is taxed under PAYE (p 90) you may only be required to complete a return about every three years.

Apart from individuals, trusts, partnerships and companies, etc., also have to submit tax returns. In the case of companies, however, provided the Revenue receive the annual accounts and tax computations they do not normally insist on the submission of corporation tax returns.

If you have not been sent an income tax return for the previous tax year and you have received income for that year apart from your wages or salary, you should request that the Revenue sends you a return form for completion. This request should be made to the Inspector of Taxes who deals with your affairs – if you are employed it will be the tax district that handles your employer's PAYE affairs. As well as including details of your income for the previous tax year your income tax return also constitutes a claim for income tax allowances and reliefs in respect of the current tax year. Thus your 1979–80 income tax return must show your income for the year to 5 April 1979 and the income tax allowances that you are claiming for the year to 5 April 1980.

A further reason for you to request an income tax return from your Inspector of Taxes is to ensure that you are granted all of the income tax reliefs and allowances to which you are entitled.

When an income tax return is issued to you it normally stipulates that it must be completed and sent back within thirty days but the Revenue usually allow further time if required.

Your 1979–80 income tax return probably will be sent to you early in April 1979 and has four main headings as follows:

Income:	Year ended 5 April 1979
Outgoings:	Year ended 5 April 1979
Capital Gains:	Year ended 5 April 1979
Allowances:	Claim for year ending 5 April 1980.

On the front page of your return you must give your private address and also sign the following declaration: 'To the best of my knowledge and belief the particulars given on this form are correct and complete.'

Table 15: Your 1979–80 Income Tax Return – Income

The following sources of income must be included in your return showing in the separate columns provided the *amounts* for your

150

Table 15 continued

wife and yourself for the year to 5 April 1979. Further rules concerning the entries are given elsewhere in this book. Include with your investment income (4–10 below) that on assets given by you or your wife to any of your children who are under 18 (p 166).

Class of Income	Details
(1) Employments or offices.	Occupation. Employer. Gross earnings (including fees, bonus, commission, tips, etc.). Benefits and expense allowances. Leaving payments, etc. Duties performed wholly abroad – state employment, whether claiming $\frac{1}{2}$ or whole deduction and dates of absence.
(2) Trade, profession or vocation.	Nature. Business name and address. Adjusted profits. Deduction for capital allowances. Other deductions for Class 4 National Insurance purposes. Relief for business abroad – dates of absence.
(3) Pensions and social security benefit.	Rates and nature of pensions. National Insurance retirement pension. Old person's pension. Widow's and other benefits. Pension from former employer and other pensions (including war widow's pension). Family allowances (give weekly amount).
(4) Property (give address, gross income and expenses).	Unfurnished lettings. Furnished lettings. Ground rents. Land (income).
(5) UK Dividends.	Show for each source separately, the amounts received, and also the tax credits.
(6) Interest, trust income, foreign dividends, etc., already taxed.	Enter the gross amounts before the deduction of tax.
(7) Interest not taxed before receipt.	National and trustee savings interest. Other banks (give names). Other sources (including war loan, defence bonds, etc.).
(8) Untaxed income from abroad.	
(9) Interest from UK building societies.	Name of society.
(10) Any other profits or income.	Include income from settlements, transfers to be treated as your income and gains on non-qualifying policies (p 208).
(11) Alterations in untaxed income or outgoings since 5 April 1978.	

Table 16: Your 1979–80 Income Tax Return – Outgoings

The amounts of outgoings for your wife and yourself for the year ended 5 April 1979 must be shown separately as follows:

Class	Details
Expenses in employment.	Give details and amounts. Include professional subscriptions.
Interest on loans (excluding bank overdrafts) for purchase or improvement of property.	*Only or main residence* To a building society or local authority – give name and Roll No. (no amounts needed). To any other person including a bank – enclose certificate. *Let property* – number of weeks let – enclose certificate. *Other property* – loan incurred before 27 March 1974 – enclose certificate. *Option mortgage* – give amount outstanding at 5 April 1979.
Interest on other loans (excluding overdrafts).	Qualifying loans. Any other loans incurred before 27 March 1974 – enclose certificates.
Other interest and outgoings.	Covenants and settlements. Alimony or maintenance. UK property rents or yearly interest paid to persons abroad.

Table 17: Your 1979–80 Income Tax Return – Capital Gains

You must give details of the gains and chargeable acquisitions for your wife and yourself for the year to 5 April 1979 as follows:

Class	Details
Chargeable assets disposed of (p 121).	Date of disposal, and description. (If your chargeable gains and proceeds are no more than £1,000 and £5,000 respectively, you need only state this fact.)
Unit trust units and shares in investment trusts – other assets.	Amount of gain for year (also show any losses) – distinguish development gains (p 140).
Chargeable assets acquired.	Date of acquisition. Description. Cost or acquisition value.

Table 18: Your 1979–80 Income Tax Return – Claim for Allowances

If you claim any personal reliefs or allowances for 1979–80 (p 6) you must enter the required details in the spaces provided on your return. These are summarised below.

Table 18 continued

Class	Details
Married man living with wife or wholly maintaining her. Children.	Wife's forenames. If you married after 5 April 1978 : date of marriage ; wife's former surname. Indicate in box if special form is required for child living outside United Kingdom. Give names of students on full grant or without grant who were on full time course at 31 December 1976. Give income for 1978–79 of children for whom allowance claimed whose earnings exceeded £500 or other income £115.
Housekeeper or person looking after children.	Give full names. Status of housekeeper (single, married, divorced, etc.). Is she resident with you ? Relationship to you (if any). If your relative, give weekly maintenance contributed by anyone else.
Additional personal allowance for children.	Does child live with you ? Wife's incapacity (if any), and whether likely to continue throughout tax year. Give names, dates of birth and details of school, etc., if child 16 or over on 6 April 1979.
Dependent relatives.	Full name and address. Relationship to you or your wife. Relative's income, separating Government and total other pensions. Contributions by you and others. Date of birth and nature of any infirmity.
Relief for persons born before 6 April 1915.	Give dates of birth of yourself and/or wife.
Son or daughter on whose services you are compelled to depend. Blind person's allowance.	Full names – status – whether resident and/or maintained by you. Details of age and/or infirmity of you or your wife. Whether claimed for you and/or wife. Local authority and date of registration. Description and amount of tax free blindness allowance for current tax year.
Death and superannuation benefits. Retirement annuity payments.	Contribution for year and proportion for death or superannuation benefit. Occupation in which non-pensionable earnings arise (employer, etc.). Name of insurance company, etc., or trust scheme. Contract number, etc. Amount to be paid in 1979–80.

(Life insurance : No details required this year.)

The Tax Inspectors and Collectors (T.M.A. S1)

The overall control and management of income tax, corporation tax and capital gains tax is exercised by the Board of Inland Revenue. They are responsible for administering the relevant law as contained in the 1970 Income and Corporation Taxes Act and the various Finance Acts. The latter are normally enacted annually about July, the main items having been announced by the Chancellor of the Exchequer in his budget speech in March or April. The Board of Inland Revenue is made up of the Commissioners of Inland Revenue. The day-to-day administration however is carried out by various Inspectors of Taxes and Collectors of Taxes who are civil servants.

The Inspectors of Taxes are organised into various tax districts to one of which you will have to send your income tax return. A district inspector heads each district under whom are a number of inspectors and clerks who obtain and verify as they think fit the information that is necessary to raise assessments to income tax, capital gains tax and corporation tax.

The Collectors of Taxes have the responsibility of collecting the tax that has been assessed. They issue demands for the tax that is due (p 160).

The office of the Inspector of Foreign Dividends handles various matters in connection with double tax relief claims.

The Assessment Mechanism (T.M.A. S29)

When you have submitted your income tax return the Inspector of Taxes will issue a 'notice of assessment' to income tax in respect of your various types of income. A separate assessment will be raised in respect of Schedule E earnings. Since the latter will have normally already been taxed under PAYE the assessment will show whether any additional payment of income tax is required or whether a repayment is due (p 158).

Your capital gains tax assessment also will be raised by your Inspector of Taxes (p 127).

If the Revenue have not received sufficient information to raise accurate tax assessments prior to the date on which the tax is due for payment, they will normally make estimated assessments in respect of the taxpayer's sources of income. Estimated capital gains tax assessments will also be raised if appropriate.

Due Dates for Payment of Tax (S4 & F2A 1975 S44, etc.)

The due date for payment of income tax assessed under the various schedules and cases (p 1), is normally 1 January in the year of assessment. Thus your Schedule D Case III income tax for 1979–80 including higher rates and investment surcharge is payable on 1 January 1980. Schedule D Case I and Case II assessments on your profits from a trade or profession are payable however in two instalments on 1 January in the year of assessment and the following 1 July.

Higher rate income tax and investment surcharge on your 'taxed' investment income is payable on 6 July following the year of assessment. This would include tax on interest, etc., taxed at source and dividends. Higher rate income tax and surcharge on other investment income however (including rents, etc.) is normally payable on 1 January in the year of assessment. (For the due dates of payment of Corporation Tax see p 173.)

If an assessment is issued later than 30 days before the respective date above however, the date when the tax becomes due and payable is delayed to a later date as follows:

(1) For assessments issued prior to 1 August 1975 the later date for payment was normally the day after that on which the agreed assessment was made.

(2) For assessments issued after 31 July 1975 the later date for payment is normally 30 days after the issue of the assessment. Note however the effect of appeals (p 156).

Discovery (T.M.A. S29 (3))

The estimated assessments will be made by the Revenue to as great a degree of accuracy as possible according to any information in their possession such as particulars for previous years. If however the Revenue make a *'discovery'* that:

(a) profits which ought to have been assessed to tax have not been assessed, or

(b) an assessment to tax is or has become insufficient, or

(c) excessive relief has been given

the Revenue may make an assessment in the amount or further amount which ought in their opinion to be charged.

Thus if your business income tax assessment for 1979–80 under Schedule D Case I is estimated at £1,000 and after submitting your accounts it becomes apparent that the correct figure is £2,000, the Inspector of Taxes will raise an additional assessment of £1,000. If however you lodged notice of appeal against the assessment (see below), your original assessment for £1,000 will be amended to £2,000.

Time Limits for Assessments (T.M.A. S34)

Normally an assessment to tax may be made at any time not later than six years after the end of the chargeable period to which the assessment relates. This means that any income tax assessment for 1979–80 may be made on or before 5 April 1986.

In the case however of any fraud or wilful default by the taxpayer (p 162) the Revenue have the right to make assessments at any time.

Appeals Against Assessments
(T.M.A. S31 & F2A 1975 S45)

If you are not in agreement with an assessment to income tax, capital gains tax or corporation tax you may appeal to the Inspector of Taxes within 30 days of the date of the assessment. Your appeal must be in writing and state the grounds on which you object to the assessment; most frequently these are that 'the assessment is estimated and excessive'. Should you not be able to appeal within 30 days, for some good reason such as absence from home or ill-health, the Revenue will normally allow you to make a late appeal.

The majority of appeals are settled by agreement. This normally follows when the accounts and/or returns have been submitted to the Inspector of Taxes and any queries that he raises are answered. If however you are not able to agree with the Revenue or if you or your accountants have not submitted all of the required information, the appeal will be listed for personal hearing before the Commissioners (p 157).

Prior to 1 August 1975 you often were required to make a payment on account of an assessment under appeal. The balance was payable when the assessment was agreed and no interest ran before that time (p 161).

For an assessment issued after 31 July 1975 however, all the tax charged by it is treated as due and payable (p 154) unless, within 30 days, you estimate how much you are being overcharged. It will then be determined by agreement with the Inspector or otherwise by the Commissioners how much of the tax should be held over and only the balance is collected. This collectible balance is payable within the 30 days after the Inspector or Commissioners have dealt with the application for postponement. Any unpaid tax normally becomes due 30 days after the date on which, following the agreement of the assessment, the Inspector issues a notice of the tax payable. The interest charge could run from an earlier date however (p 161) especially in the case of a long drawn out appeal.

The Special and General Commissioners
(T.M.A. Ss2–6)

The Commissioners before whom tax appeals are heard are of two kinds, General and Special.

The General Commissioners are not normally paid. They are similar to lay magistrates and the majority of them have no special legal or accountancy qualifications. General Commissioners are appointed in England and Wales by the Lord Chancellor. They are appointed for specific districts each of which has a Clerk to the Commissioners, who is usually a solicitor, to assist them.

The Treasury appoints the Special Commissioners who usually have practical experience of taxation matters gained either in private practice or with the Inland Revenue. The Special Commissioners are full-time civil servants.

Appeals will automatically be heard before the General Commissioners except that:

(a) You may elect within 30 days of the assessment that the appeal should be brought before the Special Commissioners. This does not apply however to questions regarding personal reliefs, valuations of quoted securities and apportionments of child allowances, which are always dealt with by the General Commissioners.

(b) Appeals against certain income tax assessments are always heard by the Special Commissioners including those on annual payments not covered by income, transactions in securities (S460) and transfers of assets abroad (S478).

In many cases you will thus have a choice as to whether the Special or General Commissioners should hear your appeal. As a general rule if your case is good in equity and its justice would commend it to average honest men you should choose the General Commissioners. If you have a good legal case (i.e. one sound according to a strict reading of the law) you should choose the Special Commissioners.

Appeal Hearings (T.M.A. Ss44–59)

The Clerk to the Commissioners will advise you of the time and place for your appeal hearing. If you are unable to attend for some good reason or if you or your accountants have not completed the required accounts, etc., it will normally be possible to have the matter adjourned at least once until a later time. If you would like an adjournment you or your agent should raise the question with your Inspector of Taxes who will usually be prepared to arrange this for you if your reasons are in order.

At the appeal hearing you may represent yourself or be represented by an accountant or a solicitor or barrister. If your appeal is on a point of law which you anticipate may go to the Courts (see below) it is wise to be represented at the outset by a barrister who can act for you in the Courts. The Revenue are normally represented by an Inspector of Taxes but on difficult legal points a person from the Solicitors' Office may act. The proceedings before the Commissioners resemble those in the Courts in many ways – for example witnesses may be summoned under oath to be examined and cross-examined.

When the hearing has been completed the Commissioners will withdraw to consider their decision. They may confirm or reduce or increase the original assessment. The decision of the Commissioners is final regarding questions of fact. If either the taxpayer or the Revenue are dissatisfied as to their decision on a point of law, they should immediately 'express dissatisfaction'. The Commissioners should then be requested to supply a 'case stated' which is a document signed by them setting out their decision. The case will then be taken on appeal to the Courts where it will first be heard before a single judge in the Chancery Division. The decision of such a court can be appealed against, following which the case will be heard before the Court of Appeal and on further appeal it may go to the House of Lords.

Before you request a 'case stated' from the Commissioners you should very carefully weigh the strength of your case and the potential tax saving if you succeed in the higher Courts against the high legal costs which would be involved.

Repayment Claims (T.M.A. Ss42 & 43 & FA 1978 S22)

Repayment claims arise in connection with many different facets of taxation. You will normally however find that any income tax repayment to which you become entitled arises in one of the following ways:

(1) Most of your income has been taxed at the source and your personal reliefs and allowances exceed your other income. If your income tax return reveals this position and you send in the required simple repayment claim form together with dividend vouchers, etc., in respect of the income tax credits, you will receive an income tax repayment. The repayment will reduce your income tax bill for the tax year to its correct level.

(2) Some of your income has been taxed both in the United Kingdom and in another country. You are frequently able to make a double taxation relief repayment claim of either UK tax or overseas tax depending on the circumstances (p 106).

(3) You may have already paid a Schedule A or Schedule D assessment for a tax year and as described elsewhere in this book, you make an election to the Revenue which results in your assessment for that year being reduced. An example of such an election is where you elect that the second and third years of your business should be assessed on an actual basis (p 61).

(4) You make a business loss which you claim to be offset against your other income for the year (p 71). Some of this income has suffered income tax by deduction at the source and on making the required claim and submitting the tax vouchers or receipts you will be repaid an appropriate amount of such tax, as well as tax credits on dividends.

(5) You discover that an 'error or mistake' has been made in a return or statement or schedule that you have previously submitted as a result of which you have been over-assessed to tax. Within six years after the end of the tax year in which the original assessment was made, you may make a claim to your Inspector of Taxes for the repayment of the tax previously overpaid.

(6) Repayment claims often arise in respect of minors (under 18) all of whom are taxpayers in their own right and so are entitled to at least the personal allowance for a single person

(£1,165).Thus if a minor's only income for 1979–80 consists of dividends of say £350 and none of the investments were gifted to him by his parents, then he can reclaim all of the relevant tax credits (i.e. 30/70 × £350 = £150). Similarly, if the trustees of a settlement apply income for the education and maintenance of a minor, that income is treated (after 5 April 1972) as belonging to the child. For 1972–73 it was treated as having suffered standard rate income tax at the source. This enabled an income tax repayment claim to be made for the minor unless he had already obtained the full benefit of his tax reliefs and allowances or the settlement had been actually created by one of his parents (p 166). Similarly after 5 April 1973 both basic rate tax and investment surcharge may be reclaimed in appropriate circumstances.

(7) Within six years of the end of the tax year in which you reach an age specified in the trust deed (at least eighteen) and thereby become entitled to accumulated income in a 'contingent trust' you may claim relief in respect of any income accumulated before 6 April 1969. You are able to obtain repayment of any unused personal reliefs and allowances for tax years up to and including 1968–69. A 'contingent trust' is one in which all or part of the income has been accumulated for you provided a certain future event takes place such as your attaining your majority.

The procedure for making repayment claims is normally very simple. If the Revenue have already received a full return of your income, or in the case of a business or company its accounts and tax computations, it will generally only be necessary to sign a short form in which you claim the tax repayment to which you are entitled. You should also send dividend vouchers or tax deduction certificates or receipts to cover the amount of your repayment.

Special forms are usually required for double tax relief claims on which you must enter particulars of the dividends. Special forms are also provided by the Revenue for use in connection with various other repayment claims, for example concerning minors.

Income tax repayment claims should normally be made to your local Inspector of Taxes. If you are for example a British subject resident abroad your repayment claims should be made to the Chief Inspector (Claims) at Bootle. The Inspector of Foreign Dividends however deals with applications from those residing abroad for the recovery of United Kingdom tax suffered on overseas dividends, etc. Normally any repayment of tax on your wife's income will be paid to you. After 30 July 1978, however, her PAYE over-deductions will be repaid direct to your wife unless she has earnings taxed under Schedule D or you are a higher rate taxpayer.

Repayment Supplement (F2A 1975 Ss47 & 48)

This applies if you receive a tax repayment more than a year after the end of the year of assessment to which it relates and after 31 July 1975. You also have to be resident in the United Kingdom and the repayment must not be less than £25. You will then get interest at 9% free of tax from normally the later of the end of the assessment year in which the tax was paid or 5 April following the year for which repayment is made; until the end of the tax month when the repayment is made. A similar rule applies for companies (p 173).

Example 24: Income Tax Repayment Claim

Miss A is 24 years of age and during the year to 5 April 1980 she only had occasional employment from which her gross earnings were £680; no PAYE being deducted. During 1979–80 she pays allowable loan interest of £515. Miss A's only other income for 1979–80 consists of £1,400 dividends (tax credit £600) and an income distribution of £550 (net) from a discretionary trust. Calculate the amount of the income tax repayment claim of Miss A for 1979–80.

Miss A – Income Tax Repayment Claim 1979–80

Details		Gross income	Tax credits
Earned income		£680	
Taxed dividends including tax credit		2,000	£600.00
Trust income – net	£550		
Grossed up equivalent at 45%		1,000	450.00
		£3,680	
Less: Personal allowance	£1,165		
Loan interest	515		
		1,680	
Taxable amount		£2,000	
Total tax credits			£1,050.00
Less: Income tax liability £750 at 25%		£187.50	
£1,250 at 30%		375.00	
			562.50
Income tax repayable for 1979–80			£487.50

The Collection of Tax (T.M.A. Ss60–64)

The collection of income tax, corporation tax and capital gains tax is done by the Collectors of Taxes (p 154).

On being notified of an assessment by the Inspector of Taxes the Collector will send out a first demand. If this is not paid within about a month of its 'due date' a second demand will be sent and after about another ten days a final demand will follow. The final demand requests payment within seven days under the threat of legal proceedings against the taxpayer concerned. It is usual for the first demand to be integrated with the notice of assessment and the payslip should be detached from the rest of the form when you make your payment.

Payments on Account

If you receive a large tax demand which you find difficult to meet out of your available funds the Collector of Taxes will in cases of hardship allow you to settle the outstanding tax by instalments payable at say monthly or quarterly intervals. You should contract the Collector of Taxes and explain to him the position. Interest will probably be payable however (p 161).

Interest on Overdue Tax (T.M.A. Ss86–92 & F2A 1975 S46)

Different rules apply depending on whether the assessment was issued before 1 August 1975 or after 31 July 1975.

(1) *Assessment issued before 1 August 1975.*

Any income tax, surtax, capital gains tax or corporation tax that was paid more than two months after the due date for payment of the respective tax was subject to interest. The interest was charged on the entire amount of the overdue tax from its due date until its date of payment. The rate of interest was 6% prior to 1 July 1974 and 9% after that date. In the case however of a back duty settlement (p 162), the rate was only 4% up to 1 July 1974 but 9% after that date.

The basic 9% charge was waived if either the total tax charged by the assessment was not more than £1,000 or the total interest was not in excess of £5. These rules still apply to assessments issued before 1 August 1975 which are currently unpaid.

(2) *Assessment issued on or after 1 August 1975.*

Interest is payable at 9% from the 'reckonable date' until the tax is settled. The 'reckonable date' is the date when the tax becomes due and payable (p 154) unless you appeal and obtain a deferment of tax. In that case the 'reckonable date' is when the tax becomes due and payable or the date given by the following table whichever is earlier:

	Description of tax	Date applicable
(a)	Schedules A or D.	1 July following the end of the year of assessment.
(b)	Additional rates of income tax.	1 January following the end of the year of assessment.
(c)	Capital gains tax.	1 January following the end of the year of assessment.
(d)	Corporation tax.	Usually 6 months after the normal payment date (p 173).

There is no longer any level of assessment below which interest is not charged. The Revenue however may excuse at their discretion the payment of interest not exceeding £10 in total for any one assessment.

No interest paid on overdue tax is allowed as a deduction from your taxable income or business profits nor is it allowed as a deduction for corporation tax or capital gains tax purposes.

Back Duty Investigations

If you have not disclosed to the Revenue your true income or if you have claimed tax reliefs and allowances to which you were not entitled the discovery of such facts by the authorities might give rise to a 'back duty' case.

It is open to the Revenue to take criminal proceedings against you resulting in fine and/or imprisonment but this is rare. The normal course will be for the Revenue to obtain full particulars of the income omitted by you and raise assessments on you in respect of the further tax that is due. You will also normally be charged interest on the tax from when it should have been paid if your income had been properly declared. The Revenue may also charge you to penalties (p 162) depending upon whether your omissions were due to pure carelessness or ignorance or on the other hand were due to some fraudulent intention.

In order to ascertain the amount of your undisclosed income the Revenue will frequently require that capital statements be drawn up at the beginning and end of the period under review. The increase in your net worth between those two dates is then added to your living expenses for the period to give your total income (subject to adjustments for known capital profits, purchases and sales, betting winnings, etc.). Your total income less income already taxed will give your total income requiring still to be taxed. This should be split between the various intervening tax years by considering your assets and living expenses, etc., for each tax year.

Fraud, Wilful Default or Neglect (T.M.A. S36)

The normal six-year time limit for making assessments (p 154) is extended indefinitely in any case where there is fraud or wilful default. This does not apply however in the case of the personal representatives of a deceased person (p 169).

In a case of 'neglect' by the taxpayer, the Revenue are empowered to make assessments for six years prior to a tax year for which an assessment has already been made. The latter must be not more than six years ago and the Revenue must obtain the leave of the Special or General Commissioners. 'Neglect' is defined as 'negligence or a failure to give any notice, make any return or to produce or furnish any document or other information required by or under the Taxes Acts'.

Interest and Penalties (T.M.A. Ss86–107)

Where an assessment has been made for the purpose of making good a loss of tax through fraud, wilful default or neglect, interest at 9% is charged on the underpaid tax from the date that the tax should have been paid (4% up to 1 July 1974).

The maximum penalties are laid down in the legislation but frequently the Board of the Inland Revenue are prepared to accept less according to the particular facts of each case.

Table 19: Penalties (T.M.A. Ss93–107)

The following are examples of some of the maximum penalties:

Offence	Penalties
Failure to submit returns.	£50 for each return plus £10 per day after a Court declaration.
Failure to submit return continuing beyond tax year following that in which issued.	£50 plus total tax based on return.
Incorrect returns.	£50 plus twice the additional tax in the case of fraud and in other cases £50 plus the additional tax.
Assisting in the preparation of incorrect returns or accounts.	£500.
Supplying incorrect information to the Revenue.	£500 in case of fraud – otherwise £250.
Failure to give notice of liability to tax.	£100.
Failure to make when required, a return of fees, commissions, etc.	£50 plus £50 for each additional day in default.
False statement made by sub-contractor to obtain exemption from tax deduction (p 115).	£5,000.

Investigatory Powers of the Revenue
(FA 1976 S57 & Sch 6)

The powers of the Revenue to obtain papers and search premises were strengthened by the 1976 Finance Act. Subject to the consent of the Board of Inland Revenue, the Inspector may require you by notice in writing to supply him with documents in your possession or power, which he considers have a bearing on your tax liability. What is more, the Inspector may require such documents from certain other people. These other people include your spouse and any of your children. In general these rules do not apply to pending appeals, nor to development land tax.

If any of your income comes from a business which you either carried on yourself or you managed, then any person who is or was carrying on a business may be directed to provide documents concerning their dealings with your business. The same applies if your wife carries on a business or manages one.

These rules also apply to a past business and any companies of which you or your spouse are or were directors.

In order for your Inspector of Taxes to obtain information about your affairs from other people, he must obtain the consent of a General or Special Commissioner (p 156) and the latter must ensure that the Inspector is justified in his request.

A barrister, advocate or solicitor cannot be compelled to yield up documents without your consent provided these are covered by professional privilege. This even applies to such a lawyer acting as your tax accountant (see below).

Tax Accountants' Papers

Your tax accountant is not obliged to reveal his working papers to the Revenue subject to the following.

Where, after 28 July 1976 a tax accountant is convicted of an offence in relation to tax by a United Kingdom court or has a penalty awarded against him for assisting in making incorrect returns, etc., subject to certain rules, an Inspector of Taxes may require him to surrender documents relating to the tax affairs of any of his clients. Notice is required in writing and the permission of a circuit judge, Scottish sheriff or Irish county court judge must be obtained. The power of the Revenue to give this notice generally ceases 12 months after the conviction or penalty award, and does not have effect whilst an appeal is pending.

Entry Warrant to Obtain Documents

If the Revenue obtain an entry warrant in a case of suspected fraud (p 162) they may enter specified premises, seizing and removing any documents or other things required as evidence for relevant proceedings. A warrant is valid for 14 days and can only be granted by a circuit judge, etc., who is satisfied on information given on oath by an officer of the Board of Inland Revenue, that evidence concerning a tax fraud is to be found on the premises in question.

Returns of Information (T.M.A. Ss13–19)

The Revenue are empowered to request returns of certain information from traders and others. For example, you may be required to give particulars of any lodgers you may have.

Your bank may be required to return details of interest paid to you during a tax year, if this exceeds £15. Furthermore, the Revenue are empowered to obtain from any business, details of its payments of fees, commissions, royalties, etc., exceeding £15 to any person during a tax year.

18. The Taxation of Trusts and Estates

Trusts

A trust is brought into existence when a person (the settlor) transfers assets to trustees for the benefit of third parties (the beneficiaries). Another word for a trust is a settlement. A trust may also be created under a will when a person (the testator) sets aside the whole or a portion of his estate to be administered (by trustees) for the benefit of his heirs or other beneficiaries.

Trusts where the Settlor or Testator is Deceased

Where the settlor or testator has died, the taxation of trusts normally follows simple rules. The trust is assessed to basic rate income tax and sometimes investment surcharge (p 25) on its income. Some of this tax will have been deducted at the source (e.g. taxed interest). Capital gains tax is charged on any capital gains of the trust (p 168).

The tax assessments are normally made in the joint names of the trustees who pay the tax out of the trust funds.

No higher rate tax is paid by the trustees but when the income is distributed to any of the beneficiaries this income is added to the beneficiaries' total income for tax purposes (p 22). The income distributions are normally treated as being net of income tax at the basic rate (30%). Thus they carry a corresponding tax credit. In the case of discretionary trusts, etc. (p 167) the investment surcharge (15%) further increases the tax credit. If part of the underlying income of the trust is building society interest however, the appropriate portion of each income distribution must be allocated to this interest which will be taxed in the beneficiary's hands in the same way as any income on his own building society investments (p 53).

For example suppose A has a life interest in a trust and receives from it income for 1979–80 made up as follows:

	Total	Building society income	Other income
Gross	£1,350	£350	£1,000
Income tax at 30% (tax credit)	300	—	300
Actual payment to A	£1,050	£350	£700

A will include in his total income £1,500 (i.e. £1,000 distribution from other income plus £350 × 100/70 grossed equivalent of building society income). If A is able to make an income tax repayment claim (p 158) he will have £300 income tax credit from the trust available for repayment.

The trustees should issue with each payment a form R.185E which sets out the amount paid and the relevant tax credit.

Trusts where the Settlor is Still Living (Ss434–459)

The taxation of trusts where the settlor is still living will follow the general rules outlined above except that in certain circumstances the settlor himself will be assessed to tax on the income of the trust. In order to avoid such assessment various rules should be observed including the following:

(a) **Period** (S434)
The settlement must be set up for a period which is capable of exceeding six years.

(b) **The Settlor must not have an Interest** (S447 & 457)
In the event that the settlor has retained an interest in the income or assets of the trust, he will be assessed to income tax on the income of the settlement to the extent that it remains undistributed. (The settlor has retained an interest in the trust if he or his wife can obtain some benefit from it.) Furthermore, if the income is distributed to others, subject to certain exceptions, the settlor and not the recipient will be charged to the excess of higher rate tax over the basic rate on the distribution.

(c) **The Settlement must be Irrevocable** (Ss445 & 446)
If the settlor or his wife has power to revoke the settlement or partially revoke it, he is assessed to income tax on its income.

(d) **Discretionary Settlements** (S448)
Discretionary settlements are those under which the application of the income and/or capital of the trust is left to the discretion of the trustees. Under such a trust the settlor or his wife must not be able to benefit from the income, or else he will be assessed to income tax on that income, whether or not any of it is actually paid to him. This does not apply if only the widow of the settlor may benefit.

(e) **Settlements for Benefit of Own Children** (Ss437–444)
Under a trust created by the settlor, his own minor children (under 18 years of age) must not receive any income nor must it be used for their upkeep or education. Otherwise the settlor will be assessed to income tax on such income. This does not apply to accumulation settlements however (p 167).

Note: In all of the above cases there are rules to prevent the double taxation of the income of the trust so it will not be assessed both on the settlor and the beneficiaries. Usually, basic rate income tax is paid by the trust or it has already been deducted at the source as in the case of, for example, interest on government securities. Dividends received by the trust carry with them tax credits which are effectively transferred to beneficiaries who are given income distributions. Also, if the trust is subject to investment surcharge, correspondingly higher tax credits attach to income distributions to beneficiaries (p 167).

Accumulation Settlements for the Benefit of the Settlor's Children

If you wish to create a trust for the benefit of your minor children without being assessed to income tax on its income (p 167) this can be done by means of an accumulation settlement. The income of the settlement should be accumulated for each child until at least the age of 18 and no payments should be made for their benefit until that age. (The trust deed must state that the trustees are empowered to accumulate income.) If it is wished to distribute income to adult beneficiaries this can be done, but the income shares of the settlor's minor children must be accumulated, or else the settlor is liable to higher rate income tax on such income.

Any income accumulated before April 1969 contingently for a minor may give rise to a repayment claim (p 158). The contingency is the attainment of a specified age or marriage and on the happening of such contingency any unused personal allowances and reliefs for tax years up to and including 1968–69 will enable a repayment claim to be made. When the income accumulations are paid to the beneficiary they are treated as capital in his hands and not subjected to higher rate income tax.

Income of Discretionary Trusts, etc.
(FA 1973 Ss16–18)

The 15% investment surcharge covers all of the income of discretionary and accumulating trusts assessable after 5 April 1973. Thus if a discretionary trust receives dividends of £700 during 1979–80 these will be imputed with £300 tax to make a total of £1,000 on which additional tax of £150 will be payable by the trustees. If however allowable expenses of say £200 are incurred then only £1,000 − £200 = £800 is liable to the additional tax and so £800 × 15% = £120 is payable.

The above applies to trusts where the income is accumulated or is payable at the discretion of the trustees but not where the income is treated for tax purposes as being that of the settlor; nor where a person is absolutely entitled to the income.

Where income distributions are made to beneficiaries, the amounts received by the latter are treated as being net of tax at 45% (30% basic rate plus 15% additional rate). The recipients can reclaim part or all of this tax if their incomes are low enough. For example if a discretionary trust pays £275 to your child (or for his maintenance) and he has no other income, there is a tax credit of

$£275 \times 45/55 = £225$ which is all reclaimable.

Beneficiaries can reclaim tax on distributions of income made to them after 5 April 1973 even if the trust received the income before that date and thus only paid tax on it at the standard rate of income tax (38.75% or previously 41.25%).

If however the tax attributable to such distributions exceeds notional tax of two-thirds of the total net accumulations at 5 April 1973, the balance is assessed on the trustees. Thus the accumulations at 5 April 1973 are treated as being net of an average tax rate of 40%. For example say on 6 April 1973 a net distribution of £550 was made out of total accumulated income of £600 at 5 April 1973. Tax on the former was £450 and tax on the latter, $\frac{2}{3} \times £600 = £400$. The trustees were assessed to additional tax of $£450 - £400 = £50$.

Trusts' Capital Gains Tax
(CGTA Ss52–55 & 126 & Sch 4)

Trusts are charged to capital gains tax at 30% on all gains from the sales of chargeable assets less (capital losses) during each tax year (p 121). The 'half income' rule for individuals did not apply to trusts. The £1,000 net gains exemption and marginal relief up to £9,500 (p 123), however, applies to trusts for the mentally disabled and those receiving attendance allowance. Other trusts formed before 7 June 1978 obtain exemption if their net gains for 1977–78 and later years are no more than £500. Up to £1,250, the tax is limited to 50% of the excess over £500 (p 123).

When any chargeable assets are introduced into the trust by the settlor this is a realisation by him on which he pays capital gains tax if applicable (p 124). For example, if A bought 1,000 shares in B Ltd for £1,000 in May 1968 and gifts them in June 1979 to a settlement that he created, the shares must be valued at that time. If the shares are then worth £2,000 he has a chargeable gain of £1,000 for 1979–80. If however the shares are worth only £600 at that time, he has an allowable loss of £400 (£1,000 − £600) which he can only set off against any capital gains resulting from other transactions between A and his trust. This is because they are treated as being 'connected persons' (p 125).

Where, after 11 April 1978, business assets, including shares in 'family companies' are settled, the trustees and settlor may jointly claim for any gain on the assets to be rolled over (p 137). The effect is that the settlor has no capital gains tax to pay on the settled business assets, etc., and the acquisition value for the trustees is correspondingly reduced.

Where a capital asset of a trust is distributed to a beneficiary this is a chargeable event which can give rise to a capital gain in the trust. Thus if a trust bought 1,000 shares in B Ltd for £2,000 in April 1970 and it distributes them to beneficiary C in July 1979 when their market value is £3,000 the trust will have a capital gain of £1,000 (£3,000 – £2,000), which is assessable for 1979–80. (An exception to this rule is where a beneficiary under a will receives his entitlement – p 170.)

Foreign Trusts (CGTA S17)

For taxation purposes a trust is generally treated as being resident abroad if a majority of the trustees are so resident and its administration and management is carried out overseas. Such a trust is exempt from capital gains tax on realisations of assets in the United Kingdom and elsewhere. There are however rules under which the Revenue can sometimes assess United Kingdom resident beneficiaries with their shares of any capital gains (provided that the settlor is UK domiciled and resident or ordinarily resident either when he made the settlement or when the capital gain is made).

United Kingdom income of foreign trusts is charged to income tax here along roughly the same lines as non-resident individuals are so charged. There is no higher rate liability however, unless distributions are made to beneficiaries resident in this country or if the anti-avoidance provisions apply regarding transfers of assets abroad (p 118). In the latter event, in certain circumstances, the Revenue may charge any beneficiaries who are resident in this country with basic and higher rate income tax and investment surcharge on the trust income.

Estates of Deceased Persons

The Tax Liability of the Deceased (T.M.A. Ss40, 74 & 77)

When a person dies, income tax and capital gains tax must be settled on all his income and capital gains up to the date of his death. Any of this tax that is not paid during his lifetime must be settled by his executors or administrators out of his estate.

If the deceased has not been assessed to tax on all his income or capital gains prior to his death, the Revenue are allowed to make assessments on such income and capital gains within three years after the end of the tax year in which death occurred. The Revenue may make assessments in this way in respect of any tax years ending within six years before the date of death in cases of fraud, wilful default or neglect of the deceased but no earlier years can be assessed (p 162).

Income Tax during the Administration Period (Ss426–433)

The administration period of an estate is the period from the date of death of the deceased until the assets are distributed to the beneficiaries according to the will of the deceased or according to the rules of intestacy. Where however a trust is set up under a will the administration period only normally lasts until the trust takes over the residue of the estate.

During the administration period, the executors or administrators pay any basic rate income tax assessments that arise on the income for that period. The tax paid by direct assessment or deduction at source is subtracted from the amounts of income paid to those entitled to the income of the estate. The latter include the income that they receive in their tax returns when the payments are made to them. They must return the gross equivalents allowing for income tax at the basic rate (30%). Once the total income payable to each beneficiary has been ascertained, it is allocated to the respective tax years for which it arose and they pay (if applicable) higher rate tax and investment surcharge on that basis.

Capital Gains Tax during the Administration Period
(CGTA Ss5 & 49 & Sch 1)

Although before 31 March 1971 all of the chargeable assets of the deceased were considered for capital gains tax purposes to be disposed of at the date of his death, no such liability arises regarding deaths on or after that date. The executors or administrators of the estate are regarded as acquiring the assets at their market value at the date of death and if they later sell any of the assets during the administration period, the estate is assessed to capital gains tax on any surplus. Thus if part of the estate of A deceased consisted of 1,000 shares in B Ltd whose value at his death on say 30 June 1975 was £2,000, if those shares are sold on 1 November 1979 for £3,000 (in order to pay capital transfer tax for example), the estate is assessed to capital gains tax on £1,000 (£3,000 − £2,000) for 1979–80.

If however assets of the estate are given to beneficiaries in settlement of their entitlements under the will of the deceased, no capital gains tax is charged on the estate on such transfers of assets. Instead, each beneficiary is treated for capital gains tax purposes as if he had acquired the assets at the same time as the personal representatives acquired them and at the same value.

Thus in the example mentioned above, if instead of selling the 1,000 shares in B Ltd for £3,000 on 1 November 1979 the executors gave them to C on that day in satisfaction of a legacy provided by the will of A deceased, C is treated as having acquired the shares on 30 June 1975 for £2,000 only. (The value of £2,000 was the probate value of the shares at the date of death.) Thus no capital gains tax is payable by the estate in respect of the transfer. If however C were to sell the shares on 1 December 1979 for £3,500 his chargeable gain will be £1,500 (£3,500 − £2,000), although the shares have only gone up in value by £500 since he received them. This is because his entitlement to the legacy is considered for capital gains tax purposes to extend back to the date of death.

For the year of assessment in which death occurs and the next two years, the special new reliefs apply for aggregate net gains not exceeding £9,500 (p 122).

Land Development (FA 1974 Sch 7 & D.L.T.A.)

The trustees of settlements and the estates of deceased persons were both liable to income tax on development gains (p 140). The rate charged was 50% being the basic rate at the time when development gains tax normally applied, plus the 15% investment income surcharge. Realisations of development value after 31 July 1976 are in general subject to development land tax (p 142). This applies to both settlements and the estates of deceased persons.

Capital Transfer Tax

See Chapter 20 (p 200) for guidelines to the capital transfer tax rules concerning settlements.

19. Companies

Introduction

The following is a general outline of the taxation of companies that are resident in the United Kingdom or are trading here through a branch or agency. In the latter case it is normally only the profits arising in this country that are taxable here. It must be stressed that the actual provisions are lengthy and many details have been omitted in this summary.

Corporation Tax on Profits, etc.
(Ss238, FA 1979 S2 & F2A 1979 S7)

The tax on the profits, etc., of companies is called corporation tax which is charged at the present rate of 52%, subject to special relief for companies with profits under £100,000 (p 175). Corporation tax is charged both on a company's profits and 15/26ths of its capital gains (p 178). Corporation tax applies not only to limited companies, but also to certain associations and unlimited companies. The company's income must be considered for each accounting period (see below). It is charged to corporation tax on the basis of the actual income assessable for each accounting period according to the rules of the various cases of Schedule D (p 2) or other Schedules if applicable.

The rate of corporation tax is fixed by Parliament in the Finance Act each year for the preceding 'financial year'. A 'financial year' commences on 1 April and for example the financial year 1973 is the year to 31 March 1974. The 1973 Finance Act provided that the corporation tax rate for the financial year 1972 should be 40%. Regarding later years the rate of 52% has been fixed for the financial years 1973 to 1978 inclusive.

The Imputation System

As mentioned above, the corporation tax rate (subject to small profits relief) went up from 40% to 52% on 1 April 1973. This increase was part of a change to a new system of corporation tax called the 'imputation system'. However, the overall tax burden of most companies was not increased, because dividend payments are now more favourably treated for tax purposes.

If a company pays dividends, these are paid gross to the shareholders, and tax at 3/7ths of the dividend must be paid over to the Revenue as what is known as 'advance corporation tax' (p 173). Prior to 6 April 1979, the Act rate was 33/67ths. This ACT can be deducted from the company's corporation tax bill, so that effectively a lower rate than 52% is paid. The shareholders are 'imputed' with tax of 3/7ths of their dividends, and are only liable for tax at the higher rates and investment income surcharge (p 25). United

Kingdom shareholders get a tax credit of 3/7ths of their dividends, but pay the higher rates on their dividends plus tax credits. Thus, if you receive a dividend of £70, you are imputed with a tax credit of 3/7ths × £70 = £30. You pay higher rates of tax and investment income surcharge (if applicable) on £70+£30 = £100, but you deduct the £30 tax credit from your total tax bill. The imputation of basic rate tax in the shareholders' hands on their dividends has resulted in the present system being known as the 'imputation system' of corporation tax.

Accounting Periods for Corporation Tax (Ss243 & 244)

Corporation tax is charged in respect of accounting periods. These usually coincide with the periods for which the company prepares its annual accounts but cannot exceed 12 months in duration. Thus, if a company prepares accounts for a period of 18 months, the first 12 months will constitute one accounting period and the remaining 6 months are treated as another accounting period. The actual tax is normally payable nine months after the end of each accounting period, or within one month from the date of issue of the assessment if this is later. In the case of a company that traded before April 1965, however, the same interval between the company's accounting date and tax due date as then existed is retained. Thus, if Company A was formed in 1960 and has always prepared its accounts to 30 April in each year, it would have paid its taxes on 1 January in the following tax year and so it must now pay its corporation tax within twenty months of its accounting date. This applies even if Company A changes its accounting date.

Repayment Supplement (F2A 1975 S48)

This applies for a company if it receives a tax repayment more than a year after the date that corporation tax is due for the relevant accounting period and after 31 July 1975. Also, the repayment must be at least £100. The repayment supplement is tax free, and is calculated at 9% from the date one year after the due date for paying corporation tax until the end of the tax month (ending fifth day of next month) in which the repayment is made. (The rate for any period before 6 April 1974 is 6%.)

ACT on Dividends, etc. (FA 1972 S84 & F2A 1979 S6)

Companies have to pay 'advance corporation tax' (ACT) on their payments of dividends made after 5 April 1973. This tax is also payable on other 'qualifying distributions'. The rate was 3/7ths to 5 April 1974, 33/67ths to 5 April 1975, 35/65ths to 5 April 1977, 34/66ths to 5 April 1978 and 33/67ths to 5 April 1979, after which it is 3/7ths.

Distributions

Under the present system there are two different classes of distributions known as qualifying and non-qualifying distributions. Qualifying distributions are dividends and similar payments. Non-qualifying distributions are those which are really distributions of special sorts of shares, etc., which carry a potential future claim on the company's profits: for example, bonus debentures or bonus redeemable shares. Whereas qualifying distributions are subjected to ACT, in the case of non-qualifying distributions, no ACT is payable by the company. The shareholder gets no tax credit at the basic rate (30%) and is not liable to such tax on the non-qualifying distribution. He is, however, liable to the excess of his higher rate tax over the basic rate on the actual value of the non-qualifying distribution. He also pays (if applicable) investment income surcharge (p 25) on this value.

Accounting Periods for ACT (FA 1972 Sch 14)

For periods after 5 April 1973 companies must account to the Revenue for ACT on a three-monthly basis. Returns were made for the period 6 April 1973 to 30 June 1973 and thereafter for each three months to 30 September, 31 December, 31 March and 30 June respectively. Also if the company's accounting period does not end on one of these dates, the period of three months during which it ends is divided into two separate periods for which returns must be submitted. Thus if a company's accounts run to 30 November each year, it submits ACT returns for the period 1 October to 30 November and 1 December to 31 December, as well as for the other three quarters each year.

The ACT return must show for the relevant period the 'franked payments' (see below) and 'franked investment income' received (see below) as well as the amount of ACT payable and certain other details. A cheque in settlement of the ACT due should normally be sent with the return. In computing the ACT due for payment, companies may deduct tax credits on receipts of 'franked investment income' during the relevant period.

Franked Payment (FA 1972 S84(3))

This is defined as being a qualifying distribution made by a company together with the relevant ACT. Thus, a qualifying distribution of £7,000 represents a franked payment of £10,000 (£7,000 + £7,000 × 3/7).

Franked Investment Income (FA 1972 S88)

This consists of income from a United Kingdom resident company (p 96) being distributions in respect of which tax credits are obtained. A company's franked investment income is the amount including the relevant tax credits. Thus if a company receives a dividend of £700, this is treated as being franked investment income of £1,000 (£700 + £700 × 3/7).

Setting Off ACT against 'Mainstream' Corporation Tax
(FA 1972 S85)

As its name suggests, advance corporation tax is a pre-payment of the main or mainstream corporation tax bill of a company. The latter is only ascertained when accounts are submitted to the Revenue after the end of the accounting period.

There is a limit to the amount of ACT which can be off-set against a company's 'mainstream' corporation tax liability. This limit is the amount of ACT which would be paid on a full distribution of the company's income excluding capital gains but before the deduction of any tax. In computing this full distribution, account is taken of the notional ACT payable. Thus, if a company makes adjusted revenue profits of £100,000 before tax, the maximum set-off for ACT is £30,000. Thus, if the company distributed £70,000 it would pay ACT of £70,000 × 3/7 = £30,000 and so its entire profit would be absorbed. After the end of its accounts year it would be assessed to £100,000 × 52% corporation tax (£52,000) from which £30,000 ACT would be deducted leaving a net amount payable of £22,000 (22%). (This is of course an arbitrary calculation because taking account of all of the corporation tax payable in this example, the distribution would produce a deficit.)

Carry-back and Carry-forward of ACT (FA 1972 S85)

Any ACT which is not relieved against corporation tax payable for the accounting period in which the relevant distribution is made, because of the restriction mentioned above, is known as 'surplus ACT'. This surplus ACT can be carried back and off-set against corporation tax payable for any accounting periods beginning in the two years preceding that in which the relevant distribution is made. A claim to this effect must be made within two years of the end of the period for which the surplus ACT arises.

If a claim as above is made to the Revenue, the surplus ACT will be allocated to one or more earlier periods and a reduction in corporation tax payable or a repayment of corporation tax will result. No allocation can be made, however, to any period prior to 6 April 1973.

Any surplus ACT which is not carried back as above, may be carried forward without time limit to be set off against future corporation tax payable.

Small Companies Rate
(FA 1972 S95 & F2A 1979 S7)

This is the term used to describe the special reduced corporation tax rate which is charged on company profits which do not exceed certain limits for a given accounting period. The profits in question comprise those on which corporation tax is paid together with 'franked investment income' (p 174) for the period.

The small companies rate applies to periods after 31 March 1973 and is 42% for the six years to 31 March 1979. This rate is to be charged on the profits of a company with no 'associated companies' (see below) provided these do not exceed £60,000. If the profits are between £60,000 and £100,000, some marginal relief is given. The tax is then broadly 52% on the profits less 3/20ths of the amount by which they fall short of £100,000. (Prior to 1 April 1978, lower thresholds applied.)

If a company has any 'associated companies', then the above-mentioned figures of £60,000 and £100,000 must be divided by one plus the number of 'associated companies' connected with the company under consideration. Thus, if five associated companies comprise a group, they will each pay 42% on their profits for the year to 31 March 1979 if these are no more than £12,000 (£60,000/5) each. If any of the companies have profits between £12,000 and £20,000 (£100,000/5), some marginal relief is obtained.

Associated Companies

These are companies which are either under common control or one controls the other. Control broadly comprises voting power or entitlement to the greater part of either the profits, or the assets on liquidation.

In considering whether two companies are under common control, shares held by a husband and wife and their minor children are considered as one. If, however, one company is controlled by an individual and another company is controlled by a more distant relative such as his brother, the two companies are not normally treated as being 'associated'.

The Computation of Assessable Profits
(Ss248–251)

It is strictly speaking necessary to compute the income assessable under each Schedule (and Case of Schedule D) and aggregate these to find the total amount chargeable to corporation tax. All corporation tax assessments are made on an 'actual' basis, however, instead of the preceding year basis that sometimes applies for income tax purposes; for example, Schedule D Case I (p 61).

The adjustments to the accounts profits that are required for corporation tax purposes follow with some modifications the normal rules for income tax assessments described earlier in the book. The following are some of the necessary adjustments:

(a) Deduct any franked investment income (p 174).
(b) Add back payments made for non-business purposes (p 57).
(c) Add back capital losses and payments and deduct capital profits and capital receipts. The capital gains less capital losses of the company must be computed for the accounting period according to the capital gains tax rules (p 121).
(d) Add back legal and other professional charges relating to capital projects.

(e) Add back business entertaining unless in connection with the company's own staff or overseas customers (p 57). Gifts of advertising articles such as diaries, pens, etc., of less than £2 value to each customer are also allowable.

(f) Add back depreciation and amortisation charged in the accounts in respect of fixed assets.

(g) Adjust the interest payable and receivable to the actual gross payments and receipts during the accounting period (if this is different to the amount charged in the accounts).

(h) Deduct capital allowances for the accounting period (see below and p 64).

(i) Add back any balancing charges and deduct any balancing allowances (p 66).

(j) Add notional income tax at the basic rate to any building society interest received. This notional income tax is calculated by multiplying the actual interest received by 3/7 (p 5). The notional tax must then be deducted from the total corporation tax payable.

(k) Deduct any stock relief which is claimed (p 184).

Special Capital Allowances Rules for Companies

The normal capital allowances rules for businesses, etc. (p 60), apply to companies subject to a number of special rules including the following:

(1) An individual in business can claim that regarding expenditure incurred after 26 October 1970, his writing down allowances should be at a lower rate than the normal rate of 25%. Companies do not have this right (FA 1971 S44(2)).

(2) Where a company obtains first year allowance (up to 100%) in respect of capital expenditure incurred after 21 March 1972 (or 26 October 1970 in a development area); if this results in an adjusted loss for corporation tax purposes such loss may be carried back and set off against profits for the three preceding years (S177(3A)).

(3) Where there is a 'company reconstruction without change of ownership' as a result of which one company takes over all of the assets and business of another company, the former continues to receive exactly the same capital allowances on the assets transferred as the old company would have got. A reconstruction without change of ownership takes place if at any time during the two years following the reconstruction, no less than 75% of the acquiring company belongs to the same people who owned no less than 75% of the old company. (This is treated for all corporation tax purposes as a continuation of the trade.) (Ss252 & 253.)

Losses (Ss177 & 179)

If for an accounting period of a company a trading loss results after the necessary corporation tax adjustments, then a repayment of the tax on an equal amount of the profits (of any description) for the previous accounting period can be obtained. The loss can only be carried back over a period equal in length to that in which it arises. A claim to the Revenue must be made within two years of the end of the accounting period in which the loss occurs.

Alternatively, a repayment of tax deducted at source from interest received and tax credits on dividends can be reclaimed. Otherwise the losses will be carried forward and relieved against future profits.

Group Loss Relief (Ss258–264 & FA 1973 S28)

In a group of companies (i.e. parent and subsidiaries) the losses of respective group members can be offset by way of group relief against the profits of others provided that:

(a) The necessary claim is made within two years of the end of the accounting period.

(b) The group relationship exists throughout the respective accounting periods of the loss making and profit making companies. Otherwise the relief is only obtained for the period during which the group relationship exists; profits and losses being apportioned on a time basis if necessary.

(c) The parent and subsidiary companies are all resident in this country and the parent has at least a 75% interest in each of the subsidiaries. Also the parent company must be entitled to at least both 75% of the distributable profits of each subsidiary and 75% of the assets available on the liquidation of each subsidiary.

(d) Subject to certain special rules group relief also applies to a consortium where five or fewer companies own between them all of the ordinary shares of a loss making company or of a holding company which owns 90% of a loss making company.

Terminal Losses (S178)

These are available to a company in a similar way to an individual who ceases trading (p 72). Thus, a company is entitled to claim to set off a loss incurred in its last twelve months of trading against its profits for the three preceding years.

Companies' Capital Gains and Capital Losses
(Ss 265–281, FA 1972 S93 & FA 1974 S10)

15/26ths of any chargeable gains of a company during an accounting period, computed according to the normal capital gains tax rules (p 121) are added to the assessable profits of the company and charged to corporation tax at 52%. Even if the lower rate (42%) is applied to the company's profits because these are low (p 163), 15/26ths of the capital gains are still subjected to the 52% rate. Before 1 April 1973 the full chargeable gains of companies were added to their assessable profits and charged to corporation tax at 40%.

Chargeable gains can be relieved by means of capital losses in the same period or those brought forward from previous periods. Trading losses can be set off against capital profits of the same period or the previous period. Capital profits can also be off-set by group loss relief claims (p 178). Note that the capital profits are first reduced by 11/26ths and the trading losses are deducted from the remainder. Trading losses brought forward from previous periods, however, can only be set off against future trading profits and not against future chargeable gains.

Capital losses (p 127) incurred by a company can only be set off against any capital gains of the company in the same accounting period or a future accounting period. Unused capital losses can be carried forward to future years even if the company has ceased trading whereas a cessation prevents trading losses from being carried forward.

After 14 April 1975 rules apply which prevent a company from manufacturing capital losses by sales from large holdings (2% upwards) of another company's shares and buying them back within a month if quoted and six months otherwise (F2A 1975 S58).

Groups of Companies (Ss 256–264 & 272–280, FA 1972 Ss 91–2 & FA 1973 S28)

Various special provisions relate to groups of companies (broadly parent and subsidiaries). A subsidiary company is classified according to the percentage of its ordinary capital owned (directly or indirectly) by its parent. Thus a 51% subsidiary is over 50% owned by its parent; and a 75% subsidiary is not less than 75% owned by its parent.

Some of the main rules relating to groups of companies are as follows:

(1) Group loss relief is available in respect of a parent company and its 75% subsidiaries subject to various rules (p 178).
(2) Provided the necessary election is made to the Revenue, dividend payments from 51% subsidiaries to the parent may be made without having to account for ACT. A similar rule relates to inter-group interest payments. These provisions only apply to companies resident in this country.
(3) Transfers of assets within a group consisting of a parent and its 75% subsidiaries (all resident in the UK) do not give rise to capital gains tax. When the asset leaves the group however, capital gains tax is paid on the entire chargeable gain on the asset whilst it was owned by any group company.
(4) For the purposes of capital gains tax 'roll-over relief' (p 137) in a United Kingdom group consisting of a parent company and 75% subsidiaries, the gain on an asset sold by one trading company may be 'rolled over' against the purchase of an asset by another trading company in the group.
(5) If a parent company holds more than 50% of the ordinary

179

shares of a subsidiary and is entitled to more than 50% of its distributable profits and more than 50% of its assets on liquidation, the parent can transfer to its subsidiary relief for ACT. Thus if the parent pays a dividend of £7,000 it gets £7,000 × 3/7 = £3,000 ACT relief, but instead of taking this itself it can surrender the relief to its subsidiary who then deducts £3,000 from its corporation tax bill.

Close Companies
(Ss282–303 & FA 1972 Schs 16–17)

Special provisions relate to 'close' companies which are broadly speaking those under the control of five or fewer persons and their 'associates'. The latter term includes close family such as husband, wife, child, father, mother, brother, sister, etc. A quoted company is not 'close' however if over 35% of its shares are owned by the general public.

A United Kingdom subsidiary of an overseas parent company is 'close' if the latter would have itself been 'close' if resident here. It is thus seen that most small or medium companies are likely to be 'close' companies unless they are subsidiaries of non-close companies. The majority of 'family' companies are 'close'.

Apportionment of Income under the Imputation System
(FA 1972 Sch 16, FA 1973 Sch 9 & FA 1978 S36)

For periods after 5 April 1973 the Revenue may apportion among the shareholders the excess of the 'relevant income' of a close company over its distributions for that period. In the case, however, of a company which is a trading company or member of a trading group, no apportionment will be made if the excess is under £1,001. (By concession, no apportionment is made for a property investment company whose excess is under £101. This applies also to an investment company which is a subsidiary within a trading group.) Also, no apportionment will be made on any individual whose share of the total apportioned amount is less than 5% and £200.

'Relevant income' consists of not more than the company's 'distributable investment income' plus 50% of its trading and property income. 'Distributable investment income' is calculated after tax and includes interest and dividends (excluding tax credits). Dividends from companies in the same group must be included. From the investment income must be deducted the lower of £1,000 (£500 for accounting periods ending before 27.10.77) and 10% of the company's trading and property income.

The 'relevant income' is reduced below the above maximum if the company can prove that it cannot distribute such income because the money is needed for business purposes including expansion and, after 26 October 1977, the acquisition of a business and the repayment of a loan originally obtained for this purpose. Income which cannot be legally distributed is also excluded. If after 23 March 1973, however, a property investment company spends its profits on the purchase of land or buildings (apart from farm or market garden improvements), this money is regarded as available for dividends.

Against the 'relevant income' are set dividends paid during the relevant accounting period and within a reasonable time thereafter (not less than eighteen months) provided they are stipulated as relating to the accounting period.

Abatement (FA 1972 Sch 16 & FA 1978 S35)

In computing 'relevant income' (p 180) you exclude a trading company's trading or property income if this is no more than £25,000 after tax and the company has no 'associated companies' (p 163). If the trading or property income after tax of such a company is between £25,000 and £75,000, you reduce this income by half of the difference between it and £75,000. This is known as abatement. For accounting periods ending before 27 October 1977, these thresholds were £5,000 and £15,000.

Thus if a trading company without any 'associated companies' has trading and property income of £50,000 after tax, it obtains abatement of $\left(\dfrac{£75,000-£50,000}{2}\right)$ = £12,500. It therefore includes with its 'relevant income' 50% × (£50,000−£12,500) = £18,750.

The above applies for 12-month accounting periods, a proportionate deduction being made in the amounts of £25,000 and £75,000 in the case of shorter accounting periods.

If a company has one or more 'associated companies' (p 176), excluding dormant and non-trading companies, the amounts of £25,000 and £75,000 are reduced by dividing them by one plus the number of the 'associated companies'. Thus if a company has four associated companies its abatement for a 12-month accounting period in which its trading profits are £10,000, is
$\frac{1}{2}×\left(\dfrac{£75,000}{5}-£10,000\right)$= £2,500.

Example 25: Close Companies

A Ltd is a close company. It has no associated companies and prepares its accounts to 31 March each year. Its pre-tax profits for the year to 31 March 1979 amount to £53,000 which includes a dividend of £400 received in December 1978 which comprised its only franked investment income for the year. The profit is after charging £6,000 depreciation. Capital allowances of £8,600 are due for the year. A dividend of £750 was paid for the year in December 1978

Assuming no other taxation adjustments are required apart from those noted above, compute:
(a)   The corporation tax liability of A Ltd for the year to 31.3.79
(b)   its ACT liability and
(c)   its excess of 'relevant income' over distributions for the year.

Example 25 continued

A Ltd

(a) *Corporation Tax Computation-Accounting Period to 31.3.79*

Profit per accounts		£53,000
Add: Depreciation		6,000
		£59,000
Less: Franked investment income (excluding tax credit)	£400	
Capital allowances	8,600	
		9,000
Adjusted profit		£50,000
Corporation tax payable at 42% (small profits rate)		£21,000

(b) *ACT Liability*

Dividends paid December 1978	£750	
Less: Dividends received December 1978	400	
	£350	
Net ACT due £350 × 3/7	£150	

(c) *Excess of Relevant Income over Distributions*

	Trading income	Investment income
Adjusted profits for year	£50,000	£400
Less: Corporation tax at 42%	21,000	
	£29,000	
Less: Abatement $\left(\dfrac{£75,000-£29,000}{2}\right)$	23,000	£400*
	£6,000	NIL
		*(maximum £1,000)
'Relevant income' 50% × £6,000	3,000	
Less: Already distributed	750	
Excess of 'relevant income' over distributions	£2,250	

Loans and Distributions from Close Companies
(Ss284–287, FA 1972 Sch 17 & FA 1976 S44)

Another special provision regarding close companies is that if they make loans to their 'participators' (see below) or associates of the latter, the companies are charged to tax at 3/7ths of the amounts. Thus if a loan of £7,000 is made to a participator which is outstanding at the company's accounting date the company will be assessed to tax of $3/7 \times £7,000 = £3,000$. This rule was extended by FA 1976 to cover loans by companies controlled by or subsequently acquired by close companies.

When the loan is repaid to the company, the tax is repaid. If the loan is repaid before any assessment has been raised, no assessment is normally made by the Revenue. Should a close company lend money to a participator or his associate and then release the debt, higher rate tax is assessed on the recipient in respect of the grossed up equivalent of the loan. Thus in the above example, if the company releases the participator from his debt he will pay higher rate tax and investment surcharge (if applicable) on £10,000 (£7,000 + £3,000). A deduction of £3,000 will be made, however, from the total tax payable.

The meaning of the term 'distribution' (dividend, etc.) is extended in the case of close companies to include the following:

(a)   Living expenses and accommodation, etc., provided for a 'participator'.
(b)   Certain interest payments made to directors and their associates excluding:
   (i)   interest paid to directors not controlling more than 5% of the ordinary share capital; and
   (ii)   interest at not more than 12% on the lower of the actual loans and the issued share capital (including share premium account) of the company. (Prior to 1.4.74 the rate was 8%.)

(A 'participator' means broadly a person having a share or interest in the capital or income of a company, including for example a shareholder or loan creditor.)

The effect of treating a payment as a distribution is that it is not deductible from the taxable profit of the company. Before 6 April 1973, the company deducted Schedule F income tax from the payments and accounted for the tax to the Revenue. After 5 April 1973, the company pays to the Revenue ACT on any 'qualifying distributions' (p 174) including the above.

Cessations and Liquidations
(S294 & FA 1972 Sch 16)

If a close company ceases to trade, its distribution requirement includes all of its trading and property income after abatement (p 181) for its final chargeable accounting period and any other chargeable accounting periods ending within a year of the date of

183

cessation. Thus if a company's accounting period ends on 31 December each year and it ceases trading on 30 September 1979, it must distribute all of its profits for the year to 31 December 1978 and from 1 January 1979 to 30 September 1979, or else an apportionment will be made on the shareholders of these total after-tax profits. The company cannot claim to retain money for business purposes in these circumstances.

The above rules apply to companies in liquidation : also any income arising after the liquidation date is subject to 100% apportionment.

Non-resident Companies trading in the United Kingdom (S246)

Where a non-resident company (p 96) carries on a trade in this country through a branch or agency here, corporation tax is charged in respect of the profits of the branch or agency. If those profits are also subject to tax in the country of residence of the company, double tax relief may be available (p 106).

United Kingdom Companies with Overseas Income

Any overseas income of a company that is resident in this country is subject to corporation tax on the gross amount of such income.

Double tax relief is frequently available in respect of overseas income that is taxed both in this country and abroad.

If a United Kingdom company receives a dividend from an overseas company from which witholding tax has been deducted, the gross dividend is included in the taxable profits subject to corporation tax. Normally, double tax relief for the witholding tax suffered is given against the corporation tax payable. (Withholding tax is tax that is 'withheld' from the dividend when the latter is paid. It is thus a form of tax deducted at the source.) In addition, if at least 10% of the voting capital of the overseas company is owned by the UK company, relief is given for the 'underlying tax' (i.e. the proportion of the total tax paid by the foreign company attributable to its dividends). In no case, however, can the double tax relief rate exceed the rate of UK corporation tax (52%).

Stock Relief for Companies
(FA 1975 S18 & Sch 3, F2A 1975 Sch 10, FA 1976 Sch 5 & F2A 1979 Sch 3)

Under the *Finance Act 1975* a company could claim stock relief for its accounting year ended within the year to 31 March 1974 subject to certain rules including the following :

(1)   Its closing stock must have been at least £25,000.
(2)   The relief was equal to the difference between the opening and closing stock less a deduction of 10% of the 'trading profits'.

(3) 'Trading profits' were broadly the profits adjusted for tax purposes excluding non-trading income and before deducting capital allowances.

(4) 'Stocks' for the purposes of the relief excluded professional work in progress.

(5) Any claim must have been made by the later of 13 September 1975 and the date that the corporation tax assessment for the year is agreed.

(6) The relief was deducted in computing the year's taxable profits.

(7) If a loss resulted from claiming stock relief, it was treated the same for tax purposes as any other company trading loss (p 165).

The *Finance No. 2 Act 1975* introduced relief for companies on the general lines described as applying to individuals and partnerships (p 60). Note the following special points for companies:

(1) The relief applied for all trading companies no matter what level of closing stock was held.

(2) The 'base period' for which the relief was given was normally the two years ended with the company's accounting date falling in the year to 31 March 1975.

(3) The time limit for claiming relief was generally two years after the end of the 'base period'.

(4) If the company made a stock relief claim under the previous rules (see above) this was deducted from the amount claimed for the two year period.

(5) Note that subject to the above rules, a company had the option of claiming both reliefs or either one of them or neither. The choice depended on the particular circumstances of the company.

(6) The special bonus of 5% (p 60) only applied to a company which did not qualify for the old (one year) relief. It did not apply to a company for which it was decided not to claim that relief.

The *Finance Act 1976* introduced a more permanent system of relief for companies.

(1) The new relief normally applies for the company's accounting period ending in the year to 31.3.76 and subsequent periods.

(2) The relief is claimed separately for each period and is the increase of closing over opening stock less 15% of trading profits after capital allowances (not changed by F2A 1979).

(3) If closing stock is less than opening stock, the company adds to its profits this shortfall. The addition is limited to unrecouped past relief however.

(4) The general rules resemble those for individuals.

(5) Claims for relief must be made within 2 years of the end of the accounting period.

(6) Special rules concern any gap between the base periods for this and the previous system, cessations (past relief is recouped) and successions.

(7) As before, the relief is deducted in computing the profit (or loss) for corporation tax purposes with similar consequences.

Finance (No. 2) Act 1979 has made several important changes.

(1) Unrecouped past relief obtained under FA 1975 and F2A 1975 will not be 'clawed-back' after the end of the company's period of account ending in the year to 31 March 1979.

(2) Any unrecouped stock relief for subsequent years will not be 'clawed-back' once six years have passed. Thus unrecouped stock relief for the year to 31 March 1976 would be written-off on 1 April 1982.

(3) If any 'claw-back' of unrecouped past relief is suffered, it is attributed to later rather than earlier periods of account so that the write-off for the previous periods is protected to some degree.

(4) Claims for periods ending after 31 March 1979 can be made for the full amount of relief available, or only part of it. Thus supposing £100,000 is the full amount claimable, only say £40,000 might be claimed; but note that in these circumstances, the remaining £60,000 would not be available to carry forward as stock relief to apply in a future period.

20. Capital Transfer Tax

The capital transfer tax is highly complicated and technical. Many of its complexities are beyond the scope of this book. The following is thus only a brief outline.

The rules for capital transfer tax are contained in Sections 1 to 9 52 and Schedules 4 to 11 of the 1975 Finance Act which received Royal Assent on 13 March 1975. Substantial changes have been made in the 1976, 1977 and 1978 Finance Acts. The tax applies to lifetime gifts made after 26 March 1974, transfers on deaths occurring after 12 March 1975 and settled property.

Estate duty does not apply to deaths occurring after 12 March 1975 (p 190). Where property passed on deaths after 12 November 1974 and before 13 March 1975, estate duty applies at capital transfer tax rates (p 251). For details of estate duty, reference should be made to Chapter 19 of the 1974–75 *Hambro Tax Guide* and earlier editions.

Property Chargeable (FA 1975 Ss19–20 & Sch 10)

Subject to various exceptions and reliefs (p 193) you will be charged to capital transfer tax on the decrease in value of your assets less liabilities which you suffer as a result of any transfer of your assets (chargeable transfer). Normally, arm's length transactions are ignored if they are not intended to convey any gratuitous benefit. Any capital gains tax which you pay is ignored in calculating the decrease.

If you are domiciled (p 95) in the United Kingdom or deemed domiciled here, capital transfer tax applies to all of your property, wherever situated. Otherwise it only applies to your property in this country.

Deemed Domicile (FA 1975 S45 & FA 1977 S49)

You are deemed to be domiciled in the United Kingdom if one of the following applies:

(a) You were domiciled here on or after 10 December 1974 and within the three years preceding the date of the chargeable transfer.

(b) You were resident here on or after 10 December 1974 and in not less than seventeen of the twenty years of assessment ending with that in which you made the chargeable transfer.

(c) Since 10 December 1974 you have become and remained domiciled in the Channel Islands or the Isle of Man (the 'Islands'), having been domiciled in the United Kingdom immediately previously; unless your domicile of origin was in the 'Islands'; or you were under 16 or otherwise incapable of having an independent domicile when you became domiciled in the 'Islands'.

Concerning those deemed domiciled in the 'Islands' (see above) there are rules exempting from capital transfer tax certain property representing or acquired from earnings there, from business or employment.

Rate Scale (FA 1975 S37 & FA 1978 S62 & Sch 10)

Capital transfer tax is charged on the cumulative total of all your lifetime transfers after 26 March 1974 together with the property passing on your death. There are, however, various exemptions from this general rule (p 193). The tax is charged at progressive rates shown in the following table. A lower scale applies to life-time gifts and a higher one to property passing on death. If you die within three years of making a chargeable transfer, additional tax is payable to bring the charge on it up to the scale applicable on death.

In general terms, if you are making a chargeable transfer, you have two options. Either you pay the tax yourself, based on the value of the transfer plus the tax; or the recipient pays your tax, calculated on the transfer value excluding the tax. If you give cash, however, you could deduct the tax, shown by the following table, from the amount given.

For example, suppose that having previously made £70,000 of chargeable transfers, you wish to make an £8,000 cash gift to your son. Tax on the £8,000 is payable at 20% and so you could keep £1,600 for the tax and pay £6,400 to your son. If you want him to get £8,000 net however, one of you would have to pay the capital transfer tax of *£2,000*; i.e. 20% × (£8,000 + £2,000).

Table 20: Capital Transfer Tax Rates after 26 October 1977

Slice of cumulative chargeable transfers	Total	Lifetime scale % on slice	Lifetime scale Cumulative total tax	On death % on slice	On death Cumulative total tax
The first £25,000	£25,000	Nil	£Nil	Nil	£Nil
The next 5,000	30,000	5	250	10	500
5,000	35,000	7.5	625	15	1,250
5,000	40,000	10	1,125	20	2,250
10,000	50,000	12.5	2,375	25	4,750
10,000	60,000	15	3,875	30	7,750
10,000	70,000	17.5	5,625	35	11,250
20,000	90,000	20	9,625	40	19,250
20,000	110,000	22.5	14,125	45	28,250
20,000	130,000	27.5	19,625	50	38,250
30,000	160,000	35	30,125	55	54,750
50,000	210,000	42.5	51,375	60	84.750
50,000	260,000	50	76,375	60	114,750
50,000	310,000	55	103,875	60	144,750
200,000	510,000	60	223,875	60	264,750
500,000	1,010,000	65	548,875	65	589,750
1,000,000	2,010,000	70	1,248,875	70	1,289,750
The remainder		75		75	

Prior to 27 October 1977, chargeable transfers were subjected to to the same rates of tax as shown in the above table except that the thresholds were all £10,000 lower. Thus only the first £15,000 of your chargeable transfers was at the nil rate, followed by 5% on the £15,000–£20,000 band, and so on. The full table appears in Chapter 24 (p 251).

In general, the new rate scale applies to events after 26 October 1977. Thus if you have paid capital transfer tax on the old scale, a transfer which you now make is taxed by reference to the new scale.

On a death within three years of chargeable transfers at the old rates, the additional tax is found by taking the difference between the tax already paid and that payable at the new rates applying on death. If the death is after 27 October 1977 and the chargeable transfer is before that date, the tax on the new death scale could be less than that already paid, but no refund is made.

Valuation (FA 1975 S38 & Sch 10)

The valuation basis for capital transfer tax purposes is broadly similar to that which applied for estate duty. Thus your assets are normally valued at their open market value at the transfer date. If the value of an asset which you keep is affected by the transfer, you will need to value your 'estate' both before and after the transfer in order to calculate its resultant fall. Your liabilities must be taken into account in valuing your total 'estate'.

Quoted Securities Passing on Death
(FA 1975 Sch 10 (14–20))

The estate duty provisions providing relief where quoted securities are sold for less than their probate values within twelve months of death, are continued for capital transfer tax purposes. Thus where any quoted shares and securities or holdings in authorised unit trusts are realised within one year of death, the persons liable to pay capital transfer tax can claim that the total of the sale prices should be substituted for the original probate values of the investments. Where however the proceeds are re-invested by those persons in quoted shares or unit trusts after the death and within two months after the last sale, the above relief may be reduced or lost.

Valuation of Related Property
(FA 1975 Sch 10 (7) & FA 1976 Ss102 & 103)

Where the value of any of your property is less than the appropriate portion of the value of the aggregate of that and any 'related property' you must value your own property as the appropriate portion of the value of that aggregate.

'Related property' is property belonging to your wife, or property in a settlement in which you or your wife has an interest in possession or a settlement made by one of you before 27 March 1974 (unless someone else has an interest in possession). Also included is any property transferred by you or your wife after 15 April 1976 to a charity or charitable trust.

This rule particularly applies to the valuation of unquoted shares. For example if you and your wife each have 40% of the shares of an unquoted company, then the value of 80% of the shares is normally much higher than twice the value of 40% of the shares. This is because an 80% holding carries with it full control of the company.

Thus the successful estate duty saving device of splitting a shareholding in a non-quoted company between your wife and yourself, so that neither of you has control, is not effective (so far as the first transfer is concerned) in producing a lower aggregate value for capital transfer tax purposes.

If you inherit any related property on a death after 6 April 1976, a special relief applies where you sell the property within 3 years of the death for less than the value on which tax was originally paid. Subject to various conditions including the requirement that the sale is at arm's length for a freely negotiated price, you can claim for the related property in question to be revalued at death on the basis that it was not related to any other property.

Land Sold within three years of Death
(FA 1976 S101 & Sch 13)

Where the person paying the capital transfer tax arising on death on certain land sells it within three years of the death for less than its probate value, he can claim that the sale proceeds are substituted in the capital transfer tax calculation. There are a number of conditions including the requirement that the shortfall is at least the lower of £1,000 and 5% of the probate value of the land. Relief is extended beyond the three years regarding a compulsory purchase notified before the end of the three years.

Abolition of Estate Duty (FA 1975 S22)

Estate duty does not apply for deaths occurring after 12 March 1975. For deaths prior to 13 November 1974 the old estate duty rules applied as did the rates (*Hambro Tax Guide* 1974–75, p 187). If the death occurred between those dates however, estate duty applied at the capital transfer tax rates (p 251); also the new exemption applied for transfers between husband and wife (p 193), and the new reliefs applied instead of the old for agricultural land (p 197), industrial property (p 195) and timber (p 197).

Gifts *inter vivos* – transitional provisions for pre-27 March 1974 gifts

The seven-year period for 'gifts *inter vivos*' is carried over to some extent from estate duty to capital transfer tax. Thus a gift made before 27 March 1974 but within seven years of death is charged to capital transfer tax on the death of the giver. Tapering relief is obtained however if the death is more than four years from the date of the gift. What happens is that the gift is excluded:

(a)   as to 15% if made at least four years before death;
(b)   as to 30% if made five years before death; and
(c)   as to 60% if made six years before death.

190

Capital Transfer Tax on Death (FA 1975 S22)

The general rule is that if you are domiciled (or deemed domiciled – p 187) in the UK at the time of your death, all of your assets, wherever they may be situated, form part of the *gross value* of your estate for the purposes of determining the capital transfer tax payable.

If you are not domiciled in the UK at your death then capital transfer tax is only chargeable on those assets which are situated in the UK (p 199).

The *net value* of your estate is determined by making certain deductions (p 191) from the *gross value* of all the property passing on your death.

Capital transfer tax on your death is charged as if immediately before your death you made a chargeable transfer equal to the *net value* of your estate, subject to certain adjustments and exemptions (p 192) if appropriate. The tax payable is calculated from the special rate scale which applies at death (p 188) taking account of your cumulative lifetime gifts after 26 March 1974 to ascertain the starting level on the scale. Thus suppose your chargeable lifetime transfers totalled £70,000, the first £20,000 of the estate passing on your death would be taxed at 40%, the next £20,000 at 45% and so on.

Gross Value of Estate (FA 1975 S23)

The gross value of your estate includes all your property situated anywhere in the world, such as land, shares, the goodwill of a business, debts owing to you, etc.

Certain other amounts must also be included in your gross estate, even though they do not belong to you or only arise after your death, such as the proceeds of a life policy held by you on your own life, or any death benefit under a pension scheme which is payable to your estate (rather than under the more usual discretionary disposal clause contained in most pension schemes).

Other amounts to be included in your gross estate are certain gifts *inter vivos* made before 27 March 1974 but within seven years of your death (p 190) and various interests in trusts (p 200). In these cases the recipients of the gifts or the trustees may pay the tax appropriate to the gifts or trusts but the rate is calculated by reference to the value of the estate including the gifts, etc.

Net Value of Estate

The more common deductions which are made from the gross value of your estate in order to arrive at its net value are as follows:
(1) Excluded property (p 192) and certain exempt transfers (p 195).
(2) Funeral expenses.
(3) Debts owing by you at the date of death which are payable in the United Kingdom.

(4) Debts due to persons outside the UK are normally only deductible from the value of assets situated outside this country.

(5) Whilst legal and other professional fees owing at the death may be deducted as debts, no deduction is given for probate and executors' expenses.

(6) Liabilities for income tax, and capital gains tax up to the date of your death, whether or not assessments were made before that time. No deduction can be made for capital transfer tax payable on your death, however, nor can tax liabilities be deducted regarding income and capital gains arising for periods subsequent to your death.

Excluded Property (FA 1975 S24 & Sch 7)

The following 'excluded property' must be left out of the value of your estate for capital transfer tax purposes, regarding both lifetime transfers and property passing on death:

(1) Property outside the United Kingdom if you are neither domiciled nor deemed domiciled in this country.

(2) A reversionary interest unless either you bought it or it relates to the falling in of a lease which was treated as a settlement (p 201).

(3) Cash options under approved retirement pension schemes (p 86), provided an annuity becomes payable to your dependents instead of the cash option itself.

(4) Those United Kingdom Government securities on which interest may be paid gross to non residents (p 50), provided you are neither domiciled nor resident here.

(5) Certain overseas pensions from former colonies. etc., including death payments and returns of contributions.

(6) Savings such as national savings certificates and premium bonds, if you are domiciled in the Channel Islands or the Isle of Man.

(7) Certain property in this country belonging to visiting forces and NATO headquarters staff.

Double Taxation Relief (FA 1975 Sch 7 (7 & 8) & FA 1976 S125)

Various other countries also operate systems of capital transfer tax and the Government of the United Kingdom is empowered to enter into agreements with them for the avoidance of the double payment of capital transfer tax both here and in the other country. Up to the date of writing, however, few such agreements have been concluded.

Concerning capital transfer tax payable on death, relief is continued for estate duty payable on the same property in other countries if there was a 'double estate duty' agreement with the countries in question as at 12 March 1975. The following countries have agreements with the United Kingdom covering estate duty and/or capital transfer tax:

France
India
Irish Republic
Italy
Netherlands
Pakistan
South Africa
Sweden
Switzerland
United States of America

Unilateral double taxation relief is available for overseas tax paid on death or a lifetime transfer. The tax must be of a similar nature to capital transfer tax and if the property is situated in the overseas country, a credit is given against the UK tax of the amount of the overseas tax. If the property is either situated *both* in the UK and the overseas country, or in *neither* of those places, the credit against the UK tax is $C \times A/(A+B)$. A is the amount of capital transfer tax, B is the overseas tax and C is the smaller of A and B.

Exempt Transfers (FA 1975 Sch 6)

Broadly, exempt transfers can be divided between those which apply both on death and during your life and those which are only exempt if the transfers are during your life. The first category includes transfers between your wife and yourself.

Transfers between Husband and Wife

Transfers between your wife and yourself both during your lives and on death are exempt from capital transfer tax. This exemption also applied for estate duty purposes on deaths after 12 November 1974. Similarly gifts *inter vivos* (p 190) between your wife and yourself prior to 27 March 1974 are outside the capital transfer tax net provided the donor survived 12 November 1974.

These exemptions do not apply however if the recipient of the property is not domiciled (or deemed domiciled) in this country (p 95). In this case, only the first £25,000 transferred to the non-domiciled spouse is exempt. This resembles the previous estate duty relief.

Under the estate duty rules, if you left property in trust for your wife for life, when you died duty was paid; but none was payable on her subsequent death. If, however, the first death occurs after 12 November 1974, the new relief will apply and so no capital transfer tax is payable on property passing to the surviving spouse. For this reason, when the latter dies, full capital transfer tax is payable on the trust property.

Exempt Transfers – Lifetime Gifts

The following transfers are only exempt if made by an individual during his life. They do not apply to trusts, nor to assets passing on death. In any one fiscal year to 5 April, you can make all of these exempt transfers cumulatively and so can your wife.

(1) *Transfers each year up to a value of £2,000*
Prior to 6 April 1976 the limit was £1,000 each year. (The period from 27 March 1974 to 5 April 1974 counted as a year for this purpose.) If you do not use up the full £2,000 allowance in one year, you can carry the unused part forward for one year only. If your transfers taken against this exemption reach £2,000 in one year, you have nothing available to carry forward, even though you may have had £2,000 carried forward from the previous year.

For example if you made no chargeable transfers prior to 6 April 1979, you have £4,000 available for exempt transfers under this category in the year to 5 April 1980. If, however, you transferred £500 in the year to 5 April 1979 you have £1,500 carried forward and so can transfer £3,500 in the year to 5 April 1980. The old estate duty small gifts relief applied up to 5 April 1975 if it produced a better result. Thus you could have made exempt transfers of up to £500 to all those who had received no gifts from you in the seven years prior to each gift.

(2) *Small Gifts*
Outright gifts to any one person not exceeding £100 for each year to 5 April are exempt. This applies in addition to the £2,000 exemption. Thus if you have say four children you can give them each £600 $\left(£100 + \dfrac{£2,000}{4}\right)$ each year, assuming you have no other transfers set against your £2,000 exemption.

(3) *Normal Expenditure out of Income*
To qualify under this exemption, a transfer must be part of your normal expenditure. This means that there must be an element of regularity. Life assurance premiums (p 205) are particularly suited for this. Further conditions are that the transfer is out of your after-tax income and you are left with enough income to maintain your usual standard of living.

Life policy premium payments will not qualify for this exemption however if they are made out of an annuity purchased on your life, unless you can show that the policy and the annuity were effected completely independently of each other. This rule even applies if you make gifts out of your annuity receipts and the donee pays the premiums on the policy on your life.

If you buy an annuity after 12 November 1974, and make transfers from it after 5 April 1975, only the income proportion of the annuity (p 220) is treated as your income for the purposes of the normal expenditure rule; the capital element is not.

(4) *Gifts in Consideration of Marriage*, made to one of the partners of the marriage or settled on the partners and their children, etc. The limits are £5,000 if the donor is a parent of one of the

marriage partners, £2,500 if a grandparent or great-grandparent or one of the parties themselves, or otherwise £1,000. (Before 13 March 1975, a grandparent or great-grandparent could give £5,000.)

Other Exempt Transfers

Subject to the particular rules, the following transfers are exempt both if made during your life and on death. They also apply to trusts (p 200).

(1) *Transfers in the Course of Trade, etc.*, are exempt if allowed as deductions in computing the profits for income tax purposes (p 57). This applies equally to professions and vocations, as well as allowable deductions against other forms of profits or gains for the purposes of income tax and corporation tax.

(2) *Gifts to Charities* are exempt without limit if made more than a year before death. If made on or within a year of death however, the first £100,000 of gifts is exempt. Gifts to settlements for charitable purposes are covered by the exemption, as are gifts to charities from other trusts.

(3) *Gifts to Political Parties* are wholly exempt if made more than a year before death, and otherwise, like for charitable gifts, a £100,000 exemption applies. For these purposes a 'political party' is one with at least two members sitting in Parliament or one member and not less than 150,000 votes for its candidates at the last General Election.

(4) *Gifts for National Purposes, etc.,* made to the National Trust, National Gallery, British Museum and similar organisations including universities and their libraries as well as museums or art galleries maintained by local authorities or universities.

(5) *Gifts for Public Benefit* of property deemed by the Treasury to be of outstanding scenic, historic, scientific or artistic merit including land, buildings, pictures, books, manuscripts, works of art, etc.

(6) *Gifts of Shares* to an employee trust provided it will then hold at least half of the ordinary shares of the company (FA 1978 S67).

Relief for Business Property
(FA 1976 S73 & Sch 10 & FA 1978 S64)

Broadly a reduction of 30% is given in the valuation of 'relevant business property' transferred from 7 April 1976 to 26 October 1977; provided the necessary claim is made, normally within 2 years. Where appropriate the relief applies to both individuals and settlements and is made on a net assets valuation basis.

'Relevant business property' includes a business or part of a business; unquoted shares owned by the controller of a company; and land, buildings, plant and machinery used in your partnership or a company which you control. Control of a company for these purposes includes shareholdings which are 'related property' (p 189) in relation to your own shares.

In general, investment company and land or share-dealing company shareholdings do not qualify for the relief. You must normally own the business property, or property which has directly replaced it for at least two years prior to the transfer or else it is not 'relevant business property' and so no relief is due.

After 26 October 1977 different rates of relief are available as follows:

(1) The whole or part of a business – 50%
(2) Unquoted company shares to be valued on a control basis – 50%.
(3) Property transferred by you which is used in a trade by a company controlled by you or partnership in which you are a partner – 30%.
(4) Shares in an unquoted trading company to be valued on a minority basis – 20%.

Waivers of Dividends and Remuneration (FA 1976 Ss91 & 92)

If you waive any remuneration to which you are entitled, this normally does not produce any capital transfer tax liability, provided the amount waived would otherwise have been assessable to income tax under Schedule E (p 75) and your employer obtains no income tax or corporation tax relief for the waived remuneration.

No capital transfer tax accrues on the waiver of any dividend to which you have a right, provided you waive the dividend within the 12 months before it is due.

The above waiver rules apply from the inception of capital transfer tax.

Conditional Exemption for Certain Objects and Buildings, etc. (FA 1975 Ss31–34, FA 1976 Ss76–85 & Sch 11 & FA 1977 S53)

Property similar to that mentioned in (4) and (5) above (p 181), is exempted from capital transfer tax on death provided the recipient undertakes to keep it in the country, preserve it and allow reasonable access to the public. If it is later sold the tax is payable unless the sale is to an institution such as the British Museum, National Gallery or National Trust.

From 7 April 1976 a similar relief applies to lifetime transfers subject to various conditions. The recipient must give the required undertaking. The relief extends to historical and artistic buildings and objects comprised in settlements. It also applies to settlements set up to maintain historic buildings.

Relief for the Agricultural Property of Working Farmers (FA 1975 Sch 8 & FA 1976 S74)

This relief applies to transfers on death and lifetime transfers by 'working farmers'. To qualify you must have been mainly or wholly engaged in agriculture as a farmer, farm worker or student in five of the seven preceding years. The relief applies to land including farmhouses and buildings occupied for farming by you for at least two years before the transfer. Before 7.4.76 the value of the property transferred was reduced to 20 times its gross rental value as agricultural land, subject to an over-riding limit of £250,000 by value or 1,000 acres, whichever produced the best result.

In respect of transfers made after 6 April 1976, this relief is altered so as to reduce the value of agricultural property by 50%. For the purpose of the 1,000 acres limit, rough grazing land is counted as one-sixth of its actual area.

The relief extends to controlling shareholdings in farming companies and also applies for estate duty in respect of deaths before 13 March 1975 but after 12 November 1974. The existing 45% relief and not the new relief applies however to gifts of agricultural property made before 13 November 1974 on which estate duty is charged on a death between 12 November and 13 March 1975. 45% relief is also obtained on a death after 12 March 1975 where the agricultural gift was before 27 March 1974 (but within seven years of death).

Concerning transfers after 26 October 1977, the new relief for business property (p 195) will be normally available, and is likely to be more beneficial.

Woodlands (FA 1975 Sch 9, FA 1976 S75, FA 1977 S52 & FA 1978 S65)

The old estate duty relief for growing timber applied in general before 13 March 1975. After that a corresponding but more restricted relief applies to the capital transfer tax charge on death provided you either owned the woodlands for at least five years, or you acquired them by gift or inheritance.

Under the relieving provisions, provided the inheritor elects within two years of it, tax is not charged on your death. If however, before the recipient dies, the timber is sold or given away, tax is charged on the proceeds or value of the gift. The tax rate is found by adding such proceeds to the estate at your death. Remember that the relief applies only to the timber and not the land on which it grows.

For a disposal after 26 October 1977, the new rates (p 188) are applied, even if the death was before that date. Furthermore, the disposal value is halved in charging the tax, if the death was after 12 March 1975 and the new business property relief would have been obtained, except that the death was too early.

Quick Succession Relief (FA 1975 S30)

This relief applies to reduce the tax payable on death where the deceased himself received chargeable transfers on which the tax was paid within four years of his death. The deduction is broadly a proportion of the original tax, being 80%, 60%, 40% or 20%, depending on whether the period between the transfer and the death is 1, 2, 3 or 4 years or less in each case. Similar relief is given where the previous transfer was a death on which estate duty was payable.

Administration and Collection (FA 1975 Sch 4)

Capital transfer tax is under the care and management of the Board of the Inland Revenue. Generally speaking the rules for administration, appeals and penalties resemble those for income tax (p 154).

Chargeable transfers must be reported to the Inland Revenue within twelve months from the end of the month of transfer (or by 13 September 1975 if the transfer was more than a year earlier).

As for estate duty, tax chargeable on death must be paid on at least an estimated figure before probate is granted.

Interest on unpaid tax runs from when the tax is due. The due date is six months after the end of the month in which death occurs. For lifetime transfers it is six months after the end of the month in which the transfer is made. In the case of transfers between 5 April and 1 October, the due date is 30 April in the following year.

The rate of interest on overdue capital transfer tax is 6% for transfers on death and 9% otherwise. This interest is not deductible for income tax purposes. If you overpay capital transfer tax you will get interest at the same rates, up to the date on which the repayment of the excess tax is made.

Payment of Tax by Instalments (FA 1975 Sch 4 (13–16))

The option of paying estate duty on certain assets in 8 yearly or 16 half-yearly instalments is continued for capital transfer tax on death. This applies to land and buildings, controlling holdings of shares in companies and certain other unquoted shares, as well as business assets.

Instalments paid on time concerning the shares and business assets mentioned above are free of interest. Land and buildings qualify for this relief only if they are held as business assets (to a limit of £250,000) otherwise interest is payable at 6%.

Payment of Tax on Lifetime Gifts by Instalments

The above provisions apply to lifetime transfers if the donee bears the tax for settled property which is retained in a settlement. If interest is payable it is at 9%. The interest free category is extended to include lifetime disposals of timber.

Capital Transfer Tax and Life Assurance (see also p 222)

If you effect a policy on your life for your own benefit, the proceeds payable on your death will be taxable as part of your net estate.

You may however effect a policy in trust for some other person or persons such as for example your wife and children. In this case the policy proceeds will not be paid into your own estate but will be paid to the trustees for the beneficiaries. Each premium payment however will constitute a separate chargeable transfer by you on which tax is payable unless an exemption applies such as the £2,000 or £100 reliefs (p 194), or the normal expenditure rule (p 194), or the policy is for your wife.

If someone else effects a policy on your life and pays the premiums, then the proceeds are not taxable on your death. This is known as a 'life of another' policy. If the person who effects the policy pre-deceases you however, then the surrender value of the policy at the date of death of that person is normally included in his taxable estate. Please refer to Chapter 21 (p 222) for further details concerning this subject.

Property Outside Great Britain

Since if you are neither domiciled nor deemed domiciled (p 187) in the United Kingdom, you will only normally pay capital transfer tax on your assets situated here, it is important to ascertain the situation of particular property. The situation of property for capital transfer tax purposes is normally deemed to be as follows:

(1) Cash – its physical location,
(2) Bank accounts – the location of the bank (or branch).
(3) Registered securities – the location of the share register,
(4) Bearer securities – the location of the title documents,
(5) Land and buildings – their actual location,
(6) Business assets – the place where the business is conducted.
(7) Debts – the residence of the debtor.

Miscellaneous Points

Close Companies (FA 1975 S39 & FA 1976 S118)

There are rules under which capital transfer tax is charged where a close company (p 180) makes a transfer of value. Broadly, tax is charged on the company as if each of the participators (p 183) had made a proportionate transfer according to his or her interest in the company.

Free Loans (FA 1976 Ss115–117)

After 5 April 1976, if you allow someone else the use of money or property at no interest or less than the market rate, you will be treated as making a chargeable transfer for each year to 5 April that the arrangement continues. The amount of the chargeable transfer is the shortfall of the interest (less tax), or other benefit which you get, compared with the market rate. This rule broadly does not apply if you lend money or property to a firm in which you are a partner or to a non close company or a close company (excluding an investment company) in which you are a participator (p 183). The rule also does not apply to money which you lend to an investment company controlled as to at least 90% by you and your spouse; or if your partnership or close company interest ended in the year of charge or in the two previous years.

Associated Operations (FA 1975 S44)

Special rules enable the Revenue to treat two or more transactions related to a certain property as forming one 'chargeable transfer'. Where transactions at different times are treated as associated operations, the chargeable transfer is treated as taking place at the time of the last of these transactions.

Family Maintenance (FA 1975 S46)

If you make any of the following gifts during your life, they are exempt:

(a) For the maintenance, education, etc., of your child, former wife or illegitimate child.

(b) For the maintenance or education of a child not in his parent's care, who has been in your care during substantial periods of his minority.

(c) For the care or maintenance of a dependent relative.

Deeds of Family Arrangement (FA 1975 S47 & FA 1978 S68)

Capital transfer tax is not charged on certain variations in the destination of property passing on death. Nor is it charged on the disclaimer of title to property passing on death. The variation or disclaimer must be within two years of the death. For deaths between 9 December 1972 and 13 March 1975 however the time limit was 12 March 1977. An election to the Revenue is required within six months of the variation or disclaimer.

This exemption operates similarly, but without time limit, where a surviving spouse's life interest under an intestacy is redeemed. It also applies if an interest in settled property is disclaimed unless there is some consideration in money or money's worth.

Settled Property (FA 1975 Sch 5 & FA 1976 Ss105–112 & FA 1978 Ss69–71 & 74 & F2A 1979 S23)

The rules concerning capital transfer tax in relation to settled property are most detailed and the following are just a few guidelines:

(1) Broadly any settlement is subject to the tax (at the lifetime

rate scale – p 188) on its world-wide assets, if at the time it was made, the settlor was domiciled in the United Kingdom. Otherwise only assets situated in this country (p 199) are caught.

(2) The settlement of any property after 26 March 1974 is itself treated as a chargeable transfer by the settlor.

(3) If you have an interest in possession in any settled property for the time being (e.g. you receive the income as of right), the property itself is treated as yours for capital transfer tax purposes. Thus if your interest ends, you will be treated as making a chargeable transfer of the value of the property concerned. The tax is calculated on the basis of your cumulative transfers to that time.

(4) No capital transfer tax is payable if you obtain an absolute interest in property in which you previously had a life interest (or other interest in possession). Similarly the tax normally is not payable on the reversion to you in your lifetime (or your spouse within two years of your death) of property which you previously settled.

(5) Special rules apply to trusts where there is no interest in possession – particularly discretionary trusts, etc., and accumulation and maintenance settlements (see below).

(6) Quick succession relief is given if an interest in possession comes to an end within four years of a previous chargeable transfer of the settled property. The chargeable value is reduced by 80%, 60%, 40%, or 20% on the second occasion of charge where the interval is not more than 1, 2, 3 or 4 years respectively.

(7) Superannuation schemes and charitable trusts are normally exempted from capital transfer tax, as are those for employees, the mentally disabled and certain 'protective trusts'.

Accumulation and Maintenance Settlements

Accumulation and maintenance settlements with no fixed interests in possession for one or more beneficiaries up to an age not exceeding 25 are not subjected to the periodic charge (below) ; nor will capital transfer tax be charged on the capital distributions to those beneficiaries. This relief covers for example a settlement under which your son obtains an interest in possession at age 25 and at 35 gets the capital, the income being accumulated up to age 25 apart from various payments for his maintenance. No capital transfer tax is payable during the currency of the trust, nor when your son becomes entitled to the income at 25 nor the capital at 35.

Special rules apply to settlements made after 15 April 1976. Relief broadly only applies if either not more than 25 years have passed since the original settlement date (or when it first became accumulating) ; or if all beneficiaries are grandchildren of a common grandparent (or their widows, widowers, etc.).

Discretionary Trusts, etc.

The following rules apply where there is no interest in possession in *all* or *part* of the *property:*

CAPITAL TRANSFER TAX

(1) Capital transfer tax is charged on distributions of capital to beneficiaries. If the settlement was made before 27 March 1974 it is charged to tax on its distributions as if it were a separate individual but without certain exemptions (p 193).

(2) For a settlement made after 26 March 1974, distributions of capital up to the original amount settled are charged at a special rate. This is the rate which would have been paid by the settlor on a gift of the amount of the original settlement at the time that the latter was made. Excess distributions over and above the original capital fall into higher rate bands as further gifts by the settlor would have done.

(3) In addition a *periodic charge* is made. This usually falls on every tenth anniversary of the date of the settlement, occurring after 31 March 1982. (The original date was 31 March 1980 but this was extended by 2 years in F2A 1979 S23). The periodic charge is 30% of the tax which would have been payable if the whole capital held on discretionary trusts were distributed. There is a proportionate abatement however for property held for nine or fewer years out of the preceding ten. Also credit is given for the periodic charge against tax on distributions of capital within the next 20 years.

(4) If the trustees of the settlement are not United Kingdom resident, an annual charge is payable starting with the anniversary of the settlement falling after 31 December 1975. The amount is 3% of the total capital transfer tax which would be payable on a distribution of the entire trust capital. The annual charge is allowed as a credit against the 10 year charge and also against tax on capital distributions. Previously, if the 10th anniversary fell between 1 January 1976 and 31 March 1980, no annual charge arose until the next anniversary. With the two year extension to 31 March 1982, 10th anniversaries during the two years up to that date are now similarly treated. Furthermore, if any prior years have been subjected to the annual charge, then a corresponding number of future years will be exempted.

(5) *Transitional relief* is given for capital distributions before 1 April 1980 out of pre-27 March 1974 settlements. Thus an old settlement can be reorganised to avoid the periodic charge — for example by creating an interest in possession, or converting it into an accumulation and maintenance one (p 201). A percentage only of the full tax is charged on such reorganisations or capital distributions, according to the following scale:

Distribution before	% of full tax
1 April 1976	10%
1 April 1977	$12\frac{1}{2}$%
1 April 1978	15%
1 April 1979	$17\frac{1}{2}$%
1 April 1982	20%

(The expiry date for transitional relief was originally fixed as 31 March 1980 but has been extended for 2 years by F2A 1979 S23).

Mutual and Voidable Transfers (FA 1976 Ss86–88)

Complicated rules have been introduced which refer back to periods before the 1976 Finance Act was passed, as well as after. Broadly, the object is to relieve both the giver and receiver from capital transfer tax, where the receiver later returns the property, etc., concerned to the original giver.

Thus, if you give money to your brother, paying capital transfer tax as a result, and he later returns it to you; subject to the detailed rules, he is not charged to capital transfer tax on his transfer of the money to you. Furthermore, you can reclaim the tax which you first paid.

(A similar rule is found in FA 1976 S88 concerning voidable transfers.)

Example 26: Calculation of Capital Transfer Tax

Mr A made the following gifts in excess of his normal expenditure:

(1)   1 April 1974 to his son B £1,100 cash
(2)   2 April 1974 to his son C £100 cash
(3)   3 April 1974 to his son D £20,100 cash*
(4)   10 April 1976 to his son B £3,000 cash
(5)   15 April 1976 to his wife W £20,000 cash
(6)   31 May 1976 to B £10,100 cash* on his marriage
(7)   30 September 1976 to C shares worth £4,600
(8)   1 December 1977 to B £10,000 cash*
*Less capital transfer tax paid by Mr A.

Mr A dies on 1 November 1979 leaving an estate worth £60,000. Assuming that the present rates apply, capital transfer tax will be paid as follows:

Capital Transfer Tax Payable During Mr A's Life

(Gifts 1, 2, 4 and 5 are completely exempt)

		Amount Charge-able	Rate	Tax Payable
(3) 3 April 1974 to D		£20,100		
Less:				
Small gift exemption		100		
		£20,000	£15,000 at Nil	—
			5,000 at 5%	£250
(6) 31 May 1976 to B on his marriage		£10,100		
Less:				
Small gift exemption	£100			
Marriage exemption	5,000			
		5,100	5,000	5,000 at 7½%
				375

Example 26 continued

	Amount Charge-able	Rate	Tax Payable
(7) 30 September 1976 to			
C shares worth	4,600		
Less:			
Small gift exemption	100		
	4,500	5,000 (grossed)	5,000 at 10%	500
(8) 1 December 1977 to B		5,000 at 7½%	
	10,000	10,000	5,000 at 10%	875
Total of chargeable gifts during life		£40,000		£2,000

Additional tax payable on (8) following A's death
within three years £5,000×15%+£5,000×20%   875
  −£5,000×7½%−£5,000×10%

Total tax on lifetime gifts   £2,875

Capital Transfer Tax on Estate at Death (value £60,000)

			Rate	
Band £40,000–£	50,000		25%	£2,500
	50,000–	60,000	30%	3,000
	60,000–	70,000	35%	3,500
	70,000–	90,000	40%	8,000
	90,000–	100,000	45%	4,500

Total capital transfer tax at death   £21,500

21. Tax Aspects of Life Assurance

by M. S. LIPWORTH

There are three broad classes of life assurance contract:
(1) life policies themselves (e.g. whole-life policies, endowment policies, term assurance);
(2) pension annuity contracts (e.g. occupational pension schemes, i.e. your firm's pension scheme and private retirement annuity plans);
(3) purchased general annuities (immediate and deferred annuities).

Each of these three classes enjoys a different tax treatment, and these will be looked at separately, both from the life company's position (to see what benefits the company is able to offer) and from your point of view, as a policy-holder, to see how your premiums and proceeds are treated.

Taxation and Life Policies

The Company's Tax Position
(Ss305–310 & FA 1972 S93 (7) & Sch 18, FA 1974 S26 & FA 1977 S45)

In respect of their life assurance business, companies are generally taxed on the excess of their investment income and realised capital gains over management expenses, and are subject to lower rates of tax than trading companies. Thus, corporation tax on all unfranked income of the life fund (i.e. income other than dividend income) is limited to 37.5%. Dividend income attributable to policyholders effectively bears tax at 30% – the life company receives dividends from investments subject to the 3/7ths tax credit, but insofar as it allocates these dividends to policyholders' funds, it is unable to utilise the credit against its mainstream corporation tax. The rate of capital gains tax in respect of policyholders' funds is the lower of the rate for individuals (currently 30%) or 37.5%. As life companies are generally able to defer realisations of assets for a long period, they usually pass on this benefit in the form of a lower rate of deduction for capital gains tax on the benefits offered under the policies. This is especially true of unit-linked policies.

Development gains tax on property development is limited to 37.5%, but if development land tax applies to disposals after 31 July 1976, the full rate is payable (p 142).

The Tax Treatment of your Premiums and Proceeds
(Ss19–21, 393–401, Sch 1, FA 1975 Ss7–10, Schs 1 & 2, FA 1976 Ss33 & 34 & Sch 4 & FA 1978 Sch 3)

Life assurance policies are divided into two classes (S19 & Sch 1):

TAX ASPECTS OF LIFE ASSURANCE

(a) Qualifying policies.
(b) Non-qualifying policies.

Various changes were introduced in FA 1975 in relation to the tests for qualifying policies and the tax consequences of various dealings with both qualifying and non-qualifying policies. Some of these changes applied immediately, and in some cases retrospectively. Other changes were deferred until an appointed day, later fixed as 1 April 1976.

Qualifying Policies

These, basically, are regular premium policies, i.e. whole-life, term or endowment policies under which premiums are payable for a period of ten years or more, annually or more frequently. There must be a fairly even spread of premiums; i.e. premiums payable in any one period of twelve months should not be more than twice the value of premiums paid in any other period of twelve months, nor more than 1/8th of the total amount of premiums payable over the first ten years.

The sum assured under an endowment policy must be not less than 75% of the total premiums payable during the term of the policy, but, in respect of insurances made on or after the appointed day, this percentage is reduced, where the life assured's age exceeds 55 years at the date of issue of the policy, by an amount of 2% for each year above 55.

The sum assured under a whole of life policy issued after the appointed day that has a surrender value must not be less than 75% of the total premiums that would be payable if death occurred at the age of 75 years; and whole life policies may provide for payments on total or partial surrender – the wording of the previous provision was unclear.

There are also rules as to the type of benefit that may be provided in policies. Certain special types of policy may vary from these general rules (e.g. mortgage protection and family income policies, shorter term policies and industrial assurance).

Where options are granted under policies issued after the appointed day, these options will be tested to ascertain whether every one of the permissible permutations would create a qualifying policy; if it does, the option is good and any subsequent exercise of the option would not be a variation. If it does not, the option would disqualify the policy. Options in policies in respect of contracts made before the appointed day will be disregarded until they are exercised. If they are exercised, the policy will then be tested to ascertain whether or not the option disqualifies the policy.

The advantages of qualifying policies are:

(a) You are eligible for tax relief on your premiums.
(b) The proceeds are entirely free of tax, provided premiums are kept up for at least ten years (or three-quarters of the term of an endowment policy, not being less than $7\frac{1}{2}$ years).
(c) While the policy is in force all income and gains attributable

to your policy and the tax thereon at the rates mentioned above are the responsibility of the life company.

Tax Relief on your Premiums
(S19, FA 1975 Sch 2, FA 1976 S34 & Sch 4 & FA 1978 Sch 3)

You are entitled to tax relief on premiums paid by you under qualifying policies (or other life assurance policies issued in respect of contracts made before 20 March 1968) up to the greater of £1,500 or 1/6th of your total Income. In order to be eligible for relief the policy must be one issued on your own life or that of your spouse, the premium must be paid by you or your spouse, and the person paying must reside in the UK. The relief will be obtained by deducting the tax relief at the rate of $17\frac{1}{2}$% from the premiums payable to the life office, resulting in a premium payment net of tax relief. The life office will recover the deficiency from the Inland Revenue. Should you over-claim (i.e. deduct in excess of both the £1,500 and the 1/6th of income limit) the Revenue have the right to recover the excess relief by assessment and disallow the future payment of net premiums on particular policies by notice to you and the life company. Alternatively, you may elect to pay your premiums gross and, if eligible, claim tax relief from the Revenue.

Tax Relief Claw-back – qualifying policies
(a)   *Claw-back on early surrender* (FA 1975 S7 & Sch 1 & FA 1976 Sch 4 Para 18)

(i)   If a qualifying policy is surrendered or made paid-up (or a bonus becomes payable in cash) during the first four policy years, the Revenue will 'claw-back' some or all of the tax relief previously obtained, subject to a ceiling. The ceiling will be calculated as follows (the percentages relating to premiums payable to that stage) :

Time of surrender	Claw-back	'Ceiling'
In the first 2 years	$17\frac{1}{2}$%	surrender value less $82\frac{1}{2}$%
In the 3rd year	$11\frac{2}{3}$%	surrender value less $88\frac{1}{3}$%
In the 4th year	$5\frac{5}{6}$%	surrender value less $94\frac{1}{6}$%

The life assurance company will be required to deduct the maximum 'claw-back', subject to the ceiling from the policy proceeds and pay the appropriate amount to the Inland Revenue.

If the tax-payer has not been allowed tax relief on these premiums, he will be able to obtain a refund from the Inland Revenue.

(ii)   Where policies are made paid-up or are partially surrendered or made partially paid-up, the same claw-

207

back principles will apply, with appropriate modifications ; and the surrender of a bonus will be treated by the Revenue like any other partial surrender of policy rights.

(iii) The new provisions apply to qualifying policies issued in respect of insurances made after 26 March 1974 ; but to prevent policies whenever they are issued from being used as a means of tax avoidance, where any policy (including a policy which has been issued on or before 26 March 1974) has its premiums increased by more than 25 per cent the increase in the premiums is to be treated as though it related to a new and separate policy.

(b) *Premiums Paid out of a Partial Surrender* (FA 1975 S8 & Sch 1)

(i) If a policyholder pays a premium on a qualifying policy and at the same time effectively recoups himself in whole or in part by withdrawing money from that policy by way of a partial surrender of policy rights (or a surrender of a bonus) tax relief will not be allowed. The life assurance company will be required to claw-back out of the sum payable to the policyholder an amount equal to $17\frac{1}{2}$% of the current year's premium (or of the amount withdrawn, if less, and if any further surrender is taken an additional claw-back will be made until the $17\frac{1}{2}$% total claw-back is reached).

(ii) The legislation applies to qualifying policies issued in respect of insurances made after 26 March 1974.

Proceeds of Qualifying Policies (S394)

If the premiums under qualifying policies are kept up for at least ten years (or three-quarters of the term of an endowment policy, if sooner) or until death if earlier, then the entire policy proceeds, whether by way of death, surrender or maturity benefit will be free of all income taxes in your hands.

Non-qualifying Policies

All other policies are non-qualifying policies. The most important category of these is single-premium policies, frequently described as single-premium bonds, where only one lump sum is paid. (Bonds issued in respect of assurances made before 20 March 1968 are, however, treated in effect as qualifying policies.) In addition, policies that may commence initially as qualifying policies, can subsequently become non-qualifying policies, where, for example, material variations occur — e.g. reduction of premiums below certain levels or alterations to the sum assured, etc.

Tax Treatment of Non-qualifying Policies (including single premium bonds)
(Ss19 & 393–400 & FA 1975 Sch 2)

(a) No tax relief is available in respect of the premium. (Note, however, that where a policy was initially a qualifying policy and later became non-qualifying, e.g. premium reduced, past tax relief obtained does not have to be repaid; only future relief is not allowable; except, however, when a policy is made paid-up or surrendered in the first 4 years – see p 207).

(b) The income and gains attributable to the policy receive exactly the same tax treatment as qualifying policies – the income and gains are those of the life company whose responsibility it is to pay the taxes and render returns, etc.

(c) The proceeds of the policy are free of income tax at the basic rate and of capital gains tax.

(d) If a 'gain' is realised in respect of the policy on the happening of a 'chargeable event' there may be a charge to income tax at the higher rates and/or the additional rate on investment income (the gain being treated as investment income), but only if the bondholder's income plus the relevant portion of the gain (see below) is sufficiently high.

(e) In general, subject to the position of partial surrenders mentioned below, the 'chargeable gain' is the investment profit element in the proceeds – the difference between the surrender value and the premiums paid. Any extra amount received by way of death benefit in the case of the death of the life assured would be a mortality profit, and would not be a chargeable gain.

A chargeable event in the case of non-qualifying policies is:

(1) Death of the life assured.
(2) The maturity of the policy.
(3) The surrender, in whole, of the policyholder's rights under the policy.
(4) The assignment of the policy for money or money's worth.
(5) Excesses arising on partial surrenders in any policy years commencing after 13 March 1975 (see p 212).

Qualifying policies may also be subject to a tax charge on a similar basis if they are dealt with prematurely (within the ten-year period) thus:

(a) Death or maturity will be a chargeable event if the policy has previously been made paid-up within the first ten years (or three-quarters of the term of an endowment policy, if less).

(b) Surrender or assignment for money or money's worth within ten years (or three-quarters of the term of an endowment policy if less) will be a chargeable event.

Assignments between spouses or as security for debts are not chargeable events.

The surrender of a right to a bonus or the taking of a bonus is now treated in the same way as any other partial surrender if it gives rise to an excess. Also, loans made on policies issued in respect of contracts made after 26 March 1974 are treated as partial surrenders, except for loans under qualifying policies, where either interest is charged at a commercial rate or the sum is lent to a full-time employee of the insurance company for the purpose of house purchase or improvement.

Measure of Tax on Gains under Non-qualifying Policies
(Ss395, 399, 400 & FA 1975 Sch 2)

No previous partial surrenders

(1)   As mentioned above, where a gain arises on the happening of a chargeable event, the gain would not be liable to income tax at the basic rate nor to capital gains tax. The only liability would be to higher rate tax and the investment income surcharge, if applicable. In order to determine whether or not a tax liability arises, the gain is divided by the number of years the policy has been held to the date of the chargeable event. For example, if a single-premium bond was purchased for £5,000, and was cashed-in five years later for £7,000, the chargeable gain would be £2,000. The 'slice' of the gain would be £2,000 divided by 5, i.e. £400.

(2)   The 'slice' is added to the bondholder's other taxable income of the year in which the chargeable event occurs, and is treated as the top part of his taxable income and of his investment income, in order to determine whether the 'slice' is subject to any higher rate tax or to the investment surcharge, and if so at what effective rate of tax.

(3)   The appropriate tax rate applicable to the 'slice' is then applied to the whole gain (i.e. £2,000) and is the difference between
   (a)   the bondholder's average rate of tax on the 'slice' when added to his other taxable income, and
   (b)   the basic rate of 30%.

(4)   Note: the gain (without top-slicing) is counted as income for the purposes of determining whether the age allowance should be reduced (see p 13).

Example 27: No Tax on the Gain

Mr A is married, aged 60, and his income consists of a pension of £7,000 per annum and investment income of £4,000. He cashes in a bond that has been held for 5 years. The original premium was £10,000 and the proceeds are £13,000. The gain on the bond is therefore £3,000, and the relevant 'slice' of the gain is £3,000 divided by 5 = £600.

Income			
	Earned	£7,000	
	Investment	4,000	
		———	£11,000
Less	Personal relief		1,815
			———
			£9,185
Add	'Slice'		600
			———
Taxable income			£9,785

Example 27 continued

The tax on the 'slice' is therefore 30% less 30% = 0.
The investment income additional rate does not apply as the 'slice' plus investment income is no more than £5,000.

Example 28: Slice Falling into Two Rate Bands, but Investment Income Surcharge not Applying

A man purchases a bond for £10,000. Five years later he cashes it in for £13,000. The gain is £3,000. In that year his taxable income after reliefs is £11,500 of which £9,000 is earned and £2,500 unearned.

Tax calculation on gain:

Gain ÷ years held	= 'slice' of £600
Taxable income + 'slice'	= £12,100
Rate on slice	
On £500 (i.e. £11,500 to £12,000) at 40%	= £200
On £100 (i.e. £12,000 to £12,100) at 45%	= £45
Therefore, £200+£45	= a total of £245

Therefore, average rate on slice $\frac{245}{600} \times 100\%$ = 41%

Rate applied to gain is 41% − 30% = 11%

With the 'slice' of £600, the total investment income is only £3,100, so no investment income surcharge is attracted.
The tax payable is £3,000 × 11% = £330

Example 29: One Rate Band and Investment Income Surcharge Applying

A man purchases a bond for £10,000; five years later he cashes it in for £13,000. The gain is £3,000. In the year of cashing-in, his taxable income is £10,000, after reliefs, of which £5,000 is earned and £5,000 unearned.

Tax calculation

'Slice' (£3,000 ÷ 5)	= £600
Taxable income + slice	= £10,600
Rate on slice	= 40%

But as investment income plus 'slice' is more than £5,000 per annum the 15% surcharge applies.
Therefore, rate to apply to gain is:

(40%+15%)−30% (i.e. basic rate)	= 25%
Tax payable on gain = £3,000 × 25%	= £750

Where a *partial surrender* (e.g. under a withdrawal plan) has been made, under the legislation prior to 1975 the gain (profit element) in each partial surrender or withdrawal received exactly the same treatment as a gain on total surrender previously referred to:

(a) The profit element is sliced by the number of years the bond has been held up to the time of the withdrawal.

(b) The 'slice' is added to the other taxable income in that year to determine whether higher rate tax or the surcharge applies at all, and if so at what rates.

(c) If any higher rate tax or surcharge arises it is applied to the whole profit element in the withdrawal.

This applies to surrenders in policy years commencing on or before the passing of FA 1975 – i.e. 13 March 1975.

New Rules for Partial Surrenders in Policy Years commencing after 13 March 1975 – 'Excesses' (see p 192)

Until FA 1975 a partial surrender of rights under a policy was automatically a chargeable event and the gain element in the proceeds received by way of partial surrender received the same treatment as a gain on a total surrender.

This system has been replaced by the following rule. At the end of each policy year an allowance will be made of one twentieth of the premium (5%). If this allowance is not used it is carried forward to the next policy year, and so on, on a cumulative basis (the limit being 100% of the premium). Every time a partial surrender is made the amount withdrawn will be compared at the end of the policy year with the cumulative allowances. If the partial surrender is less than the cumulative allowance, no chargeable event will be deemed to have occurred, and the amount withdrawn will also be carried forward.

If in any policy year the amount withdrawn, plus previous cumulative withdrawals, *exceeds* the cumulative allowances a 'chargeable event' will occur, and the *excess* will be treated as a gain, subject to higher rate tax and investment income surcharge if applicable, regardless of the actual performance of the policy.

Once an excess has occurred, all cumulative withdrawals and allowances up to that date will be deemed to have been used up, and the process of allowances (subject to the overall limit of 100% of the premium) and withdrawals will start afresh, until the next excess, being the next chargeable event. When the final chargeable event occurs (e.g. death, final surrender, assignment for value), the total profit on the policy will be brought into account, the profit being the final proceeds plus previous partial surrenders from which will be deducted the premiums paid and previous gains on past chargeable events (i.e. past excesses).

For *'top-slicing'* the periods of spread are the number of policy years since the start of the policy in the case of the first chargeable event and final termination; and the number of policy years since the previous chargeable event in the case of the second and subsequent excesses. Gains will be charged to tax in the income tax year in which the relevant policy year ends or the final chargeable event occurs.

If on final termination there is a loss, the loss can be deducted from the policyholder's taxable income in that year to the extent of any previous gains on past chargeable events (i.e. excesses), for the purposes of *higher rate tax* and *investment income surcharge* only.

Example 30: 5% Regular Withdrawals

£10,000 Bond. 5% (£500) p.a. withdrawn for 10 years.

Assume Bondholder's taxable income = £11,000 (including £5,000 investment income).

Rate between £11,000 and £12,000 = 55% (including 15% investment income surcharge).

For 10 years draws £500 p.a. paying no tax, as allowances not exceeded. In year 11 cashes in Bond for £12,000.

Gain = £12,000+£5,000 (10×£500)—£10,000
     = £7,000 (Top-slice = £7,000 ÷ 10 = £700).

Income + slice = £11,700 (55% rate) (including 15% investment income surcharge).

Tax on gain = 25% (55%−30%) × £7,000 = £1,750.

Example 31: Postpone Withdrawals

Use allowances later – e.g. to pay school fees.

£10,000 Bond.

Years 1–10 no withdrawals. 10×5% (= 50%) accumulated.

Years 11–15 withdrawals of up to 15% (total 75%) possible, tax-free at the time = £1,500 p.a. for 5 years.

If Bond cashed in after 16 years having balance of, say, £18,000, gain equals £18,000 + £7,500−£10,000 = £15,500.

'Top-sliced' by 16 to find rate of tax on gain.

Example 32: Irregular Surrenders

A £10,000 Bond; £1,200 withdrawn after 4 policy years; a further £4,500 withdrawn after 6 policy years; £1,000 after 8, and the balance of the Bond, say £10,400, is surrendered after 10 policy years.

Years	A Cumulative allowances £	B Surrender £	C Cumulative surrender between chargeable events £	D Gain (C–A) £
1	500	0	0	0
2	1,000 (2 × 500)	0	0	0
3	1,500 (3 × 500)	0	0	0

213

Example 32 continued

Years	A Cumulative allowances £	B Surrender £	C Cumulative surrender between chargeable events £	D Gain (C–A) £
4	2,000 (4 × 500)	1,200	1,200	0
5	2,500 (5 × 500)	0	1,200	0
6	3,000 (6 × 500)	4,500	5,700	2,700
7	500	0	0	0
8	1,000	1,000	1,000	0
9	1,500	0	1,000	0
10		10,400		

Final gain = (£10,400 + £4,500 + £1,200 + £1,000) —
        £10,000—£2,700
      = *£4,400*

Note:
(i) Gain of £2,700 after 6 years is divided by 6 for top-slicing.
(ii) Final gain of £4,400 is divided by 10 for top-slicing.

Existing Policies

The rules relating to excesses apply to existing as well as future policies. The new system, however, applies only to partial surrenders occurring in the first policy year falling wholly after the passing of the FA 1975 (i.e. after 13 March 1975) and the system of 5% allowances runs only from then. Withdrawals made before that Act, and between 14 March 1975 and the first policy anniversary thereafter, are governed by the old system; and no 5% allowances apply to these policy years – indeed the allowances for these years are lost altogether.

Example 33: Existing Policy

£10,000 bond taken out on 1 July 1972. 8% withdrawals of £800 per annum taken on 30 June 1973, 1974 and 1975. Profit element in each of these withdrawals is subject to treatment on old basis, and 5% allowances do not apply to any of these withdrawals, including that on 30 June 1975.

If £800 is withdrawn in new policy year commencing 1 July 1975, £500 (5%) represents allowance for policy year ending 30 June 1976; and excess of £300 subject to higher rate tax and investment income surcharge, if applicable, in the year of assessment ending on 5 April 1977.

Persons Liable for the Charge (S399 & FA 1975 Sch 2)

(a)   Where a single premium bond or other non-qualifying policy is held by an individual absolutely, or as security for a debt owed by him, the higher rate tax charge, if any, would fall on him. In cases where policies are held on trusts, the charge falls upon the settlor, if he is then alive.

(b)   If immediately before the chargeable event the rights under the policy were held in the beneficial ownership of a close company or on trust created by or as security for a debt owed by a close company, the amount of the gain is deemed to form part of the company's distributable income for purposes of FA 1972 Sch 16 and for purposes of apportionment to participators (S 399 (1) (b)). Slicing of the gain does not apply as with individuals.

(c)   If a policy is assigned for value and subsequently re-assigned to the original policyholder and a chargeable event then occurs, the original policyholder is liable for the higher rate tax charge, if any.

Where a non-qualifying policy is assigned as a gift, any chargeable excesses arising on partial surrenders made from the policy during that policy year prior to the assignment are taxed on the assignor; only gains subsequent to the assignment are taxed on the new beneficial owner.

Certificates of Chargeable Event (S402 & FA 1975 Sch 2)

When a chargeable event occurs, it is the duty of the life assurance company to submit certificates to the Inland Revenue with details of the policy and the amounts payable and previously paid by way of surrender.

Life Insurance Policies Taken Out by Companies

In certain circumstances, a company may take out life assurance policies on the lives of its directors or other key executives – 'key man' or other policies, e.g. to provide funds to repay loans or other indebtedness.

In general, if the policy that is effected is term assurance, without a surrender value, the premiums would be tax-deductible and the proceeds would be taxable in the company's hands. If, on the other hand, the policy is one that will have a surrender value, the premiums will not be tax-deductible and the proceeds are unlikely to be charged to Corporation Tax in the company's hands. There could, however, in certain circumstances, be an apportionment to participators; if, for example, a non-qualifying policy is used or a qualifying policy is prematurely dealt with (p 208) and the company cannot justify the retention of its distributable income (including the gain on the policy) on the grounds that the business needs the money, or will do in the foreseeable future (p 180). A similar case arises if the premiums paid out of after-tax profits constitute an unjustifiable use of distributable income.

Disallowance of Interest on Borrowed Monies Applied to Pay Premiums under Life Policies (Ss403, 404)

Except for certain minor exceptions, where monies have been borrowed in order to pay the single premium or regular premiums under a life assurance policy, tax relief will not be available on the interest at rates higher than the basic rate – i.e. there will be no relief for higher rate tax or the additional rate on investment income.

Pension Business

Tax Position of the Life Company

The investment income and capital gains referable to the Company's pension business are totally exempt from tax (S314). Thus, the investment income and capital gains attributable to pension annuity policies accumulate free of all taxes, excluding development gains accruing to a pension fund in respect of property developments to which the development land tax applies (p 142).

Retirement Annuity Plans for the Self-Employed and Other Persons not in Pensionable Employment

(Ss226–229, FA 1971 S20 & Sch 2, FA 1976 S30, FA 1977 S27 & FA 1978 S26)

Eligibility

(1) You would be eligible for one of these plans if you are in receipt of 'relevant earnings'. This means either earnings from non-pensionable employments, or from businesses, professions, partnerships, etc. Thus, if you have any Schedule D Case I or II earnings, you normally qualify for relief from income tax in respect of premiums paid to an insurance company on a retirement annuity policy approved by the Revenue, or under an approved trust scheme, to provide an annuity at your retirement.

This relief is also available if you have a non-pensionable employment; e.g., with a firm which does not provide a pension scheme, but not as a controlling director of an investment company. You are not eligible if you belong to a pension scheme operated by your employers, but you are eligible if you are not a member of such a scheme.

Until 1973 controlling directors could not join their company's pension scheme. They may now do so (FA 1973, S15), but if they do not they continue to be eligible for a private retirement plan.

(2) Where you have two sources of income, one being relevant earnings, and the other arising from pensionable employment, you are eligible to contribute to a private retirement annuity scheme in respect of your non-pensionable earnings, subject to certain limits (see p 217).

Tax Relief on Premiums and Limits

(3) If you have relevant earnings, and pay either single or

annual premiums in respect of an approved retirement annuity scheme within the limits mentioned below, you enjoy full tax relief on those premiums in the relevant years. The allowable premiums would be set off against your earned income.

(4) The limits of your contributions to retirement annuity plans for 1977–78 and subsequent years are restricted to the lesser of £3,000 or 15% of your 'net relevant earnings' (this means relevant earnings from your non-pensionable employment or business, etc., less certain deductions such as expenses, trading losses, capital allowances, etc.).

(5) The limits of £3,000 or 15% are increased for older tax-payers as follows: Born in

1914 or 1915	£3,600 or 18%
1912 or 1913	£4,200 or 21%
1910 or 1911	£4,800 or 24%
1908 or 1909	£5,400 or 27%
1907 or earlier	£6,000 or 30%

These higher limits do not apply to persons drawing a pension from a previous employment or who have a right thereto.

(6) If you have two sources of income, one from pensionable employment, and the other being net relevant earnings, the £3,000 limit (or the larger monetary limit for older tax payers) is reduced by 15% of the earnings from the pensionable employment (or the higher percentage for older tax payers).

For example, a person born in 1920 has pensionable earnings as a company executive of £9,000 per annum. He also has net relevant earnings from a part-time consultancy of £6,000 per annum. He can pay premiums on a retirement annuity contract of 15% of £6,000 = £900.

If, however, his pensionable earnings had been £15,000, his limit would have been £3,000 less (15% × £15,000) = £3,000 less £2,250 = £750.

(7) Under S226A, you are permitted to pay premiums, not exceeding the lesser of 5% of your net relevant earnings or £1,000, under a special policy providing for an annuity for your spouse or dependants after your death or for a lump sum payable to your estate in the event of your death before age 75. If you do so, the above limits for premiums you are permitted to pay for your own retirement contract will be correspondingly reduced.

(8) Married couples who each have relevant earnings are entitled to pay separate premiums based on their respective net relevant earnings. These premiums will be relieved against their joint earnings, except where they have elected to be taxed separately, in which event the premiums would be set off against their separate relevant earnings.

Year for which Relief Granted

(9) Normally your premiums will be offset against your earned

income in the actual tax year in which the contributions are paid. Where, however, your assessment to tax for a particular tax year becomes final after 5 October of the tax year to which it relates, you may elect to have a premium paid within six months after the assessment becomes final treated as having been paid in that earlier tax year. (An assessment under appeal which is settled by agreement normally becomes final when such agreement is signified in writing. This may be before the issue of a revised notice of assessment.) You must notify the Revenue of your election within the six months. For example, if your assessment for 1977–78 becomes final on, say, 30 June 1979 a premium paid before 31 December 1979 could be relieved against your 1977–78 relevant earnings.

(10) Moreover, you can carry forward for relief in future years any premiums paid by you in excess of the percentage limits referred to in paragraphs (5) and (6) above, but not exceeding the monetary limits.

Benefits Payable and Age at which they may be taken

(11) Your annuity may commence to be paid at any age between 60 and 75. It is not necessary for you actually to retire before the annuity may commence. In certain occupations, the Revenue allow an annuity to commence earlier than age 60 (e.g. jockeys, professional singers, newscasters, etc.). Under no circumstances may the annuity commence later than age 75.

(12) The annuity payable to you can take one of many forms: sterling or unit-linked, guaranteed or non-guaranteed, etc. In most contracts there is a provision that if you die before the commencement of the annuity, an annuity is payable to your widow or dependants nominated by you, or alternatively a lump sum would be paid into your estate, not exceeding the amount of the contributions plus a reasonable amount of interest or bonuses (this generally would include capital growth and income attributable to the premiums paid under a unit-linked plan).

(13) Should you have a contract under S226A, then on your premature death an annuity would be payable to your spouse, if she is alive (or nominated dependant), or the lump sum would be paid into your estate.

(14) Any annuity payable to the widow, widower or dependant would be free of capital transfer tax (FA 1975 Sch 7 para 2).

(15) Any annuity payable either to you, your spouse or your dependants will be treated and taxed as earned income, save to the extent to which premium contributions have been disallowed for tax relief.

Commutation and open market option

(16) If the contract so allows, you are entitled to surrender part of your annuity and receive a cash payment. This is known as 'commutation' and the amount received is tax-free. The maximum lump sum that you are allowed by way of com-

mutation is three times the annual annuity that will remain after taking the lump sum. For example, if your remaining annuity would be at least £2,000 per annum, you could receive a tax-free lump sum of 3 × £2,000 = £6,000. As a matter of practice and subject to certain conditions, the Revenue allow you to take your commuted lump sum on the basis of the maximum annuity possible under the contract provided that this is expressed as the primary annuity, allowing you by way of a subsequent election to change the remaining annuity to one of a different type that may have a lesser initial amount (e.g. commutation based on a guaranteed sterling annuity payable annually in arrears, and subsequently electing to take a unit-linked annuity as the remaining annuity). With the tax-free lump sum payment, it may be advantageous for you to purchase an annuity, because part of this would be tax-free (p 220), or you may purchase a single premium bond, operating a withdrawal scheme to provide regular cash payments to supplement your income.

(17) If the contract so provides, you are permitted, instead of taking the annuity from the life company with whom you hold the contract, to utilise the fund built up for your annuity in order to purchase an annuity from any other company, thus obtaining the best terms then available ('open market option').

Pension Provision for Directors of Close Companies
(FA 1973 S15)

Controlling directors of close companies are now eligible for inclusion in approved pension schemes established by their companies. Until FA 1973 they could not have been so included. This may now be arranged as part of a group scheme or as an individual pension arrangement for the director concerned. In general, the same rules apply to controlling directors as to any individuals in an occupational pension scheme, although there are certain limitations that apply to controlling directors – particularly to those with at least 20% control. Thus, they can now obtain benefits provided through pension plans established for their benefit by their companies, with premiums paid by the companies being deductible for corporation tax and/or personal contributions up to 15% of their incomes being allowed for income tax. They are eligible for potential benefits within the general pension limits, including a personal pension of up to $\frac{2}{3}$rds of their final salary (if they have been employed by their companies for 10 years or more), the right to commute a portion of their pension up to a maximum of $1\frac{1}{2}$ × final salary, after 20 years' service; a widow's pension of $\frac{2}{3}$rds of the individual's pension; and, in the case of death-in-service life cover, 4 × salary plus a widow's pension of 4/9ths of salary.

However, because a director of a family company is in a rather different position from an ordinary employee, the Revenue have

imposed some limitations on controlling directors, e.g. the measure-
ment of final salary is more stringent than for non-controlling
directors.

General Annuity Business

The Company's Position (Ss312–313)

If the annuities paid by the Company to general annuitants during
the tax year exceed or equal the investment income and realised
gains of the general annuity fund, the fund is not taxed on the
income and gains. Companies, therefore, try to balance the income
of the fund against their annuity payments, which explains the
special rates that are sometimes offered for different classes or
ages. Annuity rates are, as a result, generally based on gross
income, and tend to be high at times of high interest rates.

The Individual Annuitant (S230)

(1) If you purchase an annuity from a life company the annuity
     paid is regarded as consisting of a capital element (represent-
     ing a return of premium) and an income element (S230 (1)).
     The ratio between the two depends on actuarial mortality
     tables : the shorter the period (i.e. the older the age of the
     annuitant) the higher the capital content. The capital content
     is fixed from the outset.

     The effect is that the capital content is tax-free, while the
     income element is treated as ordinary investment income,
     subject to income tax at the basic and higher rates, if applic-
     able. The company pays the annuity under deduction of
     basic rate tax.

(2) An immediate annuity is one that commences to run imme-
     diately. A deferred annuity is one that runs from some time
     in the future. Some annuities are for the annuitants' lifetime ;
     others are for a limited period (temporary annuity) ceasing
     at the end of the period or death, if earlier. Some annuities are,
     however, guaranteed to run for a minimum period, and will
     continue to be paid after the death to the annuitant's personal
     representatives or assignees.

Guaranteed Income Bonds

These are a combination of two separate purchased annuity
contracts : a temporary immediate annuity and deferred lifetime
annuity. Your lump sum purchase consideration is split between
the two according to the premium for each type of contract. For
example :

(a) If you are a male aged 65 and purchased a ten year guaranteed
     income bond for a total price of £10,000 an amount of, say,
     £5,200 might be the purchase consideration of the temporary
     annuity and £4,800 the purchase price of the deferred
     annuity contracts. The temporary annuity could be as high
     as, say, £1,000 per annum for ten years, representing a gross

yield on a £10,000 outlay of 10.7% per annum. The capital content of the temporary annuity instalments would be approximately £700 and the income element £300. The income element would be paid subject to deduction of income tax at the basic rate and is treated as investment income in your hands.

(b) At the end of the ten years, the temporary annuity ceases and you then have the option of taking either a deferred lifetime annuity under the deferred contract of, say, £1,700 per annum or a lump sum equal to your initial outlay (i.e. £10,000). If you take the deferred annuity, the capital content will be relatively low; in the above example it would be £470 per annum, and the income element £1,230 per annum. The latter is fully chargeable to income tax.

(c) *Guaranteed Income Bonds issued on or before 26 March 1974.* If in the case of a guaranteed income bond issued on or before 26 March 1974 you opt to cash in the deferred annuity and take the lump sum, the difference between the lump sum of £10,000 and the purchase price of the deferred annuity (£4,800) is treated as a gain chargeable to higher rate tax and the investment income surcharge (but not to basic rate tax) in a similar way to the gain under a single-premium bond (p 208). In this case, the gain would be £5,200, realised after ten years (i.e. £10,000 cash option less £4,800 purchase consideration). A slice of £520 (£5,200 divided by 10) is added to your other taxable income in the year of cashing-in and the appropriate rate or rates applicable to the slice is applied to the total gain of £5,200 (Ss396, 397 & 399).

(d) If you choose to surrender your guaranteed income bond after, say, three years, the same principle applies, but in calculating the gain under the temporary annuity contract you deduct the capital elements of all the annuity payments you have received to that stage under the temporary annuity from the purchase price for that annuity thereby inflating the gain (S397 (1) a (i)).

(e) *Bonds issued after 26 March 1974.* In the case, however, of guaranteed income bonds and guaranteed growth bonds (deferred annuity bonds) issued after 26 March 1974, any gain arising on surrender or the taking of a cash option (£5,200 in the example mentioned in (c) above) will be subject to basic rate tax in addition to the higher rates. Moreover, the proceeds on death under an annuity contract made on or after 10 December 1974 granting a death benefit will be treated in the same way as surrender proceeds.

(f) Loans taken against these bonds will be treated as total or partial surrenders and any gains deemed to have been realised will be subject to tax as in (c) and (e) above.

Capital Transfer Tax and Life Assurance Policies

Death of Policyholder

A life assurance policy beneficially owned by the deceased is property that is subject to capital transfer tax in the same way as any other property owned by him (p 191).

Gifts of Policies (under the existing legislation)

Gifts of policies may be made in two ways:

(a) Writing the policy in trust or a subsequent declaration of trust.

(b) Assignment of the policy.

In either case the premiums may be paid: (a) by the donor direct; (b) by the beneficiary out of cash gifts from the donor; (c) by the beneficiary out of his own resources; (d) by a combination of the above.

If any of the usual capital transfer tax exemptions apply (p 193) neither the policy proceeds nor any gifts of premiums that have been made would be dutiable, viz:

(a) The gift of the premiums or policy falls within the £2,000 exemption (note if the policy is a qualifying policy and tax relief is available to the donor on the premium – e.g. policy written on life of donor in trust for beneficiaries – it is arguable that the upper limit of this exemption is £2,000 plus the tax relief available to the donor).

(b) The gifts come within the normal expenditure of the donor; or

(c) The gifts fall within the marriage settlement exemption; or

(d) The gifts fall within the small gifts exemption – outright gifts of £100 per donee (for example a premium on a policy written in trust for the absolute benefit of the beneficiary).

(e) Policies written by husband or wife in trust for the other.

If none of the exemptions apply, capital transfer tax will be payable in respect of trust or assigned policies (unless they fall within the first £25,000 of non-exempt lifetime gifts in respect of which a nil rate is payable).

If capital transfer tax is payable, the amount chargeable is the premiums paid by the donor; or, if an existing policy is gifted by assignment or declaration of trust, the greater of the premiums paid or the surrender value of the policy.

If cash gifts have been made to enable the premiums to be paid by the beneficiary, the amount of the cash gifts would be chargeable. The proceeds of the policy on death, maturity or surrender will not be subject to capital transfer tax.

Life of Another Policies

On the death of the life assured the proceeds are totally free of capital transfer tax (p 199). Clearly they do not form part of the life assured's estate, as the policy is not owned by him. The surrender value would, however, be chargeable in the policyholder's estate if he is the first to die (unless the estate passes to his spouse).

If the policyholder is enabled to pay the premiums by virtue of cash gifts from the donor, the cash gifts would be taxable, unless the exemptions mentioned above apply, but the proceeds will be free of capital transfer tax.

Use of Policies

Life assurance can be used in two main ways for capital transfer tax:

(a) to create a fund for the eventual payment of the tax; and
(b) as a vehicle for making gifts to your beneficiaries.

22. An Outline of VAT

by Professor G. S. A. Wheatcroft

Introduction

VAT was introduced into the United Kingdom on 1 April 1973. A new rate of 15% replaced the old 8% standard rate and 12½% higher rate on 18 June 1979. All the other countries now in the European Economic Community have introduced a similar tax and the coverage, but not the rates, has been (at least in theory) harmonised. It is beyond the scope of this book to give more than a brief outline of the provisions of VAT.

VAT in the UK is imposed on (1) imports of goods by any person into the UK, (2) the supply (such as sale, hire and HP) of goods and services (which together comprise virtually all supplies) by a business in the UK and (3) in certain circumstances the import of services by a business. Hence the tax is payable whenever goods or services pass from one business to another or to a private consumer, although in the former case it is normally refunded.

After the end of each accounting period for the tax (usually a period of three months) each business has to render a *return* to Customs and Excise of all its 'outputs', i.e. the supplies of goods and services it has made during the period to other businesses or to consumers; and has to account to Customs and Excise one month after the end of the period for VAT on the prices (before tax) of those outputs. Each business is, at the same time, normally allowed a credit for the VAT on its 'inputs' in that period, i.e. goods imported by it and goods and services supplied to it for the purposes of the business. Unlike income tax or corporation tax, no distinction is made between capital or revenue inputs: the credit extends to the tax on its capital purchases as well as on its purchases of stock in trade. The total of tax on the inputs of a business is ascertained from the tax invoices given to it by every other business which has supplied it with goods or services. Amongst other details a typical tax invoice shows:

To goods	£100
To VAT at 15%	15
Price payable	£115

At the end of each accounting period the business will total all the tax invoices it has received for its inputs in that period, which it must keep for production to Customs and Excise when required, together with its vouchers for tax on imports; it will also total all its outputs for the period (keeping copies of all tax invoices it has rendered to other businesses) and a typical return for an accounting period will show:

Total outputs during the period	£50,000	
VAT thereon		£7,500
Total inputs for the period	£20,000	
VAT thereon		£3,000
		————
Balance payable to Customs and Excise		£4,500

The effect of the credit mechanism is that although VAT is charged on each business in the chain of import, production and distribution, each business in the chain gets a credit for the tax on its inputs, so that the whole tax is passed on to the consumer on the final sale to him. This is best shown by an example which uses the old 10% rate for simplicity:

	Price (ex-VAT)	VAT	
Manufacturer imports raw materials	£10	£1	
Manufacturer accounts to C & E on import			£1
Manufacturer sells product to wholesaler	£100	£10	
Manufacturer accounts to C & E for VAT			£9 (10–1)
Wholesaler sells product to retailer	£150	£15	
Wholesaler accounts to C & E for VAT			£5 (15–10)
Retailer sells to consumer	£200	£20	
Retailer accounts to C & E for VAT			£5 (20–15)
Consumer bears VAT of	£20		
			————
Customs and Excise collect			£20

This example, however, only shows how VAT is collected and borne over a series of transactions: it is not necessary to trace each item in this way, as the return at the end of each accounting period will cover all the inputs and outputs of the period. Credit for the VAT on unsold stock will have been given on its purchase and it will therefore be held tax-free until sale.

Because of the credit mechanism outlined above a business does not normally bear any tax; it merely acts as a collection agency. The ultimate consumer bears all the tax, which is why VAT is described as a sales tax. The difficulty of having a retail sales tax lies in determining when the final retail takes place. With VAT it does not matter; if the purchaser is a business, he will get credit for the tax as input tax, and if he is not he will bear it. Another advantage of the credit mechanism is that the effect is neutral between supplies which go through a number of stages and those where the supplier is vertically integrated. In both cases the tax is on the amount of the final price to the consumer.

A turnover tax charges tax on tax and therefore encourages vertical integration which is not usually in the public interest.

As will be seen later (p 227), businesses which make some 'exempt' supplies do not get credit for the VAT on their inputs relating to these supplies: hence in the above paragraph we say input tax is 'normally' refunded.

VAT in Practice

All businesses (p 227) are required to be registered with Customs and Excise and they have to make returns every three months. Some businesses who are likely to have repayments of tax, however, because they make zero-rated supplies, are allowed a one-month period. The return has to be completed and the tax paid by the end of the following month. There are rules for determining into which period a supply falls. For goods it is the date when the goods are removed or made available, and for services it is the date of performance, but there are two exceptions. If an invoice (which must contain certain specified information) is issued within 14 days after that time, the date of the invoice is taken. In practice this will usually apply and the advantage is that the VAT return can be made up from the copy invoices. The other exception is for payments in advance when it is the date of invoice or payment which counts. This is the only time payment is relevant; normally it is the invoice which matters (see below under 'Special Cases' for the position of bad debts). An arrangement can also be made with Customs and Excise to use the last day of the calendar month or of a VAT accounting period as the time of supply.

The same rules apply for determining into which period the inputs fall. Consequently, relief for input tax will normally be available before the invoice has been paid. The invoices will need to be kept as proof. The VAT return will be a summary of invoices issued and invoices received. If tax is due to Customs and Excise, it will be paid with the return.

Although, strictly speaking, tax on imports by a business is due at the date of import, a business is allowed to pay the tax with the next return. No tax is due so long as the goods are in a bonded warehouse. The tax may also be paid in the following return by a business which takes goods out of the warehouse.

Zero-rating and Exemption

So far we have assumed that all the inputs and outputs of a business are taxable at a positive rate. Certain types of supply are treated specially either because they are 'zero-rated' or because they are 'exempt'. Details of these types are set out in Schedules 4 and 5 to the Finance Act 1972 and summaries of these Schedules are at the end of this chapter.

If a supply is *zero-rated* this means that no tax is charged on the supply but credit is given to the supplier for all tax on his inputs relating to that supply. Exports of goods, for instance, are zero-rated so that these leave the country free of VAT in the UK, although they may be liable to VAT in the country to which they are imported if that country imposes a VAT. Hence, a business which exports most of its products will probably find that its returns for an accounting period show more tax on its inputs than on its outputs (the majority being zero-rated). In that event, the business can claim back the difference from Customs and Excise.

The EEC requires its members to have a VAT with a similar structure although different rates are allowed. One of the reasons is that the similar treatment of imports and exports ensures equality between home-produced and imported goods.

In addition to exports, food and many other items sold within the UK (p 231) are also zero-rated.

Exemption of a supply of goods or services is not so favourable as zero-rating as whilst this means that there is no VAT on the supply (as with zero-rating) there is no credit allowed for the tax on the inputs of the business. Thus life assurance is one of the exempt items (p 232) so that there is no tax on the premium on a life policy but the life assurance company can get no credit for the tax on those inputs which it uses for its life assurance business. This introduces a hidden tax cost to its business.

A business which supplies both taxable (including zero-rated) and exempt goods and services is a 'partly exempt' business and will have an accounting problem. When claiming credit for the tax on the inputs from Customs and Excise, it is entitled to credit for the tax on those inputs which it uses for its taxable supplies but it is not entitled to credit for the tax on those inputs which it uses for its exempt supplies. Normally, a proportion of its input tax corresponding to its taxable supplies is allowed. However, many exempt items are ignored for this purpose.

Business

Central to the working of VAT is the definition of 'business' because the credit mechanism is applied only to a business. It is defined to include any trade, profession or vocation. It also includes clubs and associations, such as sports clubs and members' clubs. The charging of admission fees, for example by the National Trust, is also taxable as a business. VAT is not charged on subscriptions to political parties, trades unions or professional bodies.

Small Traders

A person whose taxable (including zero-rated) supplies are less than £10,000 (from 12 April 1978) per annum is not liable to be registered, although he can apply to be registered voluntarily. If he is not registered and his supplies exceed £3,500, £6,000 or

£8,500 in the one, two or three preceding calendar quarters, he must notify Customs and Excise, who will register him, unless he can show that his total supplies in the year will not exceed £10,000. A small trader who is not registered is in the same position as a business making only exempt supplies. He does not charge tax to his customers and has to bear any input tax.

Zero-rated Suppliers

A person whose supplies are all zero-rated can apply to be exempted from registration. He will not then be able to claim a refund of his input tax but he will not have to make VAT returns.

Groups and Divisions of Companies

A group of companies may be registered as a single business and supplies between members of the group will be ignored. One company in the group is responsible for making returns for all the members of the group. Alternatively, a company which is organised in divisions can register each division separately.

Local Authorities

Local authorities are in the position of being both in business and also carrying on non-business activities, such as welfare services. Their business activities are treated in the normal way but the input tax on the non-business activities is refunded. In this way there is no hidden tax burden in the rates.

Charities

Sales in charity shops, fetes, coffee mornings, etc. of donated goods are zero-rated if the charity is established for the relief of distress. Apart from this business supplies of a charity are treated in the normal way; there is no exemption for charities. Non-business supplies such as distribution of free goods are outside the tax unless they are exported when they are zero-rated. Where the branch of a charity makes business supplies, for example sales at a fete, it may be treated as a separate entity from the charity and be entitled to the £10,000 limit before it is taxable.

Retailers

Because retailers often cannot record each sale separately there are special schemes for calculating the amount of the tax which they pay. The schemes also deal with the difficulty of retailers which sell both zero-rated goods (e.g. food) and standard-rated goods (e.g. kitchen equipment). Details of the schemes are contained in Customs and Excise Notice No. 727 and supplements describing each scheme.

Special Cases

Motor Cars

No deduction of input tax on motor cars is allowed on cars acquired for use in the business. This also applies to the acquisition of hire cars and taxis, except London-type taxis, although the hire charge is available for credit as input tax. A car dealer is not affected and can claim a credit for input tax in the normal way, but if he takes a car out of stock and uses it in his own business, tax must be paid and it is not available for credit (see 'Self-supply', below). The definition of 'motor car' for this purpose excludes commercial vehicles, vans without rear side windows and vehicles accommodating only one or more than eleven persons.

Business Entertainment

Input tax on business entertainment (except reasonable entertainment for overseas customers) is also not deductible. Entertainment includes meals, accommodation, theatres and sporting facilities. This does not, however, prevent deduction of input tax on subsistence expenses refunded to employees.

Self-supply

It is advantageous for a business which makes exempt supplies to produce its own goods since no input tax will be charged for which it will be unable to obtain a credit. To prevent distortion, an Order charging printed stationery to tax even though supplied to oneself has been made. Thus a bank, which is exempt, printing its own stationery would be charged to tax on the value of the stationery and it could not obtain relief for the tax. An Order also applies to cars to prevent avoidance of the non-deduction of input tax mentioned above.

Second-hand Goods

Second-hand goods are chargeable to tax in the normal way, except that there are special provisions relating to cars, motorcycles, caravans, boats and outboard motors, original works of art, antiques over 100 years old, collectors' pieces, electronic organs and aircraft, which provide that VAT is payable only on the dealer's mark-up. Except in the case of cars these provisions apply only when no tax was charged on the dealer's acquisition or when tax was charged on another dealer's mark-up. Where goods are taken in part-exchange, full VAT is still payable on the new goods supplied.

Sales on Credit

A separately disclosed credit charge is exempt from VAT.

Gifts

Business gifts of goods are taxable on the cost price but items costing under £10 (in aggregate) can be ignored. Gifts of services are not taxable.

Personal Use

If a person acquires goods in the course of business and uses them for his own personal use, e.g. a shopkeeper who takes goods off the shelf, tax is payable on the cost of the goods.

Bad Debts

A limited relief for bad debts exists where the debtor goes bankrupt or goes into liquidation after 1 October 1978. The amount excluding VAT is claimed from the liquidator, etc., and the VAT from Customs and Excise. Retailers in effect obtain bad debt relief as the special schemes are based on payments.

Documentation

The legislation is contained in the Finance Acts 1972, 1973, 1974, 1975 (2 Acts), 1976, 1977, 1978 and 1979 (No. 2) and a large number of statutory instruments made under powers contained in the Acts, all of which are available from HMSO.

Detailed information is contained in the following Notices issued by Customs and Excise which are available free from any Customs and Excise VAT office:

Number

700	General Guide
701	Scope and Coverage
702	Imports
703	Exports
704	Retail Export Schemes
705	Tax-free Sales of Motor Vehicles for Use before Export
706	Partial Exemption and Self-supply (Stationery)
708	Construction Industry
709	Hotels, Catering and Holiday Services
710	Supplies by or through Agents
711	Second-hand Cars
712	Second-hand Works of Art and Antiques
713	Second-hand Caravans and Motor-cycles
714	Young Children's Clothing and Footwear
715	Construction Industry: Alterations and Repairs and Maintenance
716	Changes in the Rate of Tax (see also leaflet No. 716/1/79 in connection with the increase in the rate of VAT)
719	Refund of VAT to 'Do-it-yourself' Builders
720	Second-hand Boats and Outboard Motors
721	Second-hand Aircraft
722	Second-hand Electronic Organs
727	Special Schemes for Retailers (see also No. 735 in connection with the increase in the rate of VAT)

It should be emphasised that these Notices are guides, and, with the exception of No. 727 and the parts of the Notices relating to second-hand goods which deal with keeping records, they do not have any legal force.

Appeals

Independent VAT tribunals deal with appeals about the matters listed below. There are tribunals in London, Edinburgh, Belfast and Manchester. The tribunal consists of a chairman who can sit alone or with one or two other members. The procedure is explained in a leaflet printed by the President of VAT Tribunals which is available from Customs and Excise VAT offices.

The matters over which the tribunals have jurisdiction are as follows:

(1) Registration
(2) Registration of groups of companies
(3) Assessment of VAT by Customs and Excise
(4) The amount of VAT chargeable
(5) The amount of the deduction of input tax
(6) Apportionment of input tax by a partly-exempt person
(7) Special schemes for retailers
(8) The value of certain supplies
(9) The provision of security
(10) Repayment of VAT on certain imports
(11) Refunds to do-it-yourself builders
(12) Bad debt relief
(13) Voluntary registration of a person whose turnover is below the limit

There is an appeal from the tribunal on a point of law (there is no appeal on a question of fact) to the High Court and from there to the Court of Appeal. There is a final appeal to the House of Lords if leave to appeal is obtained. In Scotland, appeals go to the Court of Session and thence to the House of Lords.

Zero-rating

The following is a list of the more important items. Full details are contained in the booklet *Scope and Coverage* (VAT Notice No. 701) available from Customs and Excise:

Group 1: Food   All food except pet foods, alcoholic drinks and certain food products (such as ice cream, chocolate, soft drinks and potato crisps). These latter were zero-rated until 1 April 1974. Meals out are however taxable.

Group 2: Sewerage Services and Water   Water except for distilled water and bottled water; emptying cesspools.

Group 3: Books, etc.   Books, newspapers, magazines, music, maps. But diaries and stationery are taxable.

Group 4: Talking Books for the Blind and Handicapped and Wireless Sets for the Blind

Group 5: Newspaper Advertisements   Advertising in newspapers, periodicals and journals only: including advertising agency charges. Advertising in other media is taxable.

Group 6: News Services   News services supplied to newspapers.

Group 7: Fuel and Power Coal, gas, domestic heating oil, lubricating oil, electricity. Petrol and derv were zero-rated until 1 April 1974

Group 8: Construction of Buildings, etc. Sale of the freehold or grant of a lease for more than 21 years of a building by a builder; construction, alteration and demolition of buildings but not repairs. Sales by a builder's merchant, and architects' and surveyors' fees are however taxable. A person building his own house (not merely conversions and alterations) can reclaim tax paid on items purchased.

Group 9: International Services Exports of services, such as professional advice to non-residents (except individuals resident in the EEC) and overseas insurance. In some cases the 'import' of professional services is charged to VAT.

Group 10: Transport Passenger transport (inland and international) including travel agents (except in relation to hotels in the UK or package tours), and international freight transport. Taxis and hire cars are however taxable, as are pleasure boats and aircraft.

Group 11: Caravans and Houseboats Caravans which are too large to be used as trailers on the roads (22.9 feet in length or 7.5 feet in breadth). But smaller caravans are taxable.

Group 12: Gold Transactions on the London Gold Market.

Group 13: Bank Notes

Group 14: Drugs, Medicines, Medical and Surgical Appliances Drugs dispensed by a registered pharmacist on a doctor's prescription. Other drugs purchased without a prescription are taxable. Medical and surgical appliances for the disabled.

Group 15: Imports, Exports, etc. This group has limited application.

Group 16: Charities (p 228).

Group 17: Clothing and Footwear Clothing for young children, industrial protective clothing and motor-cyclists' crash helmets.

Exports of Goods This does not include exports to Northern Ireland which is part of the UK, or to the Isle of Man.

Note: Zero-rating has priority over exemption if a supply falls into both categories.

Exemptions

The following is a list of the more important items. Full details are contained in the booklet *Scope and Coverage* (VAT Notice 701) available from Customs and Excise:

Group 1: Land Sales, leases and hiring out of land and buildings (unless within zero-rating Group 8). But hotels, holiday accommodation, camping, parking, timber, mooring, exhibition stands and sporting rights are taxable.

Group 2: Insurance All types of insurance and insurance brokers and agents. Both premiums and the payment of claims are exempt.

Group 3: Postal Services Post, except telegrams. But telephones and telex are taxable.

Group 4: Betting, Gaming and Lotteries Bookmakers, charges for playing bingo. But admission or session charges, club subscriptions and takings from gaming machines are taxable.

Group 5: Finance Banking, buying and selling stocks and shares. But stockbrokers' commissions and unit trust management fees are taxable.

Group 6: Education Schools, universities, non-profit-making institutions teaching pupils of any age, or providing job training; private tuition by an independent teacher.

Group 7: Health Doctors, dentists, dental workers, nurses, midwives, registered opticians (including spectacles supplied in the course of treatment), chiropodists, dieticians, medical laboratory technicians, occupational therapists, orthoptists, physiotherapists, radiographers and remedial gymnasts, hearing aid dispensers, registered pharmaceutical chemists, medical and surgical treatment (except health farms, etc.).

Group 8: Burial and Cremation Undertakers, crematoria.

Group 9: Trade Unions and Professional Bodies

Note: Zero-rating has priority over exemption if a supply falls into both categories.

23. Tax Saving Hints

Tax Planning

This chapter deals with various ways in which you can arrange your affairs to reduce your tax bill. It must be stressed that this should not be done by means of tax evasion which is completely illegal (p 117) and may result in your tax bill being increased by the addition of interest and penalties (p 162). Thus you should always make a full disclosure of your taxable income to the Revenue in your income tax return (p 150).

You are fully entitled however, to arrange your affairs legally in such a way that your tax liability is reduced. This is known as tax avoidance (p 117). There are various anti-avoidance rules (p 117) but providing you are able to steer clear of these provisions you can effect substantial tax savings by sensible planning.

Tax planning is a very complex subject and many complicated schemes have been evolved. Such schemes are outside the scope of this book and if you have substantial income and/or assets you should obtain professional advice on tax planning if you have not already done so.

Tax Planning Don'ts

(1) DON'T save tax at the expense of commercial benefits. (It is no good losing money in your business just to pay no tax.)

(2) DON'T cause unhappiness to yourself and your family in order to save tax. (Don't emigrate if you know you will not like your new country.)

(3) DON'T enter into tax saving schemes which run on for a long time. These may be effective when you set them up but could be the target of future anti-avoidance legislation before they are completed.

(4) DON'T jeopardise your future financial security. (Do not give away all of your money just to reduce capital transfer tax.)

(5) DON'T make inflexible arrangements. It is always necessary to review your tax planning in the light of changes in your financial position and family. You must also take full account of changes in the tax system, such as the drastic cuts in the top personal income tax rates this year.

(6) DON'T forget that the law may change. Particularly remember that with capital transfer tax on death it will be the law at your death and not necessarily the law now that will govern the liability.

(7) DON'T rigidly segregate capital and income. Good tax planning sometimes involves saving income and sometimes spending capital. Each have their own taxes and you should aim to maximise both after tax.

A Basic Plan

Before examining in detail ways of saving income tax, capital gains tax and capital transfer tax, the following general guidelines are given, which are applicable to the tax and financial planning of many people :

(a) Buy your own house when you marry, or as soon afterwards as you can afford. If you remain single, house purchase is also desirable in appropriate circumstances. Tax is saved on mortgage payments as explained (p 19). Also, your home should prove a good tax-free investment.

(b) Arrange to have the maximum pension cover possible in your particular circumstances. If you are self-employed, etc., you should pay retirement annuity premiums (p 216).

(c) Arrange adequate life cover to protect your family and as an investment (p 205).

(d) Make use of deeds of covenant for your children once they reach age 18 and for your grandchildren (p 239).

(e) If you have spare funds when your children marry, make use of the capital transfer tax marriage exemptions (p 194).

(f) When your children have married, if your house is larger than you need, consider selling it and investing part of the proceeds for your retirement.

(g) If you have spare funds over and above your retirement needs you and your wife should each make use of the £2,000 capital transfer tax exemption and the £100 small gifts exemptions (p 194).

(h) Subject to there being sufficient funds for your wife, leave at least £25,000 in your will to others (p 245), otherwise the £25,000 nil rate capital transfer tax band (p 188) may be wasted.

Income Tax Saving

Personal Reliefs and Allowances

Always claim all of the personal reliefs and allowances to which you are entitled (p 6). Notify the Revenue as soon as you qualify for an additional allowance such as when you marry.

Business Expenses

Make sure that you claim all business expenses to which you are entitled (p 56). Do not overlook capital allowances. If you are able to use your car in your business you can claim a reasonable proportion of the running costs (it is often better if your business, etc., actually owns the car (p 68)).

Employments

Make sure you claim all allowable expenses (p 83). Try to obtain part of your wages or salary in tax-free ways such as lunch vouchers. Tax savings may result if for example you have a company car or are given an interest-free loan or join your firm's pension scheme. If you are not covered by an occupational scheme you should consider effecting a personal pension scheme (p 216).

Saving Tax for Your Employees (see Chapter 9, p 75)

If you are an employer you can enhance the after-tax income of your employees by various means including the following:

(a) Have a canteen for your staff or supply lunch vouchers (p 77).
(b) Provide business cars for employees (including wives who are employees) where appropriate (p 79).
(c) Grant interest-free loans to staff (but see p 80 for restrictions).
(d) Provide housing accommodation if the employees have to live close to their work (p 81).
(e) Operate pension schemes for staff (p 86).
(f) Provide recreation facilities for your staff – the cost is a business expense and the employees will not be taxed on the benefit.
(g) If you wish to make leaving payments to any employees make the payments in such form as to qualify for relief from tax under the 'golden handshake' provisions (p 88).

Note that (b), (c) and (d) above are subject to the new fringe benefit rules for directors and employees earning over £8,500 annually (p 77). It is still of considerable value to provide such benefits in most cases, however. For example, a car will involve the appropriate scale charge (if at least 10% business use is made) but the employee obtains the much larger benefit of having the use of the car. This includes its capital value, insurance, car tax, repairs and any petrol bought for him.

Repayment Claims

If you are entitled to make any income tax repayment claim (p 158), make sure that you do so at your earliest opportunity. In any event you should not allow the relevant time limit to expire. (This is normally six years after the end of the tax year concerned but is sometimes earlier.)

New Businesses and Fresh Sources of Schedule D Income, etc.

Plan your starting and accounting dates to minimise your total assessments for the opening years (p 61). Make sure you make the appropriate claims for assessment on an 'actual' basis in the second and third years if this is beneficial (p 61). Similarly employ the cessation rules and partnership changes provisions to your best advantage (p 63). These various provisions which are described elsewhere in this book enable useful tax savings to be made by skilful timing and use of the relevant elections regarding for example business commencements, changes and new sources of income assessable under Schedule D Cases III, IV and V.

If you make a loss in a new business, make the best use of it, not forgetting the option of relieving general income going back up to

3 years before you started to trade (p 72). This is particularly useful now, because of the drop in income tax rates, since your new business losses might be offset against more highly taxed income for previous years.

Wife's Earnings

If you have a business, pay your wife properly for any work that she does for it. This will enable the wife's earned income allowance to be obtained (p 8). You must be careful however that your business does not pay your wife more than the job is worth, or else the Revenue might seek to disallow part of her wages and so you will be taxed on the amount as a disallowed business expense. Also note that if your wife's wage is £19.50 per week or more, National Insurance contributions must be paid.

A satisfactory arrangement is to form a business partnership with your wife, which will give her an entitlement to a share in the profits, normally treated as earned income, and to a private retirement plan. If your wife's earnings are sufficiently high, substantial income tax savings will result from electing for the separate taxation of her earnings (p 31). Note that if your wife's share of the annual profits is over £2,250 the excess is charged at 5% (maximum £237.50) under the Class 4 National Insurance Contribution Scheme (p 74).

House Purchase

By purchasing your house or flat instead of renting it you will normally save income tax. This is because unless you make some business use of your home you obtain no tax relief in respect of rent paid whereas mortgage interest (on your main residence) is normally allowable for tax purposes (p 19). If you link your mortgage with some form of life assurance your tax bill will effectively be reduced by $17\frac{1}{2}$% of the premiums paid, subject to the relevant rules (p 10).

You must carefully consider the most favourable way to finance your house purchase from a taxation viewpoint:

(1) If your mortgage interest is likely to exceed your taxable income after allowances, so that you would have no income tax liability, you should opt for the option mortgage system. Under this you are charged a lower rate of interest but derive no tax relief from your interest payments. It is wise to take out a mortgage protection life policy for which you will get tax relief however.

(2) If your taxable income exceeds your mortgage interest so that you are liable to income tax at the basic but not higher rates, you should not use the option mortgage system. Instead you could select the conventional mortgage repayments system under which you will make normally monthly payments to the building society, etc., consisting partly of the capital advanced to you and partly of interest, and subject to the limits (p 19) get full tax relief for the latter as well as

life assurance relief on any mortgage protection life policy which you effect.

(3) If you have a comfortable income you should consider tying your mortgage to a life assurance endowment policy. Under this system you borrow a fixed sum from a building society or insurance company for a given term (20 years, etc.).

You effect a life assurance endowment policy for the sum borrowed, the policy being held by the lender as security. Every year you pay the interest and policy premiums getting tax relief as appropriate. At the end of the term your life endowment policy matures and the capital sum is paid to the lender in settlement of the mortgage.

Your policy can be with or without profits. The latter is cheaper but the former will generally prove a better investment. Indeed, most building societies will allow an endowment policy for a sum assured that is initially less than the loan, but the maturity proceeds of which will grow to equal or exceed the debt on conservative bonus assumptions. Extra decreasing life assurance covers any shortfall if you die before repayment. This type of endowment has the advantage of being cheaper than one for the full amount of the loan.

The advantages of this system are that your life is covered automatically so if you should die, the mortgage is automatically discharged. Also you get full income tax relief on your interest payments each year, as well as income tax relief in respect of the life assurance policy. Furthermore, after 5 April 1979, $17\frac{1}{2}$% is normally deductible on paying up to £1,500 of premiums each year, regardless of whether or not you pay any income tax (see also below).

Life Assurance (p 208)

As well as in connection with house purchase, life assurance provides a valuable method of coupling profitable investment and life cover with tax relief. Subject to the rules (p 10) the relief is $17\frac{1}{2}$% of your qualifying premiums. Normally, the $17\frac{1}{2}$% would be deducted from your premiums on payment.

There are many schemes in which life assurance is linked to property bonds, unit trusts, shares and combinations of these, under which you obtain life cover and tax relief. This often results in a larger investment being made on your behalf for the same net outlay compared with an investment which is not linked with life assurance.

Self-employed Annuity Contracts

If you have earned income in any year, regarding which you are not in an occupational pension scheme, and on which you pay income tax, you obtain full relief from such tax in respect of any retirement annuity premiums paid. The full rules are set out earlier in this book (p 216), subject to which you obtain relief from income tax in respect of the entire premiums paid. Thus you can obtain relief of up to 60% of your premiums if your income is sufficiently high.

If you are able to apply the premiums against your earnings for 1978–79 and earlier years, however, you would obtain relief of up to 83%, if your income was high enough.

This compares with a deduction of only $17\frac{1}{2}$% for life assurance premiums paid.

You obtain relief at your highest tax rates attributable to your earned income. Thus suppose on the top £1,000 of your earnings from your business, profession or non-pensionable employment you pay income tax of £600; if you pay an allowable premium of £1,000 under a self-employed annuity scheme, you will obtain £600 tax relief and so your net cost is effectively only £400 (£1,000–£600). This will secure for you a pension at retirement when your top tax rates will probably be lower. Self-employed annuity contracts provide a very cheap way of obtaining life cover. This is because up to one-third of the available limit each year (p 217) can be applied in temporary (term) life assurance cover. Full tax relief at your top rate is obtained.

Pension Schemes for Controlling Directors

If you are a controlling director of a family company, it can implement a pension scheme for you (p 219). Contributions paid by the company will enjoy tax relief as a deductible business expense and you can be provided with similar benefits to those of any employee under an occupational pension scheme, such as a pension of two-thirds of final salary, or a tax free cash lump sum and a reduced pension, a pension for your widow in the event of death either before or after retirement and substantial life assurance cover for your family in the event of death in service.

Deeds of Covenant

These provide an effective method of tax saving in certain circumstances (p 17). They must cover at least seven annual payments and should not be made by you to your minor children. Another relative such as a grandparent or uncle could execute deeds of covenant in favour of your minor children however.

You might usefully execute deeds of covenant in favour of any of your children who have attained age 18 and are still studying (p 17).

The covenantor who makes the payments deducts basic rate income tax and pays the net amount to the beneficiary. If the latter is not liable for income tax because his income is less than his tax allowances, he reclaims the income tax deducted by the covenantor (p 17). With the increase in personal relief to £1,165 (p 17) this advantage has been enhanced. Also the £750 lower rate (25%) band is available for a further claim of up to £37.50 (£750 × 5%).

If you wish to pay income regularly to elderly relatives with low incomes, this may profitably be done by means of deeds of covenant, so that the relatives may reclaim basic rate income tax in respect of any unused tax reliefs and allowances.

Payments under deed of covenant to charities are of benefit to them since they reclaim the basic rate income tax which you deduct on payment.

If you are considering executing a deed of covenant for more than £115 before tax each year to a minor (not your own child) remember that this may result in his father losing part or all of his income tax child relief (p 8). Note, however, that this is no longer likely, in view of the general replacement of child relief by child benefit, which is not lost.

Gifts and Settlements

If you are a higher rate tax payer and have income and capital surplus to your requirements, you can divest yourself of the surplus altogether and thereby save yourself the income tax on the income concerned. You can probably arrange that the income ends up in the hands of individuals with lower tax rates than yourself. Alternatively the income may be accumulated in a trust (p 167) where only basic rate income tax and investment surcharge is payable. If trusts are created you should take care that the settlor is not taxed on the income (p 166). Note that capital transfer tax applies to amounts settled after 26 March 1974, and so the use of settlements is now of reduced application to tax planning (p 200). Similarly watch the effect of capital transfer tax on gifts (p 187).

The Use of Overseas Income, Taxable on the Remittance Basis

After 5 April 1974 the remittance basis only applies in certain limited cases (p 99). If, however, you obtain any income overseas which is taxable here under Schedule D Case IV or V (p 101), or under Schedule E Case III (p 104), and such income is taxed on the remittance basis, do not bring the income into this country unless you need it to cover your living expenses.

The United Kingdom exchange control rules require that if you are resident here for exchange control purposes, your overseas income must be bought into the United Kingdom. The latter is defined for exchange control purposes however as including the Channel Islands and the Isle of Man, which territories are not subject to United Kingdom taxation. Thus if you open a bank account in say Jersey or Guernsey you can remit your overseas income there without incurring income tax. Any bank deposit interest or other income derived from any investment made with the funds normally is liable to UK tax on an arising basis however, if you are resident and domiciled in the UK for tax purposes, subject to the detailed rules (p 50).

You can use your Channel Islands deposits for spending on holidays abroad, etc. (p 99). Furthermore, once your overseas source of income has come to an end you can bring your funds into this country in a subsequent tax year without any charge to income tax.

Work Overseas

If your work takes you overseas, try to spend at least 30 days working there each year so that the appropriate 25% relief is obtained against the assessment on your employment (p 104), business or profession (p 103). If the employment is with an overseas company, normally no qualifying period is necessary.

Capital Gains Tax Saving

Apart from various highly complicated schemes which are beyond the scope of this book and which are only worthy of consideration in really large cases, a number of simple ways are open to you for saving capital gains tax. Some of these are described below.

£1,000 Net Gains Exemption

Make the best use of this relief. If your sales of chargeable assets produce net gains which are not normally far in excess of £1,000 in any tax year, try to spread your realisations so that your net gains are no more than £1,000 each year – you will then pay no capital gains tax.

Remember that each of your minor children (but not your wife) can also realise up to £1,000 of net gains each year and pay no capital gains tax. It is thus a good idea to spread your share dealings, etc., throughout your family.

If your net gains are less than £1,000 in any tax year, realise further profits by means of 'bed and breakfast' transactions involving the sale of shares one day followed by their repurchase the next. In this way, you will be able to make better use of the exempt band and also, if you wish, the lower rate band (see below). At the same time you will be increasing the base costs of your holdings.

Lower Rate

If you have larger gains which you wish to take, try to limit these to a net total of £5,000 in any tax year. Then your capital gains tax will be no more than £600, being £1,000 which is tax-free and £4,000 at the lower rate of 15%.

Husband and Wife

Sales and gifts of assets between yourself and your wife are not normally liable to capital gains tax (p 124). This enables you to redistribute your assets for capital transfer tax purposes without paying any capital gains tax.

Retirement Relief

If you have a family business or company and are at least sixty years of age, use the capital gains tax retirement relief (maximum £50,000) to its best advantage (p 137). This may mean waiting until you reach the age of sixty-five before selling your business and also continuing to work in it until that time. Remember that subject to the rules, your wife can also get the relief if she works in the business and owns part of it.

Timing

Timing your sales of shares or other chargeable assets can have an important bearing on your capital gains tax. If you postpone a sale until after 5 April it means that you delay the payment of your tax for one year. Also if you know that you will be incurring a capital loss during the next tax year you should defer making any potential capital profits until that year because, although capital losses can be carried forward, they cannot be set off against capital profits in earlier tax years.

Similarly if you have already made a lot of capital profits during the current tax year you should consider incurring capital losses during the same year which can then be offset. You should not normally sell investments unless it is sound to do so from a commercial point of view. A loss may be established on a shareholding however even if you buy it back one day later, but the repurchase should not be on the same day. After 14 April 1975 such transactions may be taxable, however, if done by companies (p 178).

Charities

Gifts made to charities after 21 March 1972 are completely free of capital gains tax. Thus if you wish to make a generous gift to a charity of a capital amount (rather than recurring annual amounts under deed of covenant) you will save yourself future capital gains tax if you gift a chargeable asset on which you have a large potential profit. For example if you wish to give £20,000 to a charity and own shares in A Ltd which cost £4,000 in 1968 and are now worth £20,000 you should gift those shares. (If you sold the shares and donated cash they would only produce £15,200 net of 30% capital gains tax.)

Main Private Residence

Ensure that you gain the maximum benefit from this exemption (p 135). If you have two residences, claim within two years of the date of purchase of your second abode as to which should be treated as your main private residence to be free of capital gains tax. You have a free choice in this matter and so should select the house or flat likely to increase in value the most.

Capital Transfer Tax Planning

The essence of capital transfer tax planning is the conservation of wealth. Remember that at your death the tax normally bites at a higher rate than on transfers during your life (p 188). Also, bear in mind that a future government could introduce an annual wealth tax, at some future time.

Thus in broad terms you should aim to spread assets between your family to minimise the effects of these two taxes. Do not make gifts which you cannot afford, however, nor give too much money outright to young or irresponsible children.

Reducing your Assets by Gifts

Take advantage of the various exempt transfers (p 193). By this means you can gift to your children, and others you may wish to benefit, considerable amounts over a period of years free of tax. Gifts to your wife are normally free of capital transfer tax (p 193) and are considered below.

If you have funds surplus to your requirements, you can make gifts totalling £2,000 in any year (p 194). In addition, you can make outright gifts of up to £100 each year to any number of separate individuals and, furthermore, if you have surplus after-tax income you can make normal expenditure gifts out of income (p 194). Do not overlook the reliefs applied to marriage gifts for your children and grandchildren, etc. (p 194). By means of all the above transfers you can reduce your estate without incurring any capital transfer tax liability.

Remember that the above exemptions apply to both your wife and yourself. Also, do not forget that unused portions of the £2,000 limit can be carried forward for one year only. Thus if, say, your wife wishes to give an £8,000 necklace to your daughter, it can be done free of capital transfer tax if you each give her £4,000 in cash (covering two years assuming no gifts last year) and she then buys the necklace from your wife for £8,000.

Larger Gifts and Settlements

If you have a large estate, you should consider making more substantial gifts which will entail the payment of capital transfer tax. The rate will be nil for the first £25,000 of chargeable transfers, however (p 174), and after that the lower lifetime gifts scale will apply unless you die within 3 years of the gift. (This eventuality can be covered by temporary life assurance (p 246) to pay the extra tax.) The lifetime rates are lower than the death rates at all levels up to £310,000 and so you might certainly make taxable gifts up to this level if your estate is sufficiently large. In smaller estates it is not usually advisable, however, to gift merely the £25,000 tax free band since this is equally tax free on death and it could be better to retain this sum for contingencies in your old age.

It may be desirable to make larger gifts in the form of settlements, but if these are discretionary the periodic charge (p 201) would normally apply at some future time, as well as the tax which you pay when you make the settlement and further tax when benefits are paid to the beneficiaries. Accumulation and maintenance settlements (p 201) are useful for the benefit of your minor children and grandchildren. If the beneficiaries obtain fixed interests (e.g.

in the income) which they become entitled to when they are no more than 25 years old, then no further capital transfer tax is payable (p 186), even if the payment of the ultimate capital is deferred to an older age.

Fixed trusts are also of use if you wish your grown-up children to have income but no capital until a stipulated time. Thus, if you settle money on your 20-year-old son giving him an entitlement to the annual income until he is 35 and then the capital, you are immediately divested of the capital and pay capital transfer tax on the amount settled. Your son eventually gets the capital at age 35 and no more capital transfer tax is payable. Your son is fully taxed on the income, however, and if his other income becomes high as he matures, his income tax burden could be heavy.

Gifts to Charities, etc.

Gifts to charities are exempt without limit if made more than a year from death (p 195) and otherwise the first £100,000 of gifts is exempt. A similar exemption applies to gifts to political parties. Thus you should consider making such gifts during your lifetime and bequests in your will. Both will reduce the value of your estate for capital transfer tax purposes, and capital gains tax relief applies concerning charitable dispositions (p 138).

Equalisation of Assets of Husband and Wife

Provided the recipient is United Kingdom domiciled (or deemed domiciled) no capital transfer tax is payable on transfers which you make to your wife or she makes to you, either during your lives or on death (p 193). But do not keep all of your assets until you die and then leave them to your wife because this may ultimately result in high capital transfer tax on her death which is more than the combined tax if your estates were equal and you each left your assets to your children.

Thus, suppose you have £140,000 and your wife has nothing. If you die first, leaving it all to her, no tax is then payable. But if she still has £140,000 when she dies and has made no previous chargeable transfers, the capital transfer tax at present rates will be £43,750 (p 188). If you had given your wife £70,000 before you died, however, and left your remaining £70,000 to your children, on your death £11,250 would be paid in capital transfer tax. Similarly, on your wife's death £11,250 would be paid making a total of £22,500, compared with £43,750 capital transfer tax paid if your wife inherits all your wealth.

If your wife otherwise has insufficient funds, giving her assets will also enable her to make exempt gifts to your children; thus you both take advantage of the exemptions.

A further point in favour of equalising your estate with your wife's is that wealth tax, if it is ever introduced, would be expected to apply separately to husband and wife at progressive annual rates. Thus less tax is payable on two smaller estates rather than a larger one. Of course, these tax planning considerations must be tempered by practical points such as making sure your wife ha sufficient to maintain her, should you die first. Also, a certain mutual trust is necessary. Your planning should also take account of your respective ages and states of health by arranging for a larger share to be in the hands of the one likely to live the longest.

If you are buying a new home, you should ensure that this is put into the joint names of your wife and yourself. Since the matrimonial home often comprises the major part of the assets of a married couple, this is a very useful way of equalising their respective estates.

Wills

You should think carefully about the preparation of your will and, of course, obtain good legal advice. Substantial capital transfer tax savings can result from a well drawn will. For example, you should ensure that both your wife and yourself by your separate wills leave at least £25,000 to other people so that you each get the benefit of the £25,000 nil rate band. (This presupposes the free band has not been exhausted by lifetime gifts.) Also, avoid leaving too much directly to your children if they are already wealthy; it is more beneficial for tax planning purposes to leave money in trust for your grandchildren. Such will trusts, however, should not be discretionary, but rather of the accumulation and maintenance variety (p 201).

Annuities

If you need to increase your income, annuities provide a means of doing this which at the same time immediately reduces the value of your estate. For example, if you buy an annuity for £10,000 which produces, say, £1,400 yearly until your death, no part of your original capital outlay is charged to capital transfer tax on your death. You have thus saved potential tax on your death at your top rate band. Do not overlook the effects of inflation, however; an annuity which is sufficient for your present needs soon may be worth too little to maintain you.

If you do not need the income, you may use the annuity to make gifts to your beneficiaries. For the purposes of the normal expenditure gifts exemption, however, it is only the income element and not the capital portion which is taken into account (p 220).

Protecting Family Companies

The 'related property' valuation rules (p 189) may make it costly for you to transfer valuable holdings in your family company to your children, etc. This is because capital transfer tax is payable on the transfers, normally on an assets basis. The charge on the shares on your death would be even higher, however, and so you should plan to transfer shares to your children before they become too valuable, and your wife should do the same. The best time would be on the formation of a new company or early in its development.

If you are planning a new business venture, then do not put it into your main family company. Form a new company whose shares are owned by your children (or others whom you wish to succeed to your business). The new company should be allowed to handle as much business as possible and you may even let your old company run down. In this way the next generation of your family will be left eventually controlling the major company.

In the case of a partnership, the interest of each partner is valued on the appropriate share of the underlying assets. If, however, the partnership is incorporated into a company, the value of each partner's interest is normally reduced appreciably, if it is a minority holding.

Breaking Discretionary Settlements

In view of the harsh capital transfer tax provisions relating to discretionary trusts (p 201), it is wise to consider either distributing all of the capital or reorganising a trust to avoid the periodic charge (p 202). (Make sure, however, that the trustees have the power to do this.) If the distribution or reorganisation is made now, only 20% of the full tax is payable. It may be advisable however, to wait until just before 1 April 1982 after which the full tax charge would apply. In this way the discretionary trust would be preserved a little longer, in case the adverse capital transfer tax provisions are either abolished or alleviated, as seems possible in view of the Government's stated intention to overhaul the present system. Also the income tax benefits (p 167) may somewhat compensate for the extra capital transfer tax.

Providing the Funds to Pay Capital Transfer Tax on Death

You may not be able, or indeed wish, to avoid leaving a large estate when you die. In this case you should ensure that sufficient funds are available for paying the capital transfer tax. This avoids forced realisations of assets and, for example, the sale of shares in a family company which it might be desirable to keep.

Life assurance provides one of the best means of providing money to pay capital transfer tax arising on your death, as well as being a very suitable vehicle for exempt gifts. Ensure, however, that the policy proceeds themselves are not subject to the tax, which could happen if the policy were taken out (with no trust provisions) by you on your own life. Consider taking out policies in trust for your children where you leave assets to them; this will put cash into their hands to pay the tax. This should be a 'whole of life' policy, under which a capital sum, with or without profits, or one that is unit-linked to combat inflation, is payable when you die.

If both you and your wife have large estates then you should each insure your respective lives in trust for your children, assuming that you each leave your estates to them. If however you each leave assets to the other by your will, then a joint life last survivor policy could be useful, under which a payment is made only on the second death. If the policy is correctly drawn (in trust for the eventual heirs on the second death) and the premiums are within the annual exemptions (p 193), it will not attract capital transfer tax.

Tax relief is available if the policy is written in trust for your heirs, under the Married Women's Prcperty Acts or otherwise. Take care that there is at least one trustee other than you so that the proceeds may be claimed without delay on your death.

Temporary life assurance may be used to cover the three year period following a gift or settlement on which you have paid tax at the lifetime rate. The amount covered should be the additional tax payable on that transfer should you die within three years.

Change of Residence and Domicile

Reference to the table at the beginning of Chapter 10 (p 94) will illustrate the importance of residence and domicile in ascertaining whether or not an individual is liable to income tax, capital gains tax and capital transfer tax. If you are able to become non-resident for tax purposes you will avoid liability to United Kingdom income tax on many classes of income and if you are also not ordinarily resident here you will not be liable for any United Kingdom capital gains tax on sales of assets here or abroad.

If you become neither domiciled nor deemed domiciled (p 187) in this country you will only be liable for UK capital transfer tax on assets situated here.

A very effective way of avoiding liability from United Kingdom taxes is thus to emigrate and take all of your assets out of this country. Once you have ceased to be resident and are no longer domiciled nor deemed domiciled here you will be outside the UK tax net regarding all income and assets arising and situated abroad. (You should note that if you have shares in a UK company with its registration office here, the shares are treated for capital transfer tax purposes as located in this country unless they are bearer securities.)

If you have a large potential capital gain you should defer taking this until you cease to be resident and ordinarily resident here; in this way you will avoid capital gains tax. (If you wish you may then return to this country in the following tax year.)

As a pure tax-saving exercise, you should only consider emigrating if you are a very wealthy person; and even then you should only go to a country where you feel that you will be happy. If however you wish to retire to a 'place in the sun', then in choosing to which country you should go, you should take into account the tax which you would have to pay there. Once you have established your foreign residence and domicile, in order to preserve this situation, you must avoid paying regular visits to the United Kingdom (p 110).

24. Tax Tables

Income Tax Table for 1979–80

| Income | INCOME ALL EARNED | | INCOME ALL UNEARNED | |
	Single person	Married couple	Single person	Married couple
£1,000	—	—	—	—
1,500	£84	—	£84	—
2,000	213	£46	213	£46
2,500	363	171	363	171
3,000	513	318	513	318
3,500	663	468	663	468
4,000	813	618	813	618
4,500	963	768	963	768
5,000	1,113	918	1,113	918
6,000	1,413	1,218	1,563	1,368
7,000	1,713	1,518	2,013	1,818
8,000	2,013	1,818	2,463	2,268
9,000	2,313	2,118	2,913	2,718
10,000	2,613	2,418	3,363	3,168
15,000	4,588	4,296	6,088	5,796
20,000	7,030	6,705	9,280	8,955
25,000	9,722	9,364	12,722	12,364
50,000	24,663	24,273	31,413	31,023
100,000	54,663	54,273	68,913	68,523

Notes:
(1) Married and single personal relief have been taken into account.
(2) Other reliefs such as for dependent relatives and life assurance have been ignored.
(3) No child relief has been included, since in general this only now applies to certain non-resident children and older students (p 9).
(4) The figures shown include no earned income for the wife. Otherwise extra personal relief and lower rate may be due.

Tax Rates and Allowances for 1973–74 (a), 1974–75 (b), 1975–76 (c), 1976–77 (d), 1977–78 (e) and 1978–79 (f)

	(a)	(b)	(c)	(d)	(e)	(f)
Income tax basic rate	30%	33%	35%	35%	34%	33%
Investment income surcharge (p 25)						
(Age under 65) £1,001–£1,500	—	10%	10%	10%	—	(see
£1,501–£2,000	—	10%	10%	10%	10%	p.
£2,001 upwards	15%	15%	15%	15%	15%	250)
Single personal allowance	595	625	675	735	945	985
Married personal allowance	775	865	955	1,085	1,455	1,535
Wife's earned income allowance						
(maximum)	595	625	675	735	945	985
Child relief ·						
Under 11	200	240	240	300	†170*	†100
11–15	235	275	275	335	†205*	†135
16 and over and studying	265	305	305	365	†235*	†165
Dependent relative relief	100	100	100	100	100	100
Life assurance relief–normal						
percentage of premiums allowed						
as deduction from tax payable	15%	16.5%	17.5%	17.5%	17%	16.5%

* £26 more for the first child for 1977–78.

† Relief at 1976–77 levels for certain children living abroad and students (p 9.)

Income Tax Rates for 1973–74 (a), 1974–75 (b) and 1975–76 (c)

Slice of income	Rate %			Total income	Total tax		
	(a)	(b)	(c)		(a)	(b)	(c)
£4,500	30	33	35	£4,500	£1,350	£1,485	£1,575
500	30	38	40	5,000	1,500	1,675	1,775
1,000	40	43	45	6,000	1,900	2,105	2,225
1,000	45	48	50	7,000	2,350	2,585	2,725
1,000	50	53	55	8,000	2,850	3,115	3,275
2,000	55	58	60	10,000	3,950	4,275	4,475
2,000	60	63	65	12,000	5,150	5,535	5,775
3,000	65	68	70	15,000	7,100	7,575	7,875
5,000	70	73	75	20,000	10,600	11,225	11,625
Remainder	75	83	83				

Income Tax Rates for 1976–77 & 1977–78

	1976–77				1977–78		
Slice of income	Rate %	Total income	Total tax	Slice of income	Rate %	Total income	Total tax
£5,000	35	£5,000	£1,750	£6,000	34	£6,000	£2,040
500	40	5,500	1,950	1,000	40	7,000	2,440
1,000	45	6,500	2,400	1,000	45	8,000	2,890
1,000	50	7,500	2,900	1,000	50	9,000	3,390
1,000	55	8,500	3,450	1,000	55	10,000	3,940
1,500	60	10,000	4,350	2,000	60	12,000	5,140
2,000	65	12,000	5,650	2,000	65	14,000	6,440
3,000	70	15,000	7,750	2,000	70	16,000	7,840
5,000	75	20,000	11,500	5,000	75	21,000	11,590
Remainder	83			Remainder	83		

Income Tax Rates for 1978–79

Slice of income	Rate	Total income (after allowances)	Total tax
£750 (£0–£750)	25%	£750	£187.50
7,250 (750–8,000)	33%	8,000	2,580
1,000 (8–9,000)	40%	9,000	2,980
1,000 (9–10,000)	45%	10,000	3,430
1,000 (10–11,000)	50%	11,000	3,930
1,500 (11–12,500)	55%	12,500	4,755
1,500 (12½–14,000)	60%	14,000	5,655
2,000 (14–16,000)	65%	16,000	6,955
2,500 (16–18,500)	70%	18,500	8,705
5,500 (18½–24,000)	75%	24,000	12,830
Remainder	83%		

Investment Income Surcharge 1978–79

Age up to 65		Age over 65	
£1,700	NIL	£2,500	NIL
1,701–2,250	10%	2,501–3,000	10%
over 2,250	15%	over 3,000	15%

Capital Transfer Tax Rates before 27 October 1977

Slice of cumulative chargeable transfers	Total	Capital Transfer Tax Payable			
		Lifetime Scale		On death	
		% on slice	Cumulative Total Tax	% on slice	Cumulative Total Tax
The first £15,000	£15,000	Nil	£Nil	Nil	£Nil
The next					
5,000	20,000	5	250	10	500
5,000	25,000	7.5	625	15	1,250
5,000	30,000	10	1,125	20	2,250
10,000	40,000	12.5	2,375	25	4,750
10,000	50,000	15	3,875	30	7,750
10,000	60,000	17.5	5,625	35	11,250
20,000	80,000	20	9,625	40	19,250
20,000	100,000	22.5	14,125	45	28,250
20,000	120,000	27.5	19,625	50	38,250
30,000	150,000	35	30,125	55	54,750
50,000	200,000	42.5	51,375	60	84,750
50,000	250,000	50	76,375	60	114,750
50,000	300,000	55	103,875	60	144,750
200,000	500,000	60	223,875	60	264,750
500,000	1,000,000	65	548,875	65	589,750
1,000,000	2,000,000	70	1,248,875	70	1,289,750
The remainder		75		75	

Index